Fifty Bales of Hay

By
Delilah McHenoll

Acknowledgements

I would like to say a very big thank you, to my dear friend, Maeve Dillon for her help and encouragement with this book.

Shall we ride?

Chapter 1

I groan softly, as her smooth tender hands sweep teasingly up and down the inside of my slender thighs. I thrust my pelvis forward, automatically arching my back, as her lips pleasingly caress the circumference of my right breast. Both nipples instantly rise to attention, as her tongue flicks playfully between them. My fingers entwine tightly around her long dark hair, hungrily pulling her closer. Multiple electric volts run erratically throughout every single part of my body.

My eyes unexpectedly open.

Where the heck am I?

The sunlight glistens through the slanted blinds directly onto my face and panic immediately engulfs every single ounce of my body.

"What on earth is the time?" I ask myself, feeling sweaty and flustered. I glare at the red blurry numbers on the alarm clock with squinting eyes, trying as hard as I possibly can to focus. My eyes slowly start to adjust, and I am mortified to see it's already quarter past seven.

'Shit, shit, shit. No, it can't be. Please. Not today of all days,' I

groan loudly.

Every single day throughout March, endlessly dragged by like an eternity, and today, the day I have yearned for, has at last, finally arrived. The first day of my long-awaited course at one of the most prestigious equine colleges in the country.

Trust you to have yet another erotic dream, Jazz. What the heck is wrong with you? You've got sex on the bloody brain lately!

I hurriedly scramble out of bed, swearing loudly, as I trip over my old and tatty slippers, which I'd carelessly left lying around the night before. *Oh, bloody hell, Jazz,* I think to myself sternly, racing towards the bathroom for an urgently needed shower.

In a panic, I turn on the wrong tap. I'm taken completely by surprise, as cold water shockingly blasts over every part of my young curvy body, waking me up in an instant. I haven't got the time or patience to mess about, let alone argue with the stupid temperature control this morning. Shivering and quivering, bearing a resemblance to an Eskimo, I quickly dry myself whilst glancing down at my watch on the bathroom sink in total dismay.

"Jazz, come on for goodness sake, get your arse into gear! You've only got twenty-five minutes to get to your class!" I scream at the bathroom walls.

If only Mum was here, she'd have made sure I was up in plenty of time, but she and Dad had decided to take a last-minute mini break, searching for some sun and relaxation, leaving me, the so-called adult, to look after the animals and myself!

I never oversleep.

I'm extremely grateful our two horses, one pony, and donkey live out at present. Thank goodness no mucking out for me. Still, I do need to pop by and check on them before college.

Hurriedly pulling on a pair of silky red thongs followed by my favourite black skinny jeans, I suddenly catch a glance at myself in the mirror and swear loudly once again. My long blonde hair looks a complete and utter mess. I feel totally distraught, I don't even have any time to straighten it. Quickly fastening my red silk bra, I fumble slightly with the buttons on my denim shirt whilst stomping my feet into my favourite boots, before scrunching my hair up into a tight ragged ball. Grabbing my laptop case, I race out of the door, nearly forgetting to lock it and run across to the main paddock.

Buster, Starlight, and my stunning 15.2h palomino, Breeze start to whinny, as I approach them at great speed. Buttons, our angelic little donkey, makes me smile for the very first time today, braying his usual good morning welcome. His little black legs make me laugh, trotting towards the fence as fast as they can possibly go.

"Good morning my babies," I say softly, carelessly dropping my case down onto the grass.

I'm totally aware of how late I'm running, and that I haven't really got a moment to spare, but I still make time to gently stroke each one of them in turn.

Breeze whinnies softly, as he gently places his head over my right shoulder. His warm breath blows softly against my cheek. I close my eyes, inhaling his beautiful scent, and take a deep relaxing breath before reluctantly wriggling myself out from his gentle headlock.

Glancing across at the water trough to see that it's full, I put my hands up gratefully towards the sky.

"I'm so sorry guys, but I really have to dash. Please wish me good luck on my first day. I promise I'll make it up to you all when I get back home from college," I say, before blowing each of them a kiss.

Grabbing my case, I sprint up the gravelled driveway.

"You are such a bloody idiot, Jazz, being late on your first day. Not very responsible of you, is it?" I mumble fiercely to myself, trying hard to catch my breath.

Over the last couple of years, I've thoroughly worked my socks off, studying every spare hour I could to earn my place on this course. I am determined to pass my Equine City & Guilds Diploma level 2 by this time next year and still fuming, I tut in disgust for forgetting to set my alarm. *Today of all days.*

Pretty damn irresponsible for a supposedly grown up nineteen-year-old, eh?

Finally, I reach the classroom feeling sweaty and bedraggled once again, after my crazy start to the day. I take another deep breath, before slowly and quietly opening the door. It squeaks in the echoing silence of the room. I keep my head low trying to make myself look invisible. Taking a quick glance around, I quietly sit down at the nearest empty desk. A few students turn their heads to look at me and I slowly lift my head managing a small awkward smile in greeting, as I fumble to retrieve the note pad from the side pocket of my case. *Seven minutes late, but I cannot forgive myself for being so stupid. I detest being late.* My first and most important class of the day is with a Mr Sharp.

I count four desks directly in front of me, and slowly lean forward to take a closer look at my tutor. Frustratingly, I can only see his top half, due to the other students blocking my view. My eyes glide over every inch of his masculine physique. His blonde wavy hair whirls softly around his neck, his stunning blue eyes shine like diamonds and I sigh in frustration, as he slowly turns his head away. I watch closely, as he moves towards the enormous white screen on the cream block classroom wall.

I find myself letting out a sharp gasp, as he finally turns around to face me. My eyes slowly stray from his tight-fitting shirt, and glide downwards to his revealing bulging package which is stored neatly inside his beautifully tailored cream jodhpurs. For a slight moment, my eyes feel completely stuck. I seem to have lost all control, as they embarrassingly refuse to move from the vision of this God that stands directly before me. I feel a warm glow slowly rising upwards onto my sun kissed cheeks. His black, shiny jodhpur boots look immaculate. I jump slightly, as they clonk in the eery silence against the concrete floor, as he very slowly turns around once again to point at the screen.

I take another deep breath and try hard to focus on the lesson, scribbling down notes here and there. Little beads of sweat form across my forehead and a slightly damp feeling seems to be emerging strangely between my legs. Very similar sensations to which I encountered in last night's dream. An anxious feeling starts to bubble up inside. If I don't knuckle down and try to concentrate harder, I may end up getting myself into trouble. What with being late, and now getting easily distracted, the risk of being put in detention on my very first day, is enough to make me feel queasy.

Mind you, Jazz. I suppose it could work in your favour. Spending quality one to one time with Mr Sharp could prove to be very productive indeed. Now, that could be worth risking!

Hurriedly and discreetly, I try to follow the other students out of class, but Mr Sharp carefully singles me out.

"Miss Jacobs, please could you hold on for one second? I need to have a word with you. Surely you are aware of the rules we have in place?" he asks, in a deep sexy voice.

"Yes, Sir."

"Therefore, you should really be put on detention for being late on your very first term day," he continues, raising his dark thick eyebrows.

Avoiding any eye contact, and gently biting my bottom lip in anticipation, I quickly respond. "Sir. Honestly, I truly am sorry. I can assure you it will never happen again. Is there any way I can possibly avoid detention on my first day? I would feel truly mortified explaining this to my parents."

'I seriously cannot believe I have just said that to him in such a sultry manner,' I think, feeling quite shocked at my suggestive and seductive reply.

"Well, Miss Jacobs, in your defence, I must say after reading through your entrance notes, I find it is most out of character for you to have turned up late on your very first day," he replies, in a deep, seductive voice.

"I really am truly sorry, Sir. You are right, it is totally out of character. I also dislike people being late. I have no idea or excuse, as to what came over me today. By the way, Sir, please feel free to call me, Jasmine," I reply, with a shy and apologetic look across my face.

"Well, Jasmine. This time your apology is accepted. You can be let off detention just this once, but it cannot happen again. You need to be on time, focus and listen intently, that is, if you want to achieve the best marks possible on this course," he says wryly.

"Thank you, Sir."

I hurry out of the classroom quickly. My face feels flushed, and my heart is pounding like an army of drummers. I have the most-odd sensation running throughout my body. I stop and gasp. Suddenly, I have the urge to cross my legs, as the hot flush travels all the way down past my naval.

What the bloody hell is happening to me? I cry, almost in frustration. I just cannot begin to describe how I feel at this precise moment, although dizzy and wet down below, springs to mind. I'm in a state of total confusion.

I've only ever felt these weird and wonderful sensual feelings once before in the whole of my nineteen years. This had occurred whilst staying at my Aunty's home last year. My good friend of six years Mia, who is two years older than me, had desperately needed a shower after slipping on a massive pile of fresh horse dung whilst we were busily sweeping the yard. *We both laughed so much, the tears streamed down our faces, as she laid flat out on her back on the cold concrete floor. I was no help at all, spending most of my time bent over double, as I watched her slowly and clumsily attempting to get up, but she just kept sliding around. The dung was splattered everywhere, but more so over her face, running all the way down to her waist. My ribs continuously ached from the funny faces she pulled, as she tried as hard as she could to compose herself. One minute she was dancing around the yard with a broom pretending to be a rock star and the next moment she was laid flat out spread eagled, still clinging tightly onto her broom.*

Dashing back to my room laughing continuously, whilst rummaging through my drawers to find Mia a clean change of clothes, I came to an abrupt halt, when I heard her voice calling out to me. She wanted me to pass her a bar of soap from the bathroom cabinet. Sauntering towards the bathroom, grabbling a bar of soap from inside the cabinet, I slowly turned around to hand it to her and instantly froze like a statue. With my mouth wide open, my eyes slowly and longingly took in every inch of her perfect, naked body, as she stood underneath the gushing water from the shower. I gasped in bewilderment, watching the flowing water cascade over her breath-taking pert breasts. An unfamiliar warm glow started to trickle through every single one of my veins. Slowly and shakily, I moved my right hand forward towards her, the soap nearly slipping through my trembling hands, trying hard to divert my eyes elsewhere. My heart pounded twenty to the dozen. I felt hot and flushed. The vision of her beauty took my breath away. Eventually, I managed to pull myself together, even though I knew I never wanted this moment to end. Miraculously, my trembling hand finally managed to hand over the bar of soap.

Her enchanting green eyes looked deeply into mine. "Thank you, honey," she'd said, in a very gentle voice

Electric volts ran through every part of my body, as her hand lightly brushed mine. These were the exact same sensations I had recently encountered with Mr Sharp.

Mia's smile, her lips, her body, everything about her, totally enthralled me. I remember looking away shyly, feeling guilty and confused. *Why does Mia have this erotic effect on me?* I remember every single second of that day like it was yesterday. *What on earth is wrong with me? And why, do I feel so guilty for having these warm and wonderful sensations? For goodness' sake, Jazz, Mia is one of your closest friends. She has a steady boyfriend and, as for Mr Sharp, well, he's your blinking tutor!*

Chapter 2

My first term at college flew by. I was very strict with myself, making sure I focused only on my studies. I arrived ten minutes early to class each day and had finally convinced myself, there was no way I would allow any of those confusing thoughts of Mia or Mr Sharp to creep back inside my head. I firmly dismissed them, deciding to lock them away into a secret compartment on the left side of my brain. Once this task was completed, I suddenly felt like a huge weight had been lifted. I felt positive and decided that it was now time to move forward. My full focus and concentration needed to be aimed at achieving the best possible marks on this course.

Tomorrow, is thankfully the first day of half term. Breeze and I are going to stay with my Aunty Trudy who owns a riding school in Norfolk. It's only a thirty-minute drive from here and the two of us have always been close. We text, email, even chat regularly via *Zoom*, but it isn't the same as spending quality and personal time with someone you really care about. I do have a lot of revisions to do, but I know the change of scenery will do me good and hopefully help to clear my head. Aunty has even promised to give me and Breeze some advanced dressage lessons, which is going to be a real bonus, as this could help me achieve higher grades on my course.

I've owned Breeze for almost four years. One day in June and completely on the spur of the moment, Mum and I had decided to attend a popular horse sale, which was only around an hour's drive away.

I still grimace, when I think back to the terrible and neglected state he was in. From the first moment I laid eyes on him, and I knew instantly, he urgently needed my help. With his eyes wide open in fear, looking completely lost and disorientated, he cantered wildly around the sales ring with his ribs showing through his dull cream coat. His ragged white straggly tail was so overgrown, he could easily trip over it, and shreds of twigs were entwined and knotted through the long strands of hair. With a huge lump in my throat, I knew I had to do something to help.

Eventually, I really lost it.

A gruff looking guy, wearing a long, dung splattered white coat, with his huge disgusting fleshy belly hanging out from wherever it could find any spare room, angrily raised his stick towards Breeze's head. Gasping in horror, Breeze flinched sideways whilst whinnying in pain, as the stick caught him heavily between his ears. I stood in shock with my right hand covering my mouth. A moment later Breeze reared up in retaliation, pawing the air in an angry manner with both front legs. I held my breath, both hands now covering my mouth, feeling relieved once I saw Breeze safely back down on all four legs, but he turned around, suddenly lifting his front nearside leg high up in the air, narrowly missing the evil man's head, as he went to thrash him once again. I threw my right hand up high into the air, before angrily racing towards the sale ring screaming loudly for him to stop the horrendous bullying towards this already terrified horse.

Only a couple of seconds later, a gruff sounding voice began to make an announcement over the speaker. "This highly spirited and monster of a horse is sold here and now to the lady in red. Four hundred sterling." A loud bang from a hammer followed.

Innocently and inquisitively, I looked around trying to locate the buyer. My eyes searched high and low, but I could not spot one single person wearing red. The penny eventually dropped, when I suddenly became aware of a few strange faces staring directly at me. Mum, who suddenly appeared at my side tightly grasping my arm, mumbled in shock, "Jasmine, what the F***."

At that precise moment, it had suddenly occurred to me, I was one only one around wearing a bright red hoody. I'd turned and grinned at Mum, as it finally started to sink in, still not quite believing, I'd just bought a horse.

Our intention had been to look for a sensible riding horse, one with potential to make into a top show jumping or dressage horse, as over the past few months I had sadly started to grow out of my very first pony, Buster.

At only six years old, and a complete pony nut, my parents had surprised me with the most perfect gift one Christmas. I smile, as I remember back to the red bow Buster was wearing when my Aunty proudly led him down the trailer ramp with a huge grin across her face. It was love at first sight. Buster had been with my Aunty since he was only six months old after he'd been abandoned on some nearby wasteland and she trusted him with her life. She decided he would be the perfect first pony for me. He was bomb-proof and a total gem in every possible way. He had also taught many youngsters to ride at her riding school over the years, giving them confidence and such wonderful memories to treasure for a lifetime. Buster was only ten years old when I officially became his Mum and still had plenty of years left in him.

Up until my early teens, Buster had taught me everything I know. The two of us made a strong team and became a force to be reckoned with. We had an unbreakable connection and the trust we held for each other led to us winning numerous show-jumping and cross-country events across the South East region.

When my final growth spurt arrived at the age of fourteen, my legs began to feel too long on Buster, and I started pulling up my stirrup leathers on a regular basis. In fact, they soon became so short I soon resembled a jockey. Bless my Buster, he only stood at thirteen hands, but before I knew it, I suddenly turned into a slender and lanky five foot six. My parents and I decided, with Buster just turning nineteen years old, this would be the ideal time for him to have a well-deserved retirement. He had truly earned it, serving me well and doing us both proud.

It was now time to take the next step, to find my perfect companion who would take me even further in the equestrian field, I so loved. Up until then, this was something I could only dream about, that is until the day, Breeze arrived in my life.

I giggle, as I remember the look on Dad's face that day we pulled up with the trailer. I have never seen him look so shocked and speechless, as he watched Breeze come down the trailer ramp rearing high up into the air whilst balancing majestically on his hind legs.

My phone suddenly interrupts my memories and I glance down at the screen.

Hi, Jasmine, text me when you and Breeze are on your way. We are all looking forward to seeing you. Can't wait, love you, your favourite Aunt xx.

I laugh out loud at her message. She is my one and only Aunty and the only person who still calls me by my full name, Jasmine. Most people just call me Jazz.

From out of nowhere, my thoughts return to Mia and those hidden and guilty feelings I thought I'd safely locked away, suddenly start to creep back from deep down inside, slowly bubbling away like a volcano after months of lying dormant. '*Maybe I need to share my bottled-up feelings about Mia, and Mr Sharp with someone*

I trust,' I think, whilst squeezing the last few items into a second suitcase, trying hard to lock any guilty thoughts back up into that little compartment inside my head.

What if these feelings I have for Mia and my tutor keep returning? I honestly thought I could deal with them. Should I ask to be transferred to another class next term?

During my first term at college, I'd been lucky enough to make good friends with four of the other female students in my class and two of the lads. Not surprisingly, it seems Mr Sharp also has the same sexual effect on a lot of the other students, apart from Adam and the stunning, Brooke. Jake, bless him, has no hang ups about his sexuality at all and I admire him for being so open and honest, He makes us all laugh, as he thoroughly enjoys discussing Mr Sharp's package with the girls. I get on very well with Brooke, she is only one month older than me, and we have so much in common. I always feel relaxed in her company. She has the most radiant black hair, dark chocolate-coloured eyes and her beautiful red succulent lips wait longingly to be kissed. Standing an inch taller than me, with a magnificent athletic build, she has such a warm and easy-going nature. She had told me on many occasions that the only pride and joy in her life, is her stunning Arab horse Fiery. Bizarrely, Brooke only lives a couple of miles away from me, so I was surprised when I found out, as to why we'd never bumped into each other in all these years. She'd explained to me sadly, how she'd been sent to a girls only private boarding school in Suffolk at an early age. There is something very interesting, and mysterious about Brooke, and for the life of me I cannot put my finger on it. We seem to be on the same wavelength. Sometimes, I catch her glancing at me in a very special way and occasionally those fluttering guilty feelings begin to emerge from deep within my soul.

We are just good friends, that's all.

Honestly, Jake along with the other three, Sandy, Jade, and

Felicity don't stop talking about Mr Sharp and his beloved package. They seem to be looking forward to next term when apparently, we get to see him in action, as he demonstrates his riding techniques for the very first time. Brooke has never shown any interest in boys whatsoever, and that includes Mr Sharp and his beloved package too.

Mr Sharp, Mia, and most recently, Brooke, have gradually creeped into my dreams. My dreams seem so real, and yet they feel so wrong.

Confusion overwhelms my feelings.

I'm hoping I won't see too much of Mia on my half-term break, although it's going to be hard to avoid her, as she keeps her horse on livery at Aunty's and is always popping in for a coffee and a chat. Plus, she helps Aunty around the yard and in return gets a discount on her weekly livery fee. Mind you, if I'm being completely honest with myself, I know that deep down inside, I'm yearning to see her.

I know it's wrong, but I can't help the way I feel.

Closing my eyes, I try to clear my mind of all my confusing thoughts, drifting off into a deep and pleasurable sleep.

Chapter 3

I grin at my insane Aunty who is excitedly jumping around, her hands waving frantically in the air like a complete maniac, as the horse box grinds to a halt.

"Jasmine, my girl, it's so good to see you," she says, dragging me out of the front seat of the Range Rover and into her open arms.

I laugh and hug her back, although I grimace slightly, as a couple of my ribs start to crunch with the impact of her strong, but welcoming grasp.

"Now let's get you and Breeze settled in," she says, lifting out my two suitcases as though they are as light as a feather.

"It's so good to see you, Aunty."

"Like wise. Trust me, the two of us have an amazing week ahead of us. I think we both deserve some quality Aunty and niece time, and we have so much to catch up on. I can't wait for you to tell me how college is going."

I lead Breeze slowly down the ramp. He stops for a moment, standing proudly with his head held high into the air whilst letting out a humungous whinny. He knows exactly where we are, and he loves it here. This will be his fourth holiday at Aunty's.

"Wow, Jasmine, Breeze looks in fabulous shape. He obviously wintered well. Just look at his stunning summer coat coming through," she beams, as she walks forward to greet him, caressing his strong golden neck.

I smile at her happy face. Being Mum's younger Sister there is only fourteen years difference between us, and we are lucky to share the same interests and sense of humour.

I love Breeze with every ounce of my heart, although things were far from easy when he first arrived. In fact, Mum and Dad were at their wits end, constantly worrying I'd get hurt and end up in a hospital bed. Poor Breeze was insecure and scared of almost everything. If he felt threatened in any way, he would strike out blindly and fiercely with all four legs. He would act with no hesitation at all, but I quickly learned how to read his body language. I gave him all the love, time, and patience he needed to build up our trust.

"What a difference to the poor bedraggled beggar you brought home four years ago, Jasmine. Honestly, he's a true credit to you. Your determination, eternal love, and patience has made him into the incredible specimen he is today. I cannot tell you how proud I feel of what you have both achieved," Aunty continues, seemingly with a little tear in her eye.

"Thank you." I proudly look Breeze up and down.

Standing at fifteen two hands, his once bony ragged structure is now solid and muscular. His beautiful white flowing mane and tail glisten in the late afternoon sunshine, against his glossy golden coat. I slowly rub his soft pricked ears, moving my right hand to gently stroke the striking white blaze imprinted on his forehead. My heart is full to bursting with the unconditional love I feel, for my boy.

I thank the driver and inform him we will see him at around two pm the following Sunday.

"I thought Breeze could share the field with Blossom again, as the two of them always seem to get on so well when you come to stay," Aunty says, striding ahead of us wheeling my suitcases behind her.

"Easy boy," I say softly to Breeze, as he prances and dances to my left. '*It's so good to be back,*' I think to myself, as the wonderful scent from the stable yard slowly flows up my nostrils.

A few people wave to me in the distance, as they head towards their cars, but I cannot see any sign of Mia, although it is nearly six pm and most owners would have probably gone home. The sun is still warm on this wonderful May evening and I smile as Blossom greets Breeze with a very loud whinny.

"Whoa boy," I tell him, as he starts to pull harder.

"I bet you can't wait to see your girlfriend again, hey, Breeze?' grins Aunty, as she opens the five-bar gate and gently wraps a lead rope around Blossom's neck. As soon as Breeze and I are through, I struggle to close the gate, due to him dancing continuously on the spot in anticipation of being reunited with his long-lost girlfriend.

"Let him go," calls Aunty.

I undo his headcollar as quickly as I can and at the same time Aunty lets Blossom go.

We watch in awe. The pair of them chase each other around the field in sheer ecstasy. Blossom's pure white coat against Breeze's golden coat makes a stunning sight to see. I lean over the post and rail fencing with a huge grin on my face. Breeze is showing off, leaping and cavorting around like a vision of a horse belonging to the Spanish Riding School in Vienna. His stunning white mane flows up and down with every move, like a butterfly opening and closing its wings. Blossom stays closely by his side looking thrilled to have her long-lost boyfriend back.

"Come on, Jasmine, follow me. Let's leave them to get on with their tantalising and flirting and get you settled in. You can unpack your suitcases whenever you want to," says Aunty's cheerful voice.

We walk side by side, following the winding path up towards the house. I glance all around in the hope that I may see Mia, but she is nowhere to be seen and I can't help but let out a sigh of disappointment. *Jazz. Get a grip.* I force a smile, as Aunty turns to glance at me.

It was so wonderful catching up with Aunty and when I eventually crawled into bed at eleven pm, I was totally shattered. I tossed and turned as I tried to shut out those guilty thoughts I feel for, Mia.

Chapter 4

"Oh, Breeze, you look so chilled and relaxed alongside Blossom. It looks like you've both had a lovely relaxing night. I wish I could say the same for me," I say, gently stroking his golden neck.

Very slowly he lifts his head, whinnies softly, before carefully plonking his head over my right shoulder. I wrap my arms tightly around him and inhale the wonderful smell from his coat. I adore the way he cuddles me. He gently puts his head over my shoulder, reaches down my back, and pulls me in closer towards him. He has always had the knack of being able to sense how I'm feeling, probably down to the rare and precious connection we share. What a difference to the wild and terrified horse he once was.

"I love you, my boy," I tell him.

Blossom starts to gently nuzzle my jodhpur pockets.

I start to wriggle myself free from Breeze's head lock. "Hey there young lady, I haven't got anything hidden in my pockets, I promise," I tell her with a cheeky grin.

Breeze lets out a huge sigh of disappointment, as I finally

manage to escape his strong grasp.

"I'm sorry our cuddles got interrupted, but don't you worry, it won't be too long before I'll pop back."

Placing a tender kiss onto his fleshy velvety muzzle, I feel so much happier after spending some time with my pride and joy. He never fails to lift my mood and is always there for me. I smile broadly, as I head back towards the house.

Suddenly the doorbell chimes, taking me completely by surprise. I quickly glance down at my watch to see it's only seven am. *Who on earth could that be at this time of the morning?* I firmly press the kettle switch down.

"Don't worry, Jasmine. I'll get it," calls Aunty, as I carry on getting the mugs out of the cupboard.

I'm taken completely off guard when I turn around and see Mia standing right in front of me. I hold my breath, as she smiles back at me. Her stunning green eyes look deeply into mine, as I slowly take in her cropped T-shirt, kindly showing her midriff, her skinny jeans accenting her curves. I look away shyly, as those warm and guilty feelings start to return.

"Morning, Jazz," Mia cries excitedly, embracing me in one of her bear hugs and grinning at me like she has just won the lottery.

"Erm, morning, Mia. This is totally unexpected," I say sharply, immediately regretting my tone.

Mia immediately pulls back from the embrace. "You ok, Jazz?" she asks, with a worried expression.

"I'm good, Mia," I mumble. "Sorry, I didn't sleep too well last night." I quickly turn my head to avoid her eyes.

"That's ok, Jazz. I guess it is early and it looks like you haven't had your morning coffee yet. Don't forget, I know you well. Look, you'll be ok once you've had a couple of shots of caffeine inside you," she replies, sounding slightly concerned for a moment, but then smiles and gives me a cheeky wink.

Pull yourself together, Jazz.

"Good morning, Mia," calls out Aunty from the depths of the kitchen.

"Good morning to you, too, Trudy. Is there anything you'd like me to do for you today?" Mia enquires.

"Oh, Mia. Can you believe we have run out of oat milk? I don't suppose you'd mind popping down to the shops before Nick and Charlotte arrive, would you? Pretty, pretty, please," Aunty grins.

"No problem at all. I'll pop down there right now, as I need to pick a few bits up for Mum, too," says Mia. "Jazz, would you like to come with me?"

Before I have a chance to reply, Aunty hurriedly pipes up, "Mia, if it's ok with you, I just need to borrow Jasmine for a short while. I've been meaning to ask if she'd mind giving me a hand with some of my social media pages. Well, Jasmine?" she replies, as she quickly turns to face me.

Mia turns around and gives me one of her special smiles, before heading out of the front door.

All those rushes of hidden emotion come snowballing back. 'Jazz, you should be angry and disappointed with yourself for treating Mia so badly earlier. She doesn't deserve it,' I tell myself, feeling outraged at my awful behaviour. *What is wrong with me?* My eyes start to well up with tears.

"Jasmine, Come and sit with me before Mia gets back. I need us to have a little chat," says Aunty.

I peer at Aunty through mixed emotions. Grabbing my mug of coffee, I follow her into the office, whilst dabbing my eyes on the sleeve of my shirt.

"Jasmine, I'm not sure if Mia has been in touch with you recently, but I have a delicate situation I want to talk to you about," says Aunty, in a very gentle tone.

"Is everything ok?" I ask, feeling concerned, pulling myself together in an instant.

"Mia has broken up with Jamie. To be honest, it came as a bit of a shock when I heard the news. It was completely out of the blue. Two weeks ago, Mia confided in her Mum that she has mixed and confusing feelings about her sexuality," says Aunty.

I look up at Aunty, my mouth wide open in shock. Biting my lip, still not quite understanding, I quietly ask, "What do you mean, Aunty?"

"Jasmine, I'm afraid love is not always black and white. We are all unique and love different things. Mia is just learning that she prefers girls to boys, and apparently a young lady she has known for quite a while, is the one she has fallen for," she continues.

"Who?" I ask quickly, avoiding eye contact, as I immediately regret allowing my feelings to surface in what could seem like an obvious way.

"Well, Mia hasn't said who it is yet, but her Mum thinks it's someone she's been very close to over the last few years," Aunty replies gently.

"Oh wow," is all I can manage to respond. My mind is racing nineteen to the dozen. *Could it be me? I'm totally shocked and not quite sure how I feel. This has completely thrown me. I am not sure if I'm ready to disclose my hidden fantasies yet, or am I?*

Aunty gives me a nod and a slightly knowing glance. "Look, Jasmine, you're old enough to understand that adults enjoy different things. There is no shame in it. For example, in the old days, I enjoyed," Aunty hesitates, unsure quite how to proceed.

"What did you enjoy?" I ask her, as a hundred different thoughts start racing through my head.

"Jasmine, if I tell you, I'll probably shock you and will end up going way down in your estimation," she replies.

"Never," I exclaim.

"Well, I've never told anyone this before, not even your Uncle or your Mum, so this is a secret that must be kept between you and me for always. Promise?" she asks.

"Scout's honour," I reply.

"It's a wonder your Mum hasn't told you what a terrible little tearaway I used to be," she giggles, before continuing.

"I was a very naughty girl before I met your Uncle. I was extremely mischievous and totally out of control. I remember on this one occasion I'd met a random guy in some bar. On the spur of the moment, I'd decided to jump on a bus looking for a bit of excitement and ended up thirty miles away from home. Honestly, talk about handsome, he could have been a model. We started talking, and I soon found out what an amazing and wicked sense of humour he had. Well, after numerous alcoholic drinks, we found ourselves getting totally plastered. He invited me back to his for a night cap, and I thought, '*What the heck, you only live once.*' What I hadn't envisaged, was meeting his wife who was patiently waiting at home for his safe return. I swear, I have never seen a woman so beautiful in the whole of my life. She was truly stunning and greeted me wearing a warm looking throw wrapped all around her. I was completely captivated and mesmerised by her beauty," she continues, with a faraway look on her face.

I sit with my mouth wide open not quite believing what I'm hearing, curiously waiting for her to continue.

"Hold on let me think. Now, what that guy was called? After all, it was over fifteen years ago. Oh yes, I recall it now, his name was Gerald. How on earth could I forget, Gerald? Well, he invited me inside and his wife smiled seductively, as her slender right hand slowly appeared from underneath the throw..."

I shakily offered my right hand, and within seconds she was holding it softly and firmly inside hers. Her touch made me feel something inside I would never have imagined could be possible. There was something very mystical about her, and it felt like she had put me under a magical spell. I smiled back, unable to take my eyes off her. Still feeling quite tipsy, Gerald gently took my hand and led me across to a beige reclining chair where his beautiful wife had just sat down. I gasped, as her throw started to slide slowly downwards onto the parquet floor. My eyes were glued to her sexy red lingerie, slowly following the perfect line of her legs, right the way down to the red high heels she was wearing. She eased herself up slowly and in a confident way walked straight towards me, keeping her eyes focused firmly on mine. She cupped my chin tenderly in her left hand and kissed me lovingly on my lips. I was in heaven, not only totally mesmerised by her beauty, but I had never been kissed so passionately in the entirety of my life. I was spellbound once more, as she casually turned away and walked towards, Gerald. She slowly kissed him, and then looked back at me invitingly. She walked directly towards me, signalling with her forefinger for me to follow.

"I was spellbound, as she elegantly glided across the living room. I seriously cannot believe what happened next," she confesses.

"Please tell me what happened," I cry out, in anticipation.

Chapter 5

"Drink your coffee before it goes cold," Aunty says.

I had completely forgotten about my drink. This story sounds like something out of a steamy novel.

"Well, his wife took my hand in hers and led me further into the living room. Their house was incredible."

Everywhere was open plan surrounded by solid oak beams with two large leather sofas sitting proudly against one wall. The most beautiful ornate fireplace sat neatly inside the opposite wall. I remember the warmth of the flames, the shadows dancing around the living room, and the beautiful Persian rugs which lay in front of the fire across the dark parquet flooring.

Within seconds, the dark-haired beauty gently took hold of my hands and slowly pulled me down onto the sofa next to her. She tried to kiss me again, but this time I pulled away. I cannot explain my feelings. I had butterflies dancing around crazily in my stomach, although I did also feel slightly uncomfortable, as being in a situation like this was most definitely a first for me. Not sure what I was going to do, I slowly stood up, and picked up my handbag. A sudden wave of panic engulfed me, and I yearned to go outside for some fresh air. She could see straight away how nervous I was feeling and immediately apologised. In a very soft voice, she asked if I would like to stay for a drink, obviously with no strings attached. I suddenly felt as though a weight had been lifted. I instantly relaxed, and smiled warmly at her, feeling incredibly relieved. Gerald came to sit down beside me too, also apologising wholeheartedly. They explained how awful the pair of them were feeling, as they certainly had no intentions of making me feel nervous and uncomfortable.

"Gerald said he would be more than happy to order me a taxi, although by that time it was already one am, so he suggested I could stay in their spare room just for the night," Aunty says, with a very naughty smile across her face.

"What an incredible story. What was the ladies name?" I ask, totally enthralled.

"Well, the mystical lady's name turned out to be, Ruby. Looking back, I can see how funny it was. She even told me I could lock the bedroom door if I felt concerned or threatened in any way. After her comment, we all fell about laughing. Anyway, the evening or the early hours of the morning I should say, turned out to be truly wonderful after all. We had a few drinks and nibbles and spent what seemed forever chatting about ourselves, our work, friendships, hobbies, pretty much everything, we had so much in common after all. Eventually, feeling exhausted, I'd said my goodnights at three am, thanking them kindly for their hospitality and headed off to my allocated bedroom. I didn't feel uncomfortable or scared. It felt like an adventure," continues Aunty, as she takes a sip of her coffee.

"What happened next?" I ask her, totally engrossed.

"Well, I got into bed and eventually fell asleep after the evening's extraordinary events, but it wasn't too long after, before I awoke with such a thirst. I'd drunk far too much alcohol and overindulged with the nibbles."

As quietly as I could, dressed in only my underwear and blouse, I ventured downstairs to the kitchen in search of a glass of water. I remember it so well, as I nearly lost my balance on the step outside my room. I'd completely forgotten about it! Anyway, I crept down the stairs as quiet as a mouse and there was Ruby sitting at the kitchen table with a mug of coffee. I didn't notice her at first, as the kitchen was in complete darkness apart from the gentle flicker of light shining from the fire through the stained-glass window. I only caught a glimpse of her slight frame and I remember crying out in alarm, as she turned to face me. She chuckled and apologised for frightening me twice in only a few hours! I smiled and ended up saying sorry for disturbing her. She very kindly poured me a glass of water and we both curled up at different ends of the sofa, sharing the throw between us. By now, we were both wide awake. I could hear her husbands contented snores coming from upstairs and we looked at each other and laughed.

"I remember it so clearly like it was yesterday," smiles Aunty.

"I don't know what I would have done, if I'd been in that situation," I confess.

"It's hard to explain," replies Aunty. "I'd never encountered anything quite like that in the whole of my life. The only experiences I'd had previous to this, was a quick fumble in the library or a quickie behind the bus shelter. Suffice to say, most of the time, that had always been a big let-down. Sex to me at that time was simply over-rated. It was just something every one of my age seemed to be doing. I suppose that was the reason I never stayed with anyone for too long, I just got bored."

"Aunty!" I exclaim, in a very shocked manner.

"I'm a hot-blooded woman after all, not just your Aunt," she chuckles wickedly. "Anyway, up until that evening, I'd never had any sexual encounter with a woman," she continues.

"What happened next?" I ask, now feeling extremely intrigued.

"Well, it wasn't planned at all. To be honest, I hadn't given the earlier encounter a second thought, but as we were sitting chatting about our various experiences, I remember the way the firelight made her face absolutely glow."

She had the most beautiful eyes, a deep dark bluey green in colour. She told me how she had met her first love, a young chap who had tended her parent's garden.

Apparently, he used to work along-side his dad and she had what she described as a massive crush on him. She told me, the first time she set eyes on him, she had encountered butterflies soaring through every part of her body and had daydreamed over and over about the first kiss she hoped they would share one day. I remember watching the way her hands moved animatedly as she continued her story.

Her beautiful, slender hands immaculately manicured with a soft neutral shade fascinated me. I don't recall too much about the rest of her story, as I was too focused on taking in every inch of her luscious body. I know I smiled and nodded in the right places though, because she seemed oblivious to my roaming eyes. Anyway, she eventually got up to fetch me another glass of water. My mind raced with desire and my body was on fire, as she returned with our drinks, slowly sitting back down onto the sofa. Her silk dressing gown slipped slightly as she handed me the glass of water and my cheeks felt warm with embarrassment from the naughty thoughts I was thinking. I was worried she may have noticed my reaction. She hadn't and simply sat back down opposite me.

"Her ivory silk gown casually slipped once again, this time revealing her beautiful well-defined thigh. I began choking on my drink, horrified and confused at the thoughts which were suddenly racing through my head," she continues, as she pauses to take another sip of her coffee.

"Oh Aunty. Please don't stop there," I cry out.

"I had never ever felt such a wanting need. It came as such a huge surprise and completely out of the blue. Ruby immediately grabbed my glass and leant over to pat my back."

As I felt her hand on my back, panicking I coughed again, only adding to my predicament. I think she was terrified I was going to choke to death. Eventually, I stopped spluttering and thanked her for her help and kindness. I hadn't realised, but as I'd been choking, my hands had somehow slipped down to rest on her soft and tender thighs. We both seemed to look down at the same time.

She focused on me intensely with the most beautiful smile I have ever seen and in a low sensual voice she asked me if I was feeling okay. My initial reaction was to pull my hands away, but she quickly caught them and held them close to her chest, asking me once again, if I was okay. I remember just nodding and averting my eyes from her now naked thighs. I could feel her heart beating rapidly through my now trembling hands. She slowly released one of her hands and gently took hold of my chin, carefully pulling my face up to look at hers. Her eyes looked enquiringly into mine. I could see that she felt the same way too. She carefully moved a strand of hair away from my face and rubbed her thumb across my lips. She looked deep into my eyes and moved in closer. I felt her warm breath against my face, the faint scent of her soft perfume, and the heavenly tenderness as her lips brushed mine. I responded without any hesitation, kissing her back very seductively. She then wrapped her arms gently around my waist, bringing us closer together.

For a second, Aunty looks deeply lost in her thoughts, and then the door opens slightly. I'm taken aback to see Mia standing there, with a shopping bag in hand.

Casually strolling in, Mia stops suddenly and looks quizzically at me and Aunty.

"What's wrong?" Mia enquires, with a slight note of panic in her voice.

"Nothing, Mia," I reply. "Honestly, there is nothing's wrong, I promise," I say again, more softly this time. I immediately jump up and take the bag from Mia's hand. My hand touches hers as I take hold of the handle and I immediately feel that rush of electric flowing throughout every part of my body. "Would you like another coffee, Aunty?" I ask, trying to pull myself together.

"No, thanks, I'm fine, honestly. We can catch up later. I have a lesson to teach in twenty minutes. If you like, how about meeting me in the indoor school around two o'clock? I could give you and Breeze a dressage lesson, and, Mia, please feel free to join us with Ebony," says Aunty, with a slight wink.

With that, Aunty smiles at the two of us, and promptly gets up to leave. My head is still reeling from Aunty's story and I cannot wait to hear what happened next. I try to clear my head, as Mia and I find ourselves totally alone in the kitchen.

Chapter 6

I suddenly feel panicky. *What shall I say? What shall I do?*

"Jazz, what was Trudy talking to you about?" asks Mia, in a soft voice, avoiding any eye contact, patiently waiting for the kettle to boil.

I need to be honest with Mia. I take in a deep breath before I speak. "Mia. I'm so sorry to hear about you and Jamie splitting up after all this time," I say softly.

"I'm not, Jazz," she replies, firmly turning to smile at me.

Oh, that smile. I'm finding it hard to cope with the flickers and tremors that seem to be running through every single part of my body. My face is starting to feel warm, as Mia kindly hands me a mug of coffee.

"Look, Jazz. Nick and Charlotte will be here any moment for their usual break from yard duties. Why don't we find somewhere more private so we can have a proper talk and catch up?" she proposes.

"Why don't we go to the top of the hay barn like we used to, no one will disturb us up there? I can even grab a blanket for us to sit on," I tell her. I smile and look deeply into her enchanting, emerald-green eyes. *'Get a grip, Jazz,'* I tell myself firmly. The flickers and tremors continue, and I start to feel slightly uncomfortable. I seem to have no control over them, as they begin to get stronger with every moment that passes.

"What a great idea," grins Mia, with a slightly naughty look across her face.

I quickly head towards the airing cupboard in pursuit of a blanket. I race back to the kitchen and Mia and I head off towards the barn, bumping into Nick and Charlotte on our way.

"Where are you two heading off to looking so happy?" grins Nick.

"We are just off to do a bit of revision and have a good old catch-up. Is everything okay in the yard? We can come over and give you a hand later, if you need one," I reply with a smile.

"Everything's great and hunky dory, but thanks, Jazz. Don't worry about hurrying back, most of the morning chores are done. Charlotte and I are going to put our feet up for a well-earned break for an hour or so and have a good old read of the paper," he smiles.

Cool, that means we will have plenty of time to chat. The flickers within me start to run freely once again. *Why can't I control them?*

"Have fun with your revision," smiles Charlotte.

We climb up the sweet-smelling hay bales until we find the perfect spot to sit down. "Can you believe, we've just scrambled up fifty bales of hay?" I ask her, slightly out of breath.

"Fifty bales of hay, that is a huge accomplishment, Jazz. Just look at the magnificent views from up here," says Mia.

I lay the blanket down onto four green bales of hay and we both sit down at precisely the same time.

"I absolutely adore this spot," I tell Mia.

"Me too. I always feel free, and any troubles I seem to have on my mind, quickly evaporate into thin air," she replies, with a warm smile.

I gaze over in the distance and smile, as I watch Breeze trot around the field after his beloved Blossom.

"I hope you don't mind me asking. Please feel free to say no, if it makes you feel uncomfortable, but I'm just curious to know what happened with you and Jamie," I ask softly, continuing to look straight ahead.

"Well, Jazz. I always feel at ease confiding in you; I trust you not to breathe a word to anyone. In the early days, as you know, I really enjoyed his company, but then one evening, just over three weeks ago and completely on the spur of the moment, we decided to go to the cinema. We had a very enjoyable evening and decided to pop back to his house for a drink like we often did before he drove me home. Of course, what he hadn't had the decency to tell me prior to this, was that his house was completely empty. His parents had jetted off to Florida the day before," she says, as she releases a huge sigh.

"That was a bit naughty of him," I reply.

"Anyway, we were standing in the kitchen, just chatting about normal things, when Jamie suddenly threw himself at me and forcefully kissed me. I hated every second of it and was finding it difficult to breathe. I tried to wriggle free, but he held me harshly and firmly. His stubble scratched and rubbed roughly against my face. I tried to beg him to stop, but the words refused to come out. I was frozen to the spot and felt completely helpless," she continues.

"Oh, Mia, I'm, so sorry. What a scumbag!" Suddenly, I feel angry and strangely sorrowful that I hadn't been at her side to protect her from this monster.

"Hold on, I haven't told you the rest of the story yet. He kept muttering something about seeing me kiss a girlfriend at Uni and that I needed a real man to show me exactly what I was missing. The next thing I knew, he grabbed hold of my right hand and forced it deeply down inside his trousers whilst holding my left arm in a tight lock behind his back. I was mortified. He pushed and rubbed my hand all around his hard, throbbing penis," she says, whilst pausing to take a breath.

I gasp and hold my hands across my face in horror, watching her closely, still not quite believing what she's telling me.

She takes another deep breath and composes herself before continuing. "I felt sick to my stomach but determined to fight him off. I miraculously managed to gather every single ounce of strength I had left and eventually yanked my hand free from the horror of his trousers. I was completely hysterical when I noticed my hand was covered in this horrible white, warm sort of juice and I totally freaked out. I was so angry, I punched him meaningful on his chin with my right hand. The shock of the punch made him release my left hand and I immediately bolted towards the bathroom trying to control my shaking hands as I fumbled to lock the door behind me. I scrubbed my hands trying to remove the disgusting juice, whilst puking up at the same time."

I feel mortified for her. I watch her beautiful face as it scrunches up tightly at the awful memories, and I notice tears start to well up in her eyes. "Oh, Mia. I'm truly sorry you had to go through something so traumatic. It is unacceptable and unforgivable what he did to you. I would love to get my hands on that little piece of shit," I tell her angrily.

Mia lowers her head. I slowly move closer and gently place my right arm over her shoulder to comfort her. I fight with myself from wanting to wrap both my arms tightly around her, to hold her close and keep her safe.

"How did you manage to escape?" I ask her, in a soft soothing voice.

"Jamie kept banging on the door telling me how sorry he was.

He said he hadn't a clue what had come over him. I think that is the reason why I was completely shocked, as his behaviour was totally out of character. We had kissed a few times over the last couple of years, but nothing beyond that. Anyway, thankfully I still had my phone in my trouser pocket. Still shaking like a leaf, I called Mum. Fortunately, she answered straight away and told me to stay where I was, as she was on her way to get me. It wasn't too long before she arrived, maybe ten minutes or so. She patiently and repeatedly asked me to unlock the bathroom door, and I cannot tell you how relieved I was to hear her voice. I eventually managed to unlock the door, and when she saw the state I was in, bleary mascara eyes, a tear-stained face, she instantly wrapped her arms tightly around me. With my head hung low, she guided me outside to the car. I heard Jamie's voice calling over and over again, how sorry he was. Mum kept herself calm and composed until I was safely in the car. I watched through the raindrops pattering against the car window, as she strode over towards Jamie like she was on some sort of mission. I had never seen her behave like this before. I couldn't hear what she was saying to him, but the next thing I saw, was Jamie flying through the air, landing flat out on the ground by the front door," she continues.

"Nice one," is all I can manage to say, as my right hand gently squeezes her shoulder.

"It took me a couple of days before I felt ready to tell Mum the whole story. I cannot tell you how wonderful and supportive she's been, Jazz," she says, lifting her head up to look at me.

"Oh, Mia. I wish you had told me all of this when it happened. I would have been here like a shot for you," I reply, looking deeply into her eyes.

"I know you would, Jazz, but I felt dirty and confused. It isn't the sort of thing you can explain over a text message, now is it?" she replies, holding my gaze.

Trying hard to stay focused, a burning sensation starts to flow into my cheeks and butterflies begin to flutter from deep within. I cannot control my feelings and emotions any longer. I slowly lean towards her and plant a kiss softly and tenderly onto her beautiful lips.

"Jazz, you won't believe how long I have waited for this moment," she says, her lips gently caressing mine.

This feels so right, but why do I feel guilty? I slowly pull back, feeling elated but also confused.

"Look, Jazz. We don't need to rush things. It has taken me a while to come to terms with how I feel, so it will take you time, too. Let's just have some fun and enjoy each other's company for now, with no pressure and no strings attached." Her face lightens up with a warm glow and her eyes start to sparkle once again.

I nod and smile at Mia. My stomach continues to summersault every single time I look into her hypnotising eyes, and an aching throb constantly pulsates, deep down below. *What is happening to me?*

Suddenly, Mia stands up. "If I tell you something, Jazz, will you promise not to laugh?" she enquires.

"I promise," I reply, feeling on top of the world.

"That very night after that incident with Jamie, I woke up dripping in sweat at three in the morning. I was having such an awful dream, honestly it seemed so real. Everything I had gone through, must have been playing on my mind. I had been worried I could be pregnant, what with all that white stuff he disgustingly ejaculated all over my hand," she confessed, with a straight face.

'Did Mia really just say that?' I question myself, as I start to laugh out loud.

"You promised not to laugh! Such a ridiculous dream to have," she replies, joining in with my laughter. "Do you know what? Later in my dream, I even dressed in a disguise and drove to a chemist ten miles from here to buy a pregnancy test, just in case someone recognised me," Mia continues.

I cannot control myself any longer. I am in hysterics, tears rolling down my face, as I bend over holding my ribs tightly.

"I kept telling myself over and over again, that I had got an A plus in biology and not to be so stupid. I cannot tell you how real it all seemed," she replies in between her giggles.

"Oh, Mia. I can't tell you how fabulous it's to see you laugh like this again," I tell her, in between my howls of laughter.

"I agree, Jazz, I'd forgotten what it was like to laugh like this. I'm surprised you haven't come out with any of your sarcastic, and funny one-liners yet," she grins.

"I didn't want to appear insensitive," I grin.

"Go for it," she encourages me.

"Ok, hang on, let me think. Here we go. The carpenter asked me if he could bang me with his hammer, I told him to get screwed. The fisherman asked me if I would like to see his tackle! I hit him with his rod. The footballer asked me if he could dribble his balls all over me, I gave him a red card. I met a lovely electrician, there was a definite spark between us," I reel off.

"Oh, stop it, stop it," Mia screeches, bending over holding her ribs, howling with laughter, as the tears roll down her cheeks.

"What on earth are you two laughing about? I can hear you from all the way down here," calls out Aunty, looking up at the pair of us, from thirty feet below.

"Just girlie things," Mia manages to call back, trying desperately to control her laughter.

"Don't forget your lesson at two," she waves, before heading off in the direction of the house.

"See you then," I shout back.

"That was just the tonic I needed. Thank you so much, Jazz," Mia gleams.

"My pleasure entirely, always happy to oblige," I grin back.

"Come on. I'm thirsty," she says. She holds out her right hand to help me up.

A bolt of electricity shoots directly from her hand soaring throughout every part of my body. I look into her eyes and I can tell she has felt it too. I gasp sharply, as we stand in silence under a magical spell, her hand still holding mine. Looking deeply into her longing eyes, I slowly lean forward to kiss her gently on her soft awaiting lips. She responds immediately to my urgings, and her lips gently caress mine. *I never ever want this moment to end. I cannot tell you how amazing and perfect this feels. Those guilty feelings I have fought with for all these months, have finally vanished. This feels right.*

Mia reluctantly pulls away from me, but her grin is enough to tell me she enjoyed our precious moment, too. "Come on, I'll race you down," she says, grabbing hold of the blanket, before hurriedly clambering down the bales.

"You cheat," I call after her, as I race to catch up.

"I won," she proudly announces with a cheeky grin, that makes my heart skip a beat.

I stop and stare at her in awe. How stunningly beautiful she looks standing with her hands firmly on her hips. My eyes slowly wander to her breasts. Her nipples look firm and erect through her thin white vest top. A wonderful surge of fluttering and pulsating starts to rumble from, deep down below. This is a new and pleasurable feeling. I have not got a clue what it is, or what it means, but I'm certainly enjoying the sensation and don't want it to go away.

"You ok?" Mia asks me.

"Oh, yes, I'm more than ok," I grin back.

"Come on. I'll race you to the house," she calls, before heading off at the speed of lightning.

I stand still, taking in what just happened. *It feels so right when*

I'm with Mia, but why then did I have those feelings for Mr Sharp? Still feeling slightly confused, but weirdly on cloud nine, I pull myself together and set off in hot pursuit of my gorgeous, Mia.

Chapter 7

"Jasmine, Mia, are you both ready?" bellows Aunty from across the sand school.

I turn and smile at Mia, her face is aglow, as she grins back at me. *That smile again. It is enough to drive me crazy.* I momentarily have a flashback to our first wonderful and passionate kiss this morning.

Mia looks like a professional rider, and seeing her dressed in her cream jodhpurs, brown chaps, short brown riding boots and body protector has made my blood pressure instantly rise. Ebony her pure black ex-racehorse who stands at sixteen hands, looks truly magnificent too. Her perfectly groomed mane with tiny strands of stunning auburn flecks peering through, sits perfectly against her gleaming arched neck. Her long flowing tail swishes to the left and to the right, as she attempts to get rid of a nuisance fly.

Breeze feels calm and relaxed beneath me. His muscular frame looking solid and strong against Ebony's slender body.

"Hey boy, we're going to try some more dressage moves.

Is that ok with you?" I ask him, gently patting his neck. He turns his head and licks my left jodhpur boot, making me giggle.

"I want your full attention and complete focus today," calls Aunty, bringing me back to the present moment.

I immediately sit up and move deeper into my saddle, with my shoulders back and my hands relaxed.

"First, I want you to do some gentle exercise to prepare your mounts for their forthcoming lesson. This is very important. Like all athletes, they too need to warm up. As you both should be aware by now, attempting to do any serious training without following the right procedure can have an adverse effect on your horse's well-being. Pulled or strained muscles can take weeks to heal. Mia, can you and Ebony please take the lead? Jasmine, I want you and Breeze to follow closely behind. Start with two full circuits of walk, followed by three complete circuits of sitting trot, and make sure they are at least a twenty-metre radius. Remember to breathe, and I want to see loose reins with you both sitting deep and relaxed into your saddles. Be at one with your horse," Aunty instructs.

Breeze and I follow closely behind Mia and Ebony. The golden sand beneath his strong legs feels soft and light, as he strides out beautifully. "Good boy," I praise him.

"Nice work," calls Aunty, as she moves in closer.

I watch closely as Mia asks Ebony to trot, her beautiful body sits deep and perfectly into her saddle. Sheer poetry in motion. I momentarily lose my concentration. *It's a good job Mia's wearing that body protector. I'm not sure I would be able to cope, let alone concentrate if I caught a glimpse of her incredible breasts bobbing up and down. Although what a wonderful sight that would be.*

"Jasmine, now please focus. Sit deeper into your saddle.

That's better," she says, as I eventually pull myself back together.

"As you are both aware, it is important to work on your horse's basic gaits. Walk, trot and canter, going forward and being consistent is an essential part of dressage. When you take part in dressage competitions, you will need to demonstrate to the judge how you have mastered the various gaits. Forward transitions should be smooth and well balanced and you as the rider should be riding forward from your legs and your seat. I want to see minimal hand and rein contact at the same time. Your body will be what communicates your actions to your horse. Do you understand? Oh, and don't forget to smile," Aunty continues.

Mia and I nod at precisely the same time.

"Bring your mounts slowly to a halt," she commands.

I take a long deep breath, sit deep into my saddle and with minimum contact on my reins, Breeze comes to a perfect halt. I smile and gently pat him on his neck, as a thank you for listening to me.

"Lovely work, Jasmine. Bring Ebony one step forward, Mia, so she is standing square. Good, well done," beams Aunty. "Now tie up your reins," she instructs.

Mia and I immediately glance knowingly at one another with trepidation. Her beautiful smile sends glorious somersaults and quivers throughout my body and for a moment I cannot breathe. I fumble feebly, as I attempt to tie up my reins with slightly trembling hands.

"Now stand with your horses over there by the far corner," she demands whilst pointing her finger to the right, as she walks alongside us.

"One very important thing you must always remember in dressage, is that coordination is a must. Transitions need to be prompt and occur at the exact moment you wish to change the gait. Mia, you can go first. I want you to ask Ebony to gently walk forward and keep your hands very still on the top of your legs," she continues.

My cheeks begin to glow with pride, as I watch the two of them in action.

"Beautiful, Mia. Now gently squeeze her into a trot and sit deep into your saddle. Fantastic, you are looking great. Relax your legs away from her body," she continues.

I watch in amazement as Ebony effortlessly responds to Mia's body and slows to a perfect walk.

"Excellent, now turn around. I want you to repeat what you have just done, this time riding directly towards Jasmine. Remember to get your horse going forward in front of your leg. Sit deep into your saddle and trot. Beautiful. Now relax and take a deep breath," she continues.

Watching Mia trot towards me, with a huge grin on her face is causing my hormones to go utterly crazy. More worryingly, I seem to have lost all control of my inner emotions.

"And trot, one, two, three, four, five, six. Relax, take a deep breath and slowly release it out," instructs Aunty.

Ebony immediately slows to a walk, and eventually comes to a perfect square halt. Mia's leans over Ebony's neck to give her a well-deserved hug. Her face is a picture of delight.

I gasp, as Mia slowly turns her head towards me, and gives me a naughty wink, thankfully well out of Aunty's vision.

"Top performance, Mia. Well done, you. Now untie your reins, dismount, loosen off your girth and let Ebony have a well-deserved rest. Now, I will give you a few classroom pointers to remember, and after that, you and Breeze can show me what you are capable of, Jasmine," announces a very happy looking Aunty.

As Aunty starts to talk, I only vaguely hear her words. Like a magnetic force my eyes are drawn directly across to Mia. I sigh, watching her slender body, carefully dismount from the saddle. Her beautiful backside looking at me invitingly, as she slowly lowers herself to the ground.

"It's important to know your dressage test by heart. You need to memorise the figures and movements you will be performing. Personally, I find it easier when I close my eyes and visualise myself riding Sasha through every single stride of our test over and over again, until I know it off by heart," I can hear Aunty vaguely saying.

"Now this is just unbearable, Mia, you are driving me mad," I mutter to myself, not realising I've spoken my words out loud.

Mia giggles.

"Jasmine, are you listening to what I'm saying?" Aunty asks.

"Erm, yes, of course I am, Aunty. You were saying we need to visualise the breasts, oops, I mean test," I stutter, not completing quite believing what I just said.

Mia is having an uncontrollable fit of giggles, and I feel blood instantly rush up into my cheeks.

Chapter 8

I glance out of the corner of my eye, as Mia very slowly and suggestively unclasps the Velcro fastenings on her body protector.

"It's important to practice any difficult transitions at home until you have completely perfected them. Do not be tempted to run before you can walk, so to speak," I vaguely hear Aunty say.

Mia is certainly keeping me in suspense. I try to keep one eye on Aunty and the other on Mia. I watch in a trance as Mia seductively lifts the body protector over her head, revealing her perfect, slender body. Her succulent breasts sitting perfectly and firmly inside her vest stop. Her raised nipples longing for my tongue to gently caress them.

"Here are some wonderful tips to remember, ladies," she continues, completely ignoring my little misunderstanding.

"Yes, I agree, truly wonderful tits," I mutter once again. *'What on earth is happening to me?'* I ask myself, as that wondrous warm and pulsating feeling magically reappears below. I cannot help myself from shuffling uncomfortably around in my saddle.

"Jasmine, are you ok?" Aunty asks, looking slightly concerned for a moment.

I dare not look at Mia, although I can sense her beautiful fixating eyes burning directly into me. "Just a bit of cramp, Aunty," I manage to say, whilst clearing my throat.

"Ok, we had better get you moving then, hadn't we? Time for you to shine and show me what that college has taught you to date," says Aunty, looking directly at me and Breeze.

As Mia walks past me leading Ebony, she gently squeezes my hand and the naughty twinkle in her striking green eyes, the smile that lights up the whole of her face, leaves my heart aching with desire. I am on fire.

Taking a deep breath, I close my eyes tightly trying hard to focus on the task ahead, as I patiently wait for the electric tremors to subside.

"Jasmine, the pair of you look great. Remember, keep your hands soft on your legs, sit deep and walk forward. Look straight ahead; your body needs to point in the direction you wish to go. Right off you go. Now trot. One, two, three, four. Sit deep, five, six, seven, eight. Now take a deep breath and relax those legs. Beautiful, well done," she beams.

I feel completely at one with Breeze, and he responds effortlessly to every single aid I give, just using my body alongside breathing techniques. A completely different horse, one who only four years ago wouldn't hesitate in throwing me off at any chance he got.

Breeze comes to a perfect halt. I sit deep and calm in my saddle looking directly between his golden ears, which are pricked and alert.

"Top job," beams Aunty, as Mia starts to applaud.

I feel on cloud nine. I mockingly take a bow as my eyes meet, Mia's. I move higher onto cloud ten, if that even exists.

"Jasmine, untie your reins, dismount, loosen your girth and let

Breeze have some time to relax and wind down," she instructs.

I do as she asks, and within moments I find my myself standing closely next to Mia. I'm just inches away from her, but I can feel the chemistry flowing deeply between the two of us.

"How about I give you a few more helpful tips, and then afterwards, I could pop off and get Sasha tacked up. Maybe we could hack down to the beach for an hour or so? I'm also more than happy to give you both another lesson around the same time tomorrow, if you feel that would help? I could even set up a few jumps," says Aunty.

Immediately, Mia and I turn to look at each other. Our eyes instantly lock, and I smile as the whole of her face starts to light up and my heart fills with instant warmth and joy.

"I'll take that as a yes then," says Aunty, before continuing.

I try to focus once again. Such awesome news knowing Mia and I will be spending more time together today. Bring on the beach ride.

"Like with anything you do in life, commitment and practice is the only way to improve your transitions. The key is to repeat, repeat, repeat. When you want your horse to turn, just pull up your waist slightly from the saddle and remember to turn your hips in the direction you want to go. Push your hips straight. The more you practice, the more your horse will respond without any hesitation at all. He will be able to feel your body and know exactly what your body movements require of him. Eventually, you should be able to pivot your hips very slightly and he will respond. Remember, gentle pressure with your inside leg from your seat bone. Release your outside leg whilst turning your hips and you will get there. I think you've both performed brilliantly today, so we shall end this session on a good note. I'll see you at the front of the yard in approximately fifteen minutes," says Aunty, before turning to head out of the school.

I wait until the coast is clear and slowly turn to face Mia.

Without any hesitation or prompting, she moves in slow motion towards me tenderly cupping her right hand under my chin.

I stand motionless, as her lips delicately brush mine, and the yearning I feel inside is indescribable.

Mia slowly pulls away and the loving smile she gives me, instantly warms my heart.

"Mia, I have never felt this way before. I'm totally infatuated with you in every single way," I tell her softly.

"Jazz, I know exactly how you feel. It took me quite a long time to accept the sexual feelings I was forever experiencing were not wrong in any way. I no longer needed to hide them away. Like I said earlier, there is no rush or pressure. Let's just take things slowly and go with the flow. I want us to enjoy every single precious moment we spend together. I want you to give yourself time to know for certain the feelings and emotions you are craving are the right ones for you and only you," her voice tranquil, yet sexy.

I look at her in wonderment. She completely understands the turmoil my body is presently going through, as she has been through precisely the same. I appreciate her patience, openness, and most of all her honesty. "Thanks, Mia. Your words mean a lot to me and make perfect sense. I feel so much lighter being able to talk to you about how I've been feeling, knowing that you completely understand. I can now get rid of those guilty thoughts I've been punishing myself with for so long. You're right, let's have some fun, go with the flow and enjoy our time together. After all, we do have one whole week to explore our feelings more," I tell her lovingly, as I lean forward, unable to stop my lips from firmly touching hers.

"Oh, Jazz. I want your lips to stay on mine forever, but unfortunately we only have five minutes to grab a quick drink, before your Aunty will be on our case." Our lips reluctantly part. She looks down at her watch with a cheeky smile, and suddenly I feel her left hand gently tap my backside.

Oh Lordy! Those wonderful sensations promptly flare up once again.

Chapter 9

Feeling happy and content, the three of us ride side by side through the picturesque village of Bacton. The sun glistens brightly through the leafy green trees, and a few locals tending the prized gardens of their quaint little cottages, acknowledge us with a smile and a wave.

"Even though this is classed as a small village, believe it or not the glorious sandy beach attracts numerous holiday makers and tourists from all over the country. Although there is limited accommodation available, since the static caravan site opened four years ago, the population has dramatically increased. We will ride through the magnificent Bacton woods and across the other side to the glorious village of Ferton. At the far end, lies a magnificent golden sandy beach which runs for just over three miles. Thankfully not many people apart from the locals know it exists, so it should be exceptionally quiet for us to ride on at this time of day," Aunty explains.

I glance across at Mia and a smile instantly lights up on her face.

"How is University going, Mia?" asks Aunty, as we pull over into a layby to allow a car to drive past.

"It's going very well thank you. I'm already registered with the *Health and Care Professions Council* and fingers crossed, I should pass year two of my paramedic science grade by the end of next month," she replies.

I visualise Mia's perfect body dressed in her paramedic uniform and those naughty feelings begin to stir.

"What happens after this?" enquires Aunty.

"Well, with it being my final year in September, I'll be attending a lot more placements with the local ambulance service. Once I have finally completed my three-year course, I shall then apply to various local Trusts to see what vacancies are available. I'm really looking forward to being a fully pledged paramedic by the time I'm twenty-two," grins Mia.

"Such a worthwhile career, Mia. You will be helping so many humans along the way and more importantly, saving a huge number of lives. I must say, it has been not only an honour, but a joy for me to watch you grow up from the age of seven into the beautiful and clever lady you have turned into today. I'm very proud of you," replies Aunty.

Glancing across at Mia, her porcelain cheeks glow red from Aunty's recent compliment and I suddenly feel very proud of her too.

"I do feel pretty proud when I wear my uniform," Mia confesses, with a warm caring smile on her face.

"And so, you should, Mia. None of us can do without any of the emergency services. It's such a wonderful career path for you to be on," I say.

"Thanks, Jazz. You should be proud of what you are on your way to achieving, too. I can see you being a very important member of the *British Equestrian Olympic Team,* just like you've always dreamt of," she replies in a soft tender voice, which sets my pulse racing.

The shadiness of the woods brings my attention back to the present moment. I look up at the numerous Corsican pine trees that soar high up in the sky, as the late afternoon sunshine tries to break through their magnificent twisted and majestic branches. Breeze makes a little snort. The fragrance from the wildflowers must be starting to irritate his nostrils. I slowly stroke his silky warm neck in reassurance.

"Who fancies a little canter?" calls Aunty from the front.

"Oh yes," I call out, as Mia shouts, "Bring it on." I squeeze my legs gently against Breeze's sides, and slowly shorten my reins. He immediately responds performing a perfect and well-balanced trot. I sit deeper and with one more squeeze, we effortlessly glide along the wonderous woodland path. The gentle breeze rushes across my cheeks. I feel elated as we soar along the track the two of us connected as one. Not too far ahead, I notice Mia and Ebony cantering along beautifully. Ebony resembles a rocking horse, whilst Mia barely moves in the saddle. I can't help but grin, as I slowly look around at our wonderful surroundings.

"Pulling up," bellows Aunty.

Breeze instantly responds to my body aids and within seconds we are back to a slow and relaxing walk. I urge Breeze to move upside Ebony.

"Isn't it just magical here?" asks Mia

"It's truly stunning, Mia, just like you," I whisper, our eyes slowly meeting once again.

We both start to giggle. "I think I need a cold shower," she says.

"What's so funny?" enquires Aunty, turning to look at us with one eyebrow raised.

I feel my cheeks start to redden.

Mia quickly replies, "We were just talking about that time when Breeze threw off Jazz and she ended up face down in a random water trough."

"Oh yes. I remember your Mum telling me about that little episode. By the sounds of it, you did a grand job in managing to keep hold of your reins," Aunty laughs.

"I was totally embarrassed and felt truly sorry for the couple of hitchhikers who witnessed the whole incident. I'll never forget the shock on their faces. They observed my predicament from a distance, obviously not quite sure what they could do to help. Although I must say, their faces were a real treat when I eventually managed to free myself from that dirty old trough. I remember standing there feeling completely deflated, as the green stagnant water, strands of rotten hay and numerous dead flies covered my face and chest. I must have looked like a zombie from a horror movie," I reply, wrinkling up my face, at the humiliating memory I would rather forget.

Aunty and Mia cannot control their fits of laughter. It quickly becomes infectious, and it isn't too long before I join in, too.

Aunty is the first one to compose herself, softly clearing her throat, "Did you know there are over thirty species of trees living here and numerous wildlife that hide away in the depths of this woodland?"

"Isn't it owned by the Forestry Commission?" asks Mia.

"Spot on. Can you believe Barton woods proudly stands on just over eighty acres of land and is a well-known haven for many rare birds and plants, too? Word even has it, there's an ancient burial ground, and a pond hidden somewhere deep within, although I haven't actually seen them myself," she continues.

"I'm not quite sure I'd be brave enough to venture out here in the dark. Maybe it's haunted?" I reply, as my eyes fix firmly on a fluffy grey squirrel scuttering at great speed up a tree just to the right-hand side of Aunty.

Sasha jumps slightly to the left in surprise, as Aunty sits seemingly motionless.

I watch smiling, as she gently pats her enchanting grey mare, who immediately settles back down.

Sasha stands at an impressive sixteen two hands high. She is a beautiful specimen of a horse, a Thoroughbred cross, with a powerful and solid frame. Her legs are thick and strong, her white mane flows like that of a unicorn, resembling something out of a fairy tale, fit for any Princess to ride.

I run my tongue slowly around my lips, as the taste of salt suddenly appears. We must be getting very close to the beach. I notice Mia closely watching the gentle movement of my tongue and she very naughtily winks at me. I start to glow once again.

Chapter 10

Breeze comes to a sudden halt, as Sasha and Ebony join suit. With my eyes completely transfixed, I stare ahead in awe at the endless blue ocean. It entwines miraculously with the deep blue sky, miles away into the distance. I watch totally mesmerised. The rays from the late afternoon sun, dance on the top of the flowing waves, as they gently push the sea water slowly and softly back onto the glorious grains of sand which lies like a magical and endless golden carpet.

"I'll never tire of this breath-taking view," says Aunty, letting out a huge sigh, her voice momentarily spoiling this perfect and tranquil moment.

"I can't remember the last time I saw anything so beautiful," says Mia, slowly turning her head towards me, looking inquisitively into my eyes, her eyebrows raised with an extremely warm smile.

A ripple of tiny tremors set off in readiness from deep within, as the excitement shining in her captivating eyes instantly sets my pulse racing.

"Me neither," answers Aunty, totally oblivious to the special moment Mia and I are now sharing. "Who would like a paddle in the sea?"

"Y-ye-yes," I stutter, still gazing longingly at the beautifulness of Mia.

Mia's dreamy smile gradually turns into a grin, and at this precise moment I would give anything to feel her lips firmly caressing mine.

The sexual longing every part of me has ached for over the last few hours is growing stronger by the moment. It's taken me completely by surprise, a feeling I never could have imagined experiencing.

Once again, I try hard to clear the amorous thoughts propelling through my mind.

Breeze carries me across the endless carpet of golden sand. This is just perfect. It feels like we are marooned on a dessert Island, not another human or animal to be seen. *I would love to be trapped on a desert Island with Mia.* I picture the two of us lying naked, gently caressing, and exploring every single inch of each other's bodies.

"You look as though you're deep in your own little dreamworld, Jasmine?" I suddenly hear Aunty's voice enquire.

Feeling flushed and thankful she is unable to read my mind, I quickly reply, "You're right. I was dreaming about the three of us cantering along this heavenly beach." *Great recovery, Jazz.* I need to be extra careful with what I say in front of Aunty. She is far from daft. It would be very rare indeed if she misses anything which is going on directly under her nose.

"Well, Mia, what do you think? Can we make Jasmine's dream come true?" says Aunty with a grin.

Mia eagerly nods in agreement and I watch closely as Aunty moves Sasha forward to a trot, closely followed by Mia and Amber.

"Are you ready, boy?" I ask him, before turning him around to face the others.

Breeze immediately responds and within a couple of seconds, the two of us find ourselves cantering over the rich surface of the desert looking sand beneath us. This feeling is second to none. The freedom, the wind blowing through Breeze's striking white mane can only be described as pure ecstasy. The sound of his hooves striding across the gold-plated carpet below, and the nearby waves gently crashing against the shoreline, is a moment I will treasure forever. Reluctantly, I gently ease him down to a trot, as we pull up alongside Mia and Amber.

"How exhilarating was that?" she asks, catching her breath.

Her cheeks glow with joy. I resist the deep wanting to lean towards her to kiss her tenderly on the lips. Once again, our eyes lock, and for an instant it feels like the rest of the world doesn't exist. The pulsating and throbbing, deep down below, are enough to drive me to despair.

"Shall we go for a splash and a cool down in the sea?" asks Aunty, interrupting our moment.

I think you need a good cooling down in certain areas, don't you, Jazz?

"You'd like that my boy, wouldn't you?" I ask Breeze, who nods his head up and down in response, as I shuffle slightly uncomfortable around in my saddle. The texture beneath us gradually starts to change, as we head towards the tranquil and calmness of the sea. I smile, as the foamy froth of the waves slowly melt before my eyes, completely disappearing out of sight. The powerful, and endless miles of deep blue water seductively invite me towards it.

Breeze snorts at the coldness of the first incoming waves touching his front hooves. He bravely walks forward, as the cold sea spray gets to work attaching itself to any exposed skin on my body. My arms, my neck, my cheeks feel moist and damp. '*A bit like, deep down below,*' I think with a grin. Breeze and I stand in silence taking in another wonderous moment. Very slowly, I close my eyes to take in a deep and relaxing breath. The sound of the waves gently splashing all around has an instant calming and therapeutic effect on my soul.

"Hey, Jazz," I hear Mia's soft voice. I open my eyes to see her and Ebony right by my side. Her left leg brushes against my right one and a sudden bolt of chemical electricity races through my veins. I watch, as Mia turns her head away and I quickly look in the direction of where she is glancing.

Aunty is facing the other way, around twenty feet away from us with Sasha looking to be having an awesome time splashing and pawing her front foreleg into the delightful blue sea.

Instantly, I feel Mia's lips burning against mine. I immediately respond with no hesitation at all. Her tongue seductively teases the underside of mine. I am on fire. Eventually, and very reluctantly Mia drags her lips from mine, before quickly turning her head to check on Aunty's location.

No change. Sasha is still busy playing in the sea and Aunty seems oblivious to anything else around her, she looks to be happily locked away in her own little world.

Mia sighs with relief and smiles at me warmly. I take in every inch of her soft, tender skin, with an uncontrollable yearning and longing to want to kiss her once again. I casually touch her hand giving it a gentle squeeze. That smile, oh that stunning hypnotic smile is enough to send me completely crazy.

Our tender moment is interrupted as Breeze suddenly paws the water with his front off-fore, splashing droplets of sea water over Ebony and Mia. He continues to play around in the water, so I let him have his head, glancing quickly to see if Aunty is still turned the other away.

I grin, knowing the coast is now clear and lean slowly towards, Mia. Tenderly, my right finger caresses the top of her cheek bone moving teasingly down towards her luscious red lips. I momentarily hear her gasp, before she slowly wraps her right hand firmly around mine, guiding my finger down to her chin, the length of her slender neck and seductively down towards her breastbone. I close my eyes and let out a quiet moan with the softness of her skin. I feel her lips lightly caressing my cheek, as she holds my hand securely against her throbbing chest.

"Are you both ok?" Aunty calls from a distance.

I am unable to speak. The precious moment we have just shared has totally overwhelmed me.

"Yes, Trudy, we are fine, thank you. Jazz thought she had something in her eye, but I can't see anything," calls back Mia, smiling at me with a naughty wink.

"Probably a grain of sand, that's all. Don't worry, it'll work its own way out eventually. Make sure you don't rub it, Jasmine, or you'll make your eye sore," says Aunty, pulling up by the side of me and Breeze.

"It'll be fine," I tell her with a smile, turning my head slightly, so she doesn't notice my hot, flushed cheeks.

"I suppose, we ought to start heading back. I have one more lesson booked at seven o'clock and I bet the pair of you have got plenty of revision to do?" she asks.

"Yes, I suppose you're right. Unfortunately, I have a mountain of studying to get through, although I would rather stay here in this special and magical place," sighs Mia.

"I know how you feel. Every time I ride over here, any busy thoughts in my mind completely vanish and my body feels totally revitalised. Jasmine, now what are your plans for this evening?" enquires Aunty.

"Well, sadly, I too have revision to do, but maybe once you have finished your lesson, the two of us could sit down with a nice glass of something spicy and you can continue to explain what you need me to do with your social media pages?" I reply, with a naughty grin across my face, raising one eyebrow at the same time.

Aunty snorts and giggles, whilst Mia looks at us both enquiringly.

"Sounds like a plan," Aunty blurts out with a nod and a wink.

Chapter 11

"There we go, my boy," I tell Breeze, releasing him into the field so he can continue his flirting with his beloved Blossom. I stand leaning over the post and rail watching the two of them cavorting around, although to be honest my head is completely elsewhere. It's full to bursting with red hot naughty thoughts of Mia. Suddenly, I feel heated breath against my right ear and shivers instantly run throughout my body.

"I wondered where you'd got to," whispers Mia, in a low and sultry voice, gently nibbling my ear.

"Mia, you're driving me crazy," I reply, gasping in delight. I throw my head back in ecstasy. Her lips caress me slowly, yet purposely, as they make their way down the nape of my neck, her tongue circling and teasing me seductively. My body is on fire. Goosebumps start to appear over every part of my body, making the hair on my arms stand upright. My stomach is revelling in the somersaults it's performing, and that deep pulsating feeling has returned, deep down below.

"Does this feel good?" she asks.

Her lips gently begin to smother mine, and I moan in delight. "Please, don't stop," I manage to plead, holding her beautiful face, as we kiss in the most sensual way imaginable.

"I'm just off to teach my lesson now. I've left your dinner in the oven on low, Jasmine, so it'll be ready when you are," we hear Aunty shout. "Are you both ok?"

"Don't you worry, Trudy, we're fine. I was just checking Jazz's eye again. It still seems to be irritating her slightly," Mia swiftly calls back.

"Try washing it out will cold water, Jasmine. You should know this, Mia, being a trainee paramedic and all," she calls back laughing.

"I've got to dash. I'll see you later, Jasmine, and you tomorrow, Mia. Happy studying," she waves.

"Wow, now that is what I call a close call," I say, finally letting out a long deep breath. I look up to see Mia grinning naughtily at me.

"Naughty, but very nice," she drools.

"Jazz, I can't bear the thought of leaving you, but I do have to get home," she says sadly.

My body begins to ache and cry out for her magical touch to return. "No, Mia. I want you to stay where you are and continue to seduce me until you drive me to over the edge," I reply, in a soft alluring voice.

"Me, too, babe," she murmurs back.

She just called me babe. Now, I like the sound of that.

"We have plenty of time. If we take things slowly, the build up to what I have eventually got planned for the two of us, will not only be well worth the wait, but truly mind blowing too. Trust me," she assures me, with a rather wicked glint in her eyes.

I quickly check no one is around before leaning in for one last kiss. "Bring it on."

"Oh, my gorgeous, Jazz. You know how crazy I am about you, don't you?" she asks in a soft and tender voice, looking deep down into my eyes, one hand slowly running through my long blonde hair.

"I certainly do, and I think you know I feel the same. I just hate the thought of us being apart," I reply sadly.

"Me, too. Look, I really need to dash, but I promise, I'll message you later. Missing you already," she says, giving me one last kiss on the lips, before disappearing out of sight.

I stand and let out a long sigh, as I slowly walk along the pathway towards the house. My head is spinning with so many wild thoughts. My body aches and yearns for Mia's touch, so much so, it hurts.

Sitting on the cosy beige sofa with a well-deserved gin and tonic, I look at the pile of theory pages I should be concentrating on, but they continue to stare back at me blankly. Momentarily, I close my eyes and a fabulous image of Mia appears before me. Her smile, her beautiful long silky black hair, her perfectly shaped nose, her come to bed eyes, her heavenly breasts, the list is endless. I let out a sigh, and open my eyes, as I hear a door closing in the distance.

"There you are. How's the studying going? I see you've already made a start on the gin. Nice one," laughs Aunty, as she stands towering over me.

"Very slowly," I reply, taking a sip of my gin and raise my glass.

"What a day. Let me grab a bottle of red. If you don't mind, I'd love to come and join you, that's if I'm not interrupting you?" she asks.

"Oh yes, please do. To be honest, I'm finding it hard to concentrate on anything at all. It'll do my brain good to shut off and just chill out for a while," I sigh.

My phone beeps, and I lift it up to read the message, *'I can't wait to feel your lips firmly on mine tomorrow babe. Sweet dreams, missing you xx'*

I smile warmly and reply, *'I feel so lost and empty without you. When I'm all alone in bed later, my only thoughts will be of you lying naked beside me, imagining your lips slowly caressing mine. My dreams may be very hot and steamy later. Miss you too xx'*

'I don't want you getting hot and steamy without me, so behave yourself! Counting the hours till I see you,' replies Mia.

I chuckle.

"You look a lot happier. Is there anything you want to tell me?" asks Aunty, sitting opposite me in her armchair with a large glass of red.

I feel my cheeks start to redden, as she holds her crystal glass up into the air.

"Cheers," she salutes, before taking a very large swig of wine. "Anyway, first things first. You haven't told me if you have someone special in your life. Is there anyone I should know about?" she queries, with one eyebrow raised.

I move my eyes down to my glass, trying hard to avoid her gaze and think carefully before I reply. "To be honest, I'm going through a bit of a confusing stage. I feel mixed up and sometimes guilty about some of the thoughts I have," I confess.

"Jasmine, you can confide in me at any time, you know that don't you? Blimey, I've confessed some of my innermost and naughty secrets to you," she replies, her glass already beginning to look half empty.

"You mean there's more to tell? You still haven't finished telling me the rest of your story about, Ruby, now have you?" I question, with a naughty grin on my face, trying to change the subject.

"Believe you me, I have many, many more stories to tell you. I bet some would even make your toes curl," she replies laughing, as a nice warm glow starts to form on her cheeks.

"Come on Aunty, please finish telling me about, Ruby," I plead, watching her top up the empty wine glass.

"Are you really sure you want to know?"

"Yes."

Chapter 12

"I can't even remember where we got to," Aunty says, taking another large gulp of her wine.

"It was just after you'd stopped choking on your glass of water. Ruby had then wrapped her arms around your waist."

I watch Aunty closely. Her face looks to soften, as a dreamy look appears.

"Oh yes, what a great memory you have. How could I forget!" she grins. "I can tell you now, my body was in a state of hunger and wanting for this stunning lady who had managed to somehow set my body alight."

Very slowly, still firmly holding my right hand, she guided me across to the awaiting deep pile rug which sat invitingly in front of the roaring fire. It was like I'd been hypnotised. I watched her, feeling totally besotted, as she pulled two cushions from the sofa and took hold of the throw. She walked slowly towards me, not taking her eyes off mine, as she laid the two cushions at the top of the rug and placed the throw down by her side. She then knelt down in front of me, her sparkling blue eyes looking deeply into mine.

"I remember gasping in ecstasy, as she slowly kissed my neck, her teeth gently nibbling at my skin, as her lips caressed me in a way I had never experienced before," she continues, as she slowly releases a huge breath.

I await eagerly for the next account, as she takes another mouthful of wine. I sip at my gin and tonic. A clear and wonderous vision of Mia is firmly imprinted in my mind.

"She asked me to lay down on the rug."

"Let me take you to a magical place, somewhere you have never ever been before," she told me in a low sexy voice.

I was truly captivated and without any hesitation at all, I immediately obliged. I was in heaven, as I laid down on the soft deep pile rug which felt warm, inviting and cosy. Her eyes focused back on mine, her long shiny black hair falling towards me, as she leaned downwards and began to kiss me tenderly once again. Her lips,

brushed the top of my forehead, very slowly making their way down
to my mouth, her tongue gently searching for mine. Never, had I felt
anything so sensual and sexy in the whole of my life.

"I sincerely hope these descriptive events aren't getting too much for you, Jasmine. Maybe a tad too much information?" Aunty suddenly asks.

"Don't be silly. We are both adults," I tell her in a positive voice, not wanting her to stop.

Her hands suddenly started to roam, as her kissing got more
intense. I closed my eyes tightly, I felt her lips leave mine and very
slowly she lifted my T-shirt up and over my head, her fingers lightly
brushing my stomach. The sensation I felt is indescribable. I
couldn't move and to be honest, I didn't want too. I could have
stayed in that magical moment, forever. I groaned with pleasure at
the way how she was making me feel, her lips gradually working
down my neck, to my chest, pausing whilst she slipped her hands
carefully under my back unclipping my bra with ease. Very slowly,
she pulled my arms gently through the straps before tossing my bra
across to the other end of the lounge. I moaned, as she cupped my
breasts softly in both hands, I heard her gasp too. She lowered her
head allowing her tongue to seductively circle the tip of my nipples.
I was putty in her hands and never wanted it to end.

She continued to caress my breasts with one hand, whilst the
other one unhurriedly made its way down to my thong. I remember
arching my back, pushing myself up towards her, as she teasingly
plucked at the slender straps before unhurriedly sliding my thong
down over my knees, past my ankles, eventually throwing it high into
the air in the same direction as my bra. I've no idea what came over
me, but I suddenly had the urge to do precisely the same to her. I
know she was taken completely by surprise by my sudden actions. I

slowly sat up and commanded her to lie down on the rug. She didn't even try to resist. Leaning over, I looked into her eyes whilst running my right hand lightly through her silky draping hair. My lips slowly, but hungrily caressed hers, whilst I took my time seductively removing her clothes and it wasn't too long before she was lying naked at my side. She moaned with delight, as my body gently laid on top of hers. The second our breasts touched, I had the most mind-blowing wanting for this stunning sexy lady to make love to me there and then. She must have read my mind.

"I'm sorry, Jasmine, but seriously, I cannot tell you anymore. You'll just have to use your imagination, although I can honestly say it was one of the most amazing and sexual experiences I have ever encountered," she finishes, with a faraway look in her eyes.

"Aunty, so why on earth did you go ahead and marry Uncle, if you felt this way about Ruby?" I ask, suddenly feeling sorry for her.

"Things were a lot different back then. No one ever talked about being in love with someone of the same sex. It was all a bit of a taboo subject," she replies.

"But that's so unfair. You always tell me to follow my heart, whatever the consequences," I gasp.

"I know, Jasmine, and that is only because I don't want you to go through what I did and regret for the rest of your life not following your heart," she says sadly.

"Oh Aunty, I really am so sorry. Did you fall in love with Ruby?" I ask.

"Oh yes, Jasmine, one hundred percent, but unfortunately the timing was all wrong. She was married and I was just eighteen, not really knowing what I wanted in life. As I reluctantly got dressed and ready to leave, she did ask me if we could see each other again. Very seductively, she slid her phone number into the front pocket of my jeans, whilst placing a pen and piece of paper right in front of me, whispering into my ear to scribble down mine. This might shock you, but it far from ended there. In fact, she messaged me the very next day. She told me what an amazing time she'd had and how would I fancy a repeat performance? She asked, if I'd like to pop around the following evening, as she had a very close friend visiting for a couple of days and thought I would thoroughly enjoy meeting her. I enquired about Gerald, but she told me not to worry about him, as he worked two hundred miles away during weekdays," she continues, before getting up to top up her glass.

"Oh my God. Did you go back to Ruby's?"

"I couldn't resist, but that's a story for another day," she replies, with a very wicked look across her face.

"Aunty, you are such a dark horse. I seriously cannot wait to hear all about your second visit. Do you love Uncle?" I suddenly blurt out.

"Gosh, Jasmine, of course I love him, but it was a completely different type of love I felt for Ruby. The love I felt for her was one of sexual longing and lust, although sadly, it is something I doubt I'll never experience again in my lifetime. Don't get me wrong, me and your Uncle tend to get along fine most of the time. It also helps, him working away for weeks at a time. I concentrate on my work and have the freedom to do whatever I want. Your Uncle gets on with his life and we're both happy with the way this works. Promise me now, you will never repeat any single thing I have confided in you to anyone? Even if they were to pin you down and torture you," she asks, with a giggle.

"Cross my heart, Aunty. I seriously can't wait for the next instalment of Ruby."

"When on earth did you grow up so fast?" she smiles.

"I haven't a clue," I grin back.

"Now what about you? What is happening in your love life?" she enquires, with a cheeky smile.

I start to feel the blood rush quickly into to my cheeks, just as Aunty's mobile phone rings loudly.

"Hold on one second. Speak of the devil, it looks like your Uncle's trying to call," she says, glancing down at her screen.

"Hello. Yes, we are both doing fine, thank you. Just hold on for one second," I hear her say, in a flat sounding voice.

"I'd better get some revision done before it gets too late," I tell her, feeling thankful for the perfect timing of Uncle's call.

"You haven't answered my question yet though?"

"I will do, another time. Night, night."

I blow her a kiss.

I toss and turn, thinking all about today's events with Mia, eventually managing to drift off into a deep and fulfilling dream.

Chapter 13

The sunlight trickles in through the half-closed blinds, as I slowly star to stir. My body feels damp and flushed, although I'm not at all surprised after the dream I just had. Lying still, with my eyes firmly closed, my mind quickly rewinds back to some of the naughty, but pleasurable moments.

Mia dressed in skin-tight black leather trousers, long boots, and a very revealing bodice had somehow managed to pin me down. She very slowly, but firmly moved my hands high above my head grasping them tightly in one of hers. She leaned forward, and I moaned in utter joy at the sight of her beautiful breasts, as they landed softly on top of mine. Her lips drove me crazy, teasingly nibbling every single part of my neck, gradually making her way downwards. I couldn't move, and to be honest I didn't want to. The look in her eyes was one of wanting and pure lust, the magical sensations flowing throughout my body drove me completely to oblivion. Her right hand very slowly and seductively moved between my legs. "Take me now Mia," I whispered.

The sudden urge to touch myself, deep down below takes me completely by surprise. My right hand without any prompting or guiding from me gradually slowly starts to move downwards to my thigh. '*Jazz. What on earth are you doing? Get a bloody grip,*' a voice suddenly shouts in my head. Sitting up quickly, I vigorously shake my head, before heading to the bathroom for a well needed cold shower. My sponge caresses every single part of my sticky body, and my thoughts start to run wildly once again. I imagine Mia's hand guiding the soapy sponge seductively across my breasts, and her other hand... *Jazz, are you turning into a sex maniac?*

I grin to myself, thinking how much I have changed in just over twenty-four hours. I decide to pull myself together, and hurriedly get dressed before rushing out to see my boy.

***

"Oh Breeze," I sigh, wrapping my arms tightly around his golden neck. "What the heck is happening to me?" He seems to understand my confusion, and gently wraps his head tighter into my back. I stay completely still, thoroughly enjoying the deep connection and true understanding we share. *This is priceless.* "Now my boy, we're going to be doing some jumping today. Are you up for showing Aunty and Mia how much we've improved?" I ask him. The sheer mention of Mia's name has sent spectacular tingles directly down my spine.

Breeze nods his head up and down my back in agreement, as I gently try to escape his head lock, before happily crunching away on the carrot I've just offered him.

I love the sound of horses crunching, it fascinates me, although to be honest if a human started crunching directly in front of me, I would want to bloody strangle them.

Breeze's crunching seems to have attracted Blossom's attention and she arrives at my right gazing lovingly in the hope she will get one, too. "How can I forget you, my little beauty?" She gratefully, but politely takes the carrot I offer. "Right, time for a shot or two of caffeine for me. I'll see you this afternoon," I tell them, before slowly making my way back to the house.

I enter the kitchen. "Well, there you are and a very good morning to you, sexy girlfriend," beams Mia.

Sexy girlfriend? Now, I like the sound of this. I turn around anxiously looking for Aunty, my cheeks instantly turning bright beetroot in colour.

Walking directly towards me with a beautiful loving smile on her face, Mia laughs. She slowly touches my cheek with her right hand, her lips touching mine feeling hungry and passionate. I

75

respond urgently, wrapping my arms tightly around her waist, my legs wobbling like jelly. I gasp, as her body touches mine. My hands slowly move upwards inside her vest top to touch her soft and silky skin. I feel her take a sharp intake of breath, as her lips caress my neck, her hand gently pulling my hair back, so she can move downwards towards my breastbone. The loud ringing from the house phone, rudely interrupts our magical moment. Very reluctantly, Mia eases herself away from me. "Damn it. I'd better get that Jazz, as your Aunt is busy teaching," she says, with a long frustrating sigh before rushing off towards the hallway.

I stand in a daze. My body slowly trying to recover from our recent sensual encounter. Now, that is what I call a good morning welcome. I head eagerly towards the kettle, feeling relieved my legs have finally lost their wobbles and can at last move forward again.

"I hope you slept well," says Aunty, striding through the kitchen, directly towards the sink to wash her hands.

I try hard to avoid her gaze. "I slept like a log, thank you."

"Mrs Potter has booked her daughter in for a lesson on Dapple at ten o'clock tomorrow. I hope that is ok with you. It's the only slot I could find, as your diary looks fairly full this week already," says Mia, as she reappears.

"That's fine, Mia, thank you. Yes, May half-term is a busy time of the year. What with parents booking extra lessons for their kids, to get them up to speed in time in readiness for the Summer camps," she replies with a smile.

"Thank you," says Aunty, as I pass her a mug of hot coffee. "Just what I need right now."

Placing Mia's mug down on the breakfast bar, my right hand accidently touches hers. Little electric volts start to fire up, and I quickly pull my hand away, trying hard to keep a straight face. Mia smiles at me naughtily with a wink.

"What's on the agenda today?" asks Mia, turning to face Aunty.

"I have endless lessons booked in throughout the day. My next one is not until ten, followed by twelve, four, five o'clock and finally my last one of the is at seven. I don't suppose you two would mind giving me a hand today, would you? Betsy and Starsky both need a groom and thirty minutes lunging. Spirit needs a slow and relaxed twenty-minute walk around the village and Emperor desperately needs a bath before his owner returns from Greece. How about, in return I set up a full jumping course for you in the school, say for around two o'clock? Well?" she asks.

Mia and I look at each other with a smile and nod our heads in agreement.

"Fabulous, thank you both. I really appreciate your help," she replies gratefully.

"You are more than welcome; it's the least we can do," I say, with a grin.

"By the way, when you get chance, I want you to pop into my office. You'll find a schedule on my desk for a fun show which is being held this coming Saturday in the next village to ours, so just a twenty-minute hack from here. I'm teaching most of the day, although I should be finished by four o'clock, so I thought it would be a nice little outing for the two of you to do on Jasmine's last day. Oh, and by the way, a bit unexpected I know, but your Uncle has decided to home for a couple of days and will be arriving Saturday evening. A colleague of his, is thankfully giving him a lift from the airport, and I have agreed to meet him at what used to be one of our favourite restaurants. It's only a forty-minute drive from here and he's reserved a table for seven," she replies.

My heart felt like a ship gradually sinking deep into the ocean, as she mentioned the words, my last day here. *'How am I going to cope without seeing Mia every day?'* I ask myself in panic.

Mia must have sensed the sudden sadness on my face, and immediately gives me a warm and loving glance. "A nice romantic meal with William, hey, Trudy?" she teases.

"Definitely not romantic, Mia. You know only too well what William's like," she sighs, with a hint of sadness across her face.

I wonder what all this is about. Surely, Aunty should feel happy that Uncle is coming home?

"Come on, Jazz, shall we go and have a look at that schedule? I think it would be fun to enter a couple of classes, don't you?"

"Yes, you're right. It would be fun. Why not? Let's do it." My mood immediately starts to lighten.

Chapter 14

I can feel Mia's eyes burning intensely through me, as I ask Starsky to trot nicely around the schooling ring. "Good boy," I tell him, as he quickly responds to my voice. I smile, watching this stunning looking Arab in full action. His chestnut coat gleams in the glorious morning sunshine, as his knees thrust up high, resembling a top-class dressage horse. He owns the ring, floating around majestically, looking like a king.

"What a lovely mover," I hear Mia say.

"He certainly is," I agree, trying to concentrate on the job in hand.

"I wasn't talking about Starsky. I meant you," she laughs back.

"Oh, Mia, please behave yourself. You'll make me lose my concentration," I call back, gradually easing Starsky to a walk, and eventually to a halt. "Well done," I tell him, reeling in the long lunge line. Walking towards him, I congratulate him with a gentle kiss on his very sweaty muzzle. "Your work for today is now done. You did great." I bend over, my backside pointing into the air, in a final attempt to retrieve the lunge whip from the ground.

"What a spectacular view," calls out Mia. I giggle out loud, as I turn walk towards her, but suddenly stop.

Her smile, her eyes, her face, every single part of her instantly melts my heart and once again those erotic feelings begin to erupt.

"Would you like a hand?" she asks, grinning at my flushed face.

"I'll tell you what sort of hand would be very helpful at this present moment. For a start, I would like both your hands to slowly caress every single inch of my body," I reply being sultry.

"Well, I suppose I'll have to see what I can do accommodate you then, Miss," she replies, with a naughty looking grin.

"Come on boy," I tell Starsky, as we walk through the gate, which Mia has kindly opened.

We stop and wait, for Mia to close it, and suddenly I feel two warm hands gently squeezing my buttocks.

The pumping sensation way down below takes me completely by surprise. Mia's hot breath gently blows on the right side of my neck, and I gasp once again as her luscious warm lips eagerly get to work, turning my legs into wobbling jelly. Thankfully, Starsky is oblivious to us both. He stands obligingly, casually taking in his surroundings. Small beads of sweat begin to prickle across my forehead, and onto the top of my head which is holding the weight of my skull cap. "Mia, you are driving me crazy," I whisper, closing my eyes to treasure this wonderous and sensual moment.

"There you two are. How's it going?" asks Aunty, striding towards us.

"Er, well, yes, he did a grand job. Such a lovely mover," I stutter.

"There we are, Jazz," says Mia, handing me four brushing boots, she's quickly removed from off Starsky's legs.

"Now, that's great teamwork, ladies, just what I like to see. Starsky is looking fabulous and in top form. Chanelle will be thrilled with the way he is progressing. In fact, I must call her this evening with some updates. Now, Jasmine, remember to drink lots of water, I know it isn't overly hot today, but we can't have you getting dehydrated, now can we? I must say you do look slightly flustered. Mia, please make sure you keep a very close eye on her for me, and I'll see you both in the school shortly," she says, with a wink, before turning to walk in the opposite direction.

"Don't worry, I will," calls back Mia.

My heart is pounding ten to the dozen. *How close was that?*

"Phew," says Mia, as her lips press pleasingly against mine.

"Oh, Mia, I now know where that saying comes from, you know the one, when someone says you have the hots for someone. Well, that is an understatement, as I'm on fire," I say, as her lips reluctantly leave mine.

We slowly head back towards the yard. "Come on, Jazz. Let me give you a hand," she says, with her ravishing smile. "Why not let me remove his cavesson and wash him down for you? It will do you good to take a break. Go and sit on that bale over there and relax with a cold drink, whilst you watch me in action," she grins.

I gratefully remove my skull cap feeling relieved, although my hair is completely drenched with sweat. I smile, as a very slight breeze runs across the yard catching my face on its travels. I readily remove a cold lemonade can from the fridge, holding it firmly against my flushed and reddened cheeks. *This feels so good.* Thankfully, I begin to feel the heat of my blood gradually cooling down, that is until I glance over at Mia. I watch her with great pleasure, as she bends over holding the hosepipe. The cool water trickles down Starsky's legs, reminding me of a mini waterfall. Mia's fabulously shaped backside tucked away neatly inside her tightly fitted cream jodhpurs pointing nicely in my direction, makes my blood pressure rise once again. The smile she gives me, as she turns to look at me is enough to drive me to despair and I glance away quickly whilst taking in a long, deep breath.

"All done," she cheerfully says, leading a fresh looking Starsky towards his stable.

"I owe you big time," I grin.

"That's right, you do. I have a fabulous idea as to how you can thank me," she informs me, removing the headcollar and standing back.

We watch Starsky rolling around in delight amongst the deep golden straw. He looks thrilled with himself, and when he eventually gets up, he resembles a scarecrow. Honestly, there isn't a single part of him which isn't covered in straw.

"And just how can I thank you?" I ask seductively, my tongue slowly circling the perimeter of the lemonade can.

"Oh, wow, Jazz. You really are teasing me now, aren't you? Come on, follow me," she says, in a whisper, gently grabbing my free hand after bolting the stable door, quickly checking the coast is clear, before leading me towards the tack room.

Glancing around, I'm relieved to see there isn't a single soul in sight. All I can hear is the awesome sound of horses crunching contentedly on their hay. Mia gently grasps the can from my hand. I take a short breath. In a slow, and teasing manner, she slowly lifts my T-shirt and places the cold metal can firmly against my stomach. I yelp out as the coldness hits my skin.

"This should help to cool you down, Jazz," she says, in a low sexy voice.

"Oh yes, it certainly will, but I have another slight concern, Mia. Your warm tender touch is making me feel hot, all over again. Now, how do you think you can you help out with this?" I whisper.

Her right hand slowly moves up towards my right breast. I hold my breath, as her fingers pleasantly slide into the cup of my bra.

I gasp and throw my head back, as her fingers teasingly circle my erect nipple. I am on fire. The uncontrollable and fierce throbbing commences, deep down below and can only be described as one of pure ecstasy. I hear Mia moan with delight, as she replaces her teasing fingers with her tongue. I thrust my pelvis towards hers, wanting to feel her body pushed tightly against mine. I have never experienced anything like this before. I long for her tongue to tease and explore every single part of my body, and I mean every single part. "Oh, Mia. Please don't stop," I moan, as her lips tenderly kiss my nipple before slowly making their way all around the outline of my breast. I can vaguely hear a loud whinny seemingly coming from somewhere close by. Mia pulls away quickly. The can drops quickly down onto the floor and the sound of the tin hitting the concrete startles me, as I urgently try to place my right breast back firmly inside my bra.

Our breath-taking episode sadly and quickly comes to an unexpected and abrupt end. This can only mean one thing. One of the livery owners must be arriving. To my complete surprise, Mia doesn't seem to be phased at all. The warm glow and the dreamy expression across her beautiful face, warms my heart instantly. I struggle to pull my T-shirt back down into place, her enchanting eyes slowly follow my every move

"Great, thanks, Jazz. I'll see you over at the school in half an hour then," Mia says loudly, casually walking out through the tack room door.

"Good afternoon, Mia. What a lovely day it is," I hear a woman's voice reply.

"I totally agree, Brenda. It's certainly turning out to be a fabulous day," replies Mia in a very cheerful manner.

I let out a long, huge sigh. *What just happened? Wasn't it me who was supposed to be thanking her, not the other way around? 'I need to find some way of making it up to her,'* I tell myself, with a naughty grin, as my body tries to recover from our recent and unforgettable encounter. I reluctantly bend over to pick up the empty can. My head is spinning with so many magical thoughts, as I try hard to urge my legs to walk towards the rubbish bin.

Chapter 15

As I near the end of my grooming session with Breeze, I stand back to admire how stunning he looks. His golden coat glistens with health, his mane and tail look like strands of white silk, his four white socks gleam, his light blue mystical eyes dazzle wide, as he stares contently ahead, looking like a true King crowned in a halo of gold. *How did I get so lucky?* "Hey boy, the two of us can now head over to the school and get cracking with a bit of jumping. Also, how would you fancy doing a preparation warm up at a local show this weekend, before our big quarter final knockout which is coming up in just under four weeks-time? What do you think?" I ask him, as I finish tightening his girth.

He nods his head up and down in agreement.

"That's a deal then," I tell him, before adjusting my body protector and securing my skull cap. I slowly lead him across to the mounting block and within moments I'm sitting comfortably and confident on my pride and joy. I check his girth and tighten it slightly before we make our way across to the indoor school. I eagerly look around for Mia, but she is nowhere to be seen, although

I suppose I am five minutes early.

I peer inside the school. Seeing the eight jumps ready and waiting makes my heart skip a beat, as I look around in awe. To me show jumping gives me a sense of power and such an incredible adrenalin rush. The intense concentration and timing required to glide effortlessly over the huge jumps gives me a complete sense of true accomplishment. That magical feeling of being totally at one with your horse is priceless and addictive. These sensations which take over the whole of my body, are second to none, although I must admit, my earlier encounter with Mia, does come very close.

"Hey sexy girlfriend," I hear Mia's, soft, seductive voice coming from close behind me.

I look her up and down, longing to be able to feel her tongue circling around my nipple once again.

Mia and Ebony move in closer. "Are you ok, Jazz?"

"Oh yes, I'm more than ok, and that's all thanks to you," I grin. *Oh, that smile, her lips, her mesmerising eyes, her cheekbones, her slender body, her soft hands, her breasts, her stunning backside.* There isn't a single part of her I don't yearn for.

"Are we ready then?" asks Aunty, striding towards us in a very authoritative manner.

Mia and I look at each other and grin with a nod.

"Right, firstly we need to get you all warmed up. Jasmine, you can take the lead today. I want to see two full circuits of walk around the edge of the school, then two trots, followed by two full circuits of collected canter," she commands.

I urge Breeze forward, as I glance around at the colourful jumping course which looks so tempting and inviting. I can feel Mia's eyes on my back, as her and Ebony follow closely behind.

Breeze feels in magnificent form beneath me. His stride is relaxed and supple, as he occasionally glances towards the awaiting jumps.

"Looking good all of you. Now trotting," Aunty calls out.

I rise lightly up and down in my stirrups to the rhythm of Breeze's strides. He moves like a professional dressage horse with no effort required. *I wonder if Mia is watching my backside.* I suddenly think, as I instantly miss one bounce. *Jazz. Get a grip and concentrate on the job in hand. You have sex on the brain!*

"And canter," instructs Aunty.

Breeze and I glide around the edge of the school effortlessly. It's like being on a beautiful rocking horse, as I sit deep into my saddle hardly moving at all.

"Fabulous work," grins Aunty, as I slowly ease Breeze back down to a walk and finally display a perfect square halt.

Mia and Ebony arrive close by my side and we look at each other and smile.

"Mia, please could you and Ebony to go first? I have set the poles at two foot for now and will raise them once you've both completed the course and feel comfortable in going higher," instructs Aunty.

"Good luck," I whisper, tenderly stroking the top of her leg, knowing it is completely out of Aunty's view.

"Don't forget, you still need to thank me later," Mia whispers, with a naughty wink, before she and Ebony head off towards the start.

I watch the two of them in action, as they clear jump after jump with ease. No hesitation at all, just poetry in motion. My heart skips a beat, as she pulls Ebony up at my side. She has a huge grin on her face, as she continuously pats Ebony congratulating her on their faultless round. "Off we go my boy," I tell Breeze, as Mia cheekily squeezes my right bum cheek. *'Just wait until I get my hands on her later,'* I say to myself, with a mischievous smile.

"Off you go, Jasmine," calls Aunty.

I can feel the concentration running throughout every single inch of Breeze's body. His ears are pricked high and ready for action. We clear the eight jumps with ease. Breeze is used to much higher jumps, so this must feel like a little warm up to him.

"What an awesome round," calls out Aunty. "Just give me five minutes or so to higher them."

"Would you like a hand?" I call out.

"No, thank you, I'm fine. Why don't you just sit and chat amongst yourselves?" she calls back, before immediately getting to work.

"Nice round, Jazz. The two of you make it look so easy. Anyway, changing the subject whilst your Aunt is out of ear shot, have you thought about how you are going to thank me later?" she asks, leaning towards me, gently kissing my lips.

"Oh, Mia. Don't you worry on that score, I have a few ideas up my sleeve that I think you might like," I reply, as I quickly turn to check on Aunty, who is scurrying around, oblivious to our goings on.

"Give me a clue," she asks, looking me deep into my eyes. Her hand slowly glides up from my knee, seductively and slowly to the inside of my thigh.

I moan in delight at the touch of her hand, as the dull throbbing starts to strike up from, deep down below. "Oh, Mia. What on earth are you doing to me? I can't think, my mind has gone completely blank," I manage to mumble.

"I suppose I'll just have to wait and see then," she replies, slowly moving her hand back onto her reins.

"Ok, Mia, are you ready?" calls Aunty.

"Oh yes. I'm ready in more ways than one, hey, Jazz?" she replies in a sensual whisper.

I try hard to pull myself together, but my pulse is racing and more worryingly, I feel slightly damp between my legs. Breeze shuffles around impatiently beneath me, so I ask him to walk forward, just in time to see Mia and Ebony complete another clear round.

"Well done, Mia," shouts Aunty, who looks to be thrilled with their performance.

Mia is literally glowing, as her and Ebony walk directly towards me. "Wasn't that awesome, Jazz? That is the highest we have ever jumped," she says in excitement.

"Well done, that was a superb display. See, I told you, you can do anything you put your mind to," I reply encouragingly.

Mia gently touches my hand, her face still beaming with delight. "Good luck."

I smile, as I urge Breeze forward. "Are you ready boy?" I ask him, as I concentrate fully on the job ahead, erasing any other thoughts completely from my head. We soar over the eight jumps, clearing every single one of them with ease. I am proud of his performance and my adrenalins in full flow, as I bring him down to a halt. "Aunty. Please could you put them up to one hundred and twenty-five centimetres?" I call across to her, feeling enthusiastic.

"Bloody hell, Jazz. Please tell me you are not going to jump higher?" asks Mia, looking slightly concerned.

"Oh yes, Mia. Breeze and I can jump much higher. Once I get offered a place in the Olympic team, we will be expected to jump at least one hundred and sixty centimetres, so that is a foot and a bit higher than what we are about to tackle now," I tell her with a grin.

"But that's so high," gasps Mia. I can't help but laugh at the worried expression across her face.

"Ready for you both to show us what you can do, Jasmine," bellows Aunty.

"I can't watch," I vaguely hear Mia say, as Breeze and I stride towards the start.

"Let's show them all we can do this," I tell him positively. Over the cross rail we fly. Up and over the vertical with ease. We turn towards the combination and Breeze soars high into the air, then I count one stride, two strides, three strides and lean forward as he times it to perfection. I ease him back a stride as we head towards the false wall, he effortlessly clears it by inches. Back and along to the right, we jump the triple bar like it's a piece of cake, over the solid board which two parallel poles sit high above, and sail over the final vertical leisurely, to earn us a clear round. I'm feeling on top of the world, as I ask Breeze to slow down to a trot continuously patting him down his neck.

"Oh, my word, that was a top performance, way beyond belief. Never in a thousand years would I have expected you to be able to reach this kind of standard at your age. The two of you looked like a top-class act and it's no wonder the team scouts have been following the pair of you. You jumped that with so much ease, clearing them easily by at least a foot," babbles Aunty, not stopping to take a breath, as I eventually ask Breeze to stand.

I look across at Mia, whose mouth is wide open in amazement and I can't help but grin back.

"There is no way, me and Ebony are competing against the two of you on Saturday," she eventually manages to blurt out. "That was so blinking thrilling to watch. I'm so proud of the two of you."

Chapter 16

"You did me proud today, my boy," I tell Breeze, giving him one last hug before turning him out to his awaiting girlfriend. I walk slowly back to the yard in search of Mia. Feeling chilled and relaxed, I lean over Ebony's stable door, with a dreamy look across my face. Standing before me, Mia stands like the vision of beauty she is. I let out a long satisfying sigh, as she bends over to place her grooming kit neatly back in the box.

She instantly looks up, as though she can sense I'm close and as our eyes meet, the love and wanting need, I yearn for her is indescribable. "Hey sexy girlfriend," she drawls in a wonderous sexy voice.

"Do you need a hand?" I ask, with a naughty smile.

"Oh yes. I need both your hands, Jazz," she teases, with a cheeky wink.

"Your wish is my command," I reply, making my way into the stable, quickly bolting the door securely behind me. "There's no one around, Mia, just you and me."

"Amazing, but haven't we still got work to do?" she queries, in a cheeky manner.

"Oh yes, we have," I nod, slowly making my way towards her.

Ebony seems oblivious to my presence and is happily munching on her sweet-smelling hay. I take hold of Mia's left hand and guide her seductively across to the corner of the stable. My heart is beating loudly, and my body is riddled with so many sensual sensations.

"Mia, just feel what you are doing to me," I groan, gently guiding her hand upwards towards my left breast.

She lets out a muffled moan, as her hand presses against my firm and well-developed breast. Very slowly, I run my fingers through her long dark hair, carefully moving it to one side to reveal her long, elegant neck. My lips brush lightly over her soft, silky skin and at the same time I inhale the sensational taste of her body. My lips hungrily move down towards her chest bone, as my left hand delicately makes its way teasingly behind her back, to the top line of her jodhpurs.

"Oh, Jazz," she moans. "If this is your way of thanking me, then please don't ever stop."

My fingers slowly move upwards inside the back of her T-shirt, lovingly caressing every single inch of her satin flesh.

Mia throws her head back in ecstasy, with her eyes fully closed. My lips and fingers continue to wander, as she gasps with delight.

I allow both my hands to run tenderly, but teasingly from her hips to her bra straps, whilst her lips continue to press lovingly against mine. I push my body tightly against hers, as our breasts finally touch. I moan and murmur in delight. I find it hard to believe the amount of electricity fluently flowing between our bodies. The two of us become locked away in a world of our own, allowing our love and emotions to fly freely like a bird.

"I think you are booked in this Thursday," says Aunty's voice, sounding not too far away.

Mia and I instantly freeze. She very slowly puts one finger to her lips, as we stay where we are, not daring to move. I have the urge to giggle, as we stand like statues with my hands still firmly stuck inside the back of her T-shirt.

"Yes, that's correct. Thursday at five pm. I look forward to seeing you then," says Aunty, as we hear the clonk of her riding boots along the concrete floor just outside Ebony's stable.

I hold my breath, as I look deeply into Mia's eyes.

We listen carefully. The footsteps eventually recede into the distance, and I let out a huge sigh of relief before we both drop down onto the deep golden straw.

"That was too close for my liking," Mia says, as she looks deeply into my eyes once again.

"I totally agree," I reply, trying hard to get my breathing back to some sort of normality.

Suddenly, Mia leans towards me and gently pushes me backwards into the straw. She lightly lies on top of me, cupping my chin in both her hands. Her tasty red lips reach out to touch mine, I wrap my arms around her and pull her in closer. She reluctantly pulls away, her striking green eyes looking intensely into mine.

"What's the matter?" I whisper, as I look lovingly and questioningly into her eyes.

"I love you, Jazz," she smiles warmly, as her lips gently brush mine.

"Oh, Mia, I love you, too. I cannot tell you how long I have waited to hear you say those words," I reply, feeling ecstatic. We kiss tenderly for what seems ages, our hands slowly caressing and exploring each other bodies.

I jump slightly, as I hear Ebony snort from what sounds to be very nearby. I grudgingly open my eyes. Ebony's gorgeous black head looks enquiringly down at the pair of us, as she chomps on a mouthful of hay. I cannot help but laugh at the funny inquisitive face staring directly at me. "Turn around slowly," I whisper.

"Oh, Ebony. What are you like spoiling our fun like this?" Mia asks her, in between her giggles.

"Maybe she was concerned about the two of us rolling around in the straw moaning and groaning," I tell her, in between my laughs.

"Come here, let me give you a hand," Mia says softly, as she holds her right hand towards me, once she is safely back on her feet.

Ebony lightly sniffs both of Mia's cheeks, tickling her with the tiny strands of hay that are dangling from her mouth.

Back on my feet, I feel slightly hot and flustered. Mia refuses to take her eyes off me, as she unhurriedly removes the grains of straw embedded in my long golden hair. I reach up to her forehead, and with my finger and thumb I slowly extract a single strand of straw sitting at an upright angle from the front of her hair. My fingers gently wander down across to her stunning cheekbones, as she leans forward tenderly covering my lips with hers.

"Oh, Jazz. What is happening to us? I feel like I'm ready to explode at any second," I whisper.

"Me, too, my darling, but don't worry. That special moment we've both been patiently dreaming of and waiting for, will happen when the time is right. Trust me,' she whispers, her teeth seductively nibbling my earlobe.

"I honestly don't know how much longer I can wait. My body is aching and longing to be naked next to yours. I want to caress and explore every single inch of you," I moan.

"Oh, Jazz. I don't think you have a clue how much you are turning me on. I want our first time to be one of the most precious moments either of us could ever dream of experiencing," she whispers.

"But when?" I ask, in a begging voice.

"We just need to be patient for a little while longer. Trust me, the right time will come along for us, my love," she replies softly, as she cups my chin in her right hand, whilst looking deeply and lovingly into my eyes.

I kiss her longingly and hold her close to me, never wanting to let her go.

"Come on, Jazz, back to reality I'm afraid. We still have work to do. How about I turn Ebony out into her field whilst you get Spirit bridled up, so we can take him for his thirty-minute walk? When we get back, we can complete our final task and give Emperor his bath," she smiles, reluctantly releasing her arms from around my waist.

"I suppose," I sigh, brushing myself down, before straightening up my clothing.

"See you in fifteen minutes then," she says with a grin, as I unbolt the stable door.

"Missing you already," she calls back. I walk in a daydream towards one of the fields to locate Spirit. My body is still tingling from the intensity of our recent and intimate encounter.

Chapter 17

Thankfully, Spirit is being very well behaved. Standing at sixteen two hands, his hunter frame is bulky and solid, but unlike his name, underneath he is a gentle giant.

"I can't remember if I told you or not about one of my Uni friends, Josh. The one having an affair with his tutor. It was all over the local news," Mia asks, as we make our way along the old fashioned, windy lanes down towards the village.

"No, you didn't. What on earth happened?" I reply, feeling slightly shocked.

"I truly feel sorry for the pair of them. I mean, no one can help who they fall in love with, now can they?" she replies, although I can't see her face, hidden on the other side of Spirit's huge neck.

"Do you know how long the affair had been going on for?" I ask.

"Apparently, for well over a year. Josh is such a wonderful and caring guy. He's in the same year as me, although studying a different course. His tutor, Mr Barnes, believe it or not, is only thirty-one and such a handsome guy. In fact, all the girls constantly drooled over him, even though we all knew he was gay. He was a well-respected teacher in his profession and now it sadly looks like his career is finished," she continues.

"That's so awful. How on earth did they get caught?" I ask, feeling sorry for both, Mr Barnes, and Josh.

"It was wholly by accident. Apparently, the two of them had been enjoying a meal at a restaurant which is a good forty miles away from here. A fortieth birthday party was in full swing that evening too and lots of photos as usual had been taken. They were oblivious, just in a world of their own, and completely uninterested in anything happening around them. The two of them being in love had kissed and unfortunately this moment had been caught on camera. It was only a few days before the photo circulated not only around Uni, but also on all the social media sites, too," she replies sadly.

"How terrible. Their chances of being caught like this must have been one in a million," I reply.

"I know, such a shame and a such a waste. Josh immediately dropped out of Uni and as for Mr Barnes, well I haven't a clue what's going to happen to him," she replies.

"Such a sad story, Mia. Two people falling in love, desperately wanting to spend time with each other and to get caught out like that. I feel sorry for them too, even though I don't know them. I wonder if they'll ever see each other again?" I say, as we head up the pathway leading back to the yard.

She stands to face me when we come to a halt in the yard. "Who knows, Jazz? Fingers crossed for the two of them. I hate to think what poor Josh is going through. I should really send him a message of support."

"Josh will probably appreciate any support you and his other friends can offer him at this very difficult time," I tell her with a smile, thinking how wonderful and caring she is.

Mia glances at her watch. "Shall I go and get Emperor ready for his bath whilst you finish sorting out Spirit? Seriously, I can't believe where the day has gone. It's nearly four o'clock."

"I cannot believe tomorrow is Wednesday already," I reply, glumly.

Mia looks quickly around, to check the coast is clear before tenderly kissing my sulky looking lips. I can't resist their urgings, responding in a passionately and urgent way.

"Look, we still have four full days together, so let's make the most of them and have some fun," she says with a big grin.

"You're right. I'll give Spirit a quick groom, pick out his feet and see you shortly at the bathing area," I smile, feeling much happier, as I lead Spirit back towards his stable.

"Hey there, gorgeous boy," I say, heading towards the beautiful grey gelding who is standing quietly nibbling on his hay net. Mia stoops down under his neck to face me. "He's all washed down and ready for the shampoo."

"To be honest, I don't know who looks the wettest, you or him," I laugh, slowly looking her up and down.

I hold my breath, as my eyes suddenly stop at her breasts. The cold water looks to have done such an eye-catching and magnificent job. Her erect nipples point at me, bulging from her bra and through her soddened T-shirt. I am so tempted to lean forward to give them a gentle stroke. *Surely it would be rude not to?*

Mia must have read my mind. "I know exactly what thoughts are running through your mind, 'Miss sex on the brain,' but we do have our work to complete," she informs me, with a mischievous smile.

"Oh, please?" I plead, my eyebrows frowning in disappointment.

"Maybe later," she winks, as I reluctantly pick up the shampoo and get down to work.

"How much blinking shampoo have you put on?" asks Mia.

The bubbles constantly keep reappearing, as I massage my hands deeply into Emperors smooth silky coat. "A bit too much, by the looks of it," I reply, quickly grasping a handful of bubbles patiently biding my time, waiting for the right moment. Emperor only stands at thirteen hands high, which means I can easily see Mia's every move. I wait until she leans over his back once again, and in an instant I place the large handful of bubbles directly onto the top of her head.

"Oh, so you think that is funny, do you?" she laughs.

"I was just giving you a helping hand. You mentioned to me earlier, your hair was in desperate need of a wash," I reply, biting my bottom lip in a very seductive manner, staring into Mia's eyes, slightly raising my eyebrows, waiting for her to retaliate.

She glares back at me wickedly. "Don't you worry. I'll get my own back," she calmly replies.

My tongue slowly rolls around the outside of my lips. "Bring it on."

"How are you both getting on?" Aunty's voice asks, coming from somewhere behind me.

I instantly put my tongue away, as I turn to face Aunty with a smile.

"We just need to rinse off, Emperor, wash his tail, wait for him to dry and all our chores will be completed," replies Mia, with a grin, as her hands continue to massage Emperors back.

I watch her hands slowly rub and caress his back. *I wish Mia could massage my body all over like that.*

"Great work and thank you both so much. My day has been completely manic and there is no way I could have coped without your help," Aunty says gratefully, and tiredly.

"You look shattered," I reply.

"I feel it. I'm just going to pop back to the house to grab a quick sandwich and coffee before my last lesson at six. To be honest, I seriously can't wait to put my feet up with a large glass of red later. I hope you'll be joining me for a tipple or two, Jasmine," she says, turning to look at me.

"It would be rude not to."

She turns to make her way back towards the house. "Right, I'll leave you to it. Have fun and thank you once again."

I glance over at Mia. *Oh, don't worry we will.*

"If you take charge of the hose, Jazz, I'll follow behind with the scraper," Mia says, occasionally glancing at me, as though she could be planning her revenge.

I let the water run wild over Emperors body, the bubbles eventually beginning to disappear. I watch Mia's every move, with a playful look across my face. The lust I have for her is getting stronger and stronger.

"Nearly done," she says, as she finishes wringing out his tail, by continuously swirling it around in a circle. Droplets of water splatter across my face.

"Are you ready for me to turn off the tap yet?"

"Not yet, Jazz," she says, gently removing the hosepipe from out of my grasp, aiming it down towards his hooves. "That's better. Now you can turn it off," she says with a grin.

As I head off in the direction of the tap, I'm totally unaware that Mia is following closely behind.

"Jazz. I really don't think you look wet enough," I hear her voice whisper from behind my right shoulder.

Feeling slightly confused, I immediately turn around to face her. Before I know what has happened, Mia has somehow managed to push the hosepipe firmly down the top of my T-shirt. I gasp, as water trickles slowly down the middle of my cleavage and all the way down to my feet. I am completely drenched. Quickly bending over, so it looks like I've hurt myself, I discreetly pull out the hosepipe without Mia seeing.

Her laughter suddenly stops, and I feel a soft hand leaning tenderly on my back.

"Oh, Jazz, I'm so sorry. Are you ok?" I hear her ask, in a very soft voice.

As quickly as I can, I stand up and turn to face her. I raise my right hand, pushing the hosepipe firmly down the back of her T-shirt. I laugh, as she jumps up and down in shock, as the water flows down her back and I laugh even more, as she struggles to remove the hose. Her arms are not long enough to reach it.

"Please help," she begs.

"What's it worth?" I ask, standing with one hand firmly on my hips.

"Whatever you want. I promise," she replies, with a cheeky grin.

I walk slowly towards the tap, placing my right hand on the top whilst glancing back towards Mia.

"Please," she asks again, with her hands closed tightly together, as she begs.

I cannot help but laugh at her face, as I turn off the tap and slowly head back towards her.

She slowly turns around with her back facing towards me, whilst I carefully remove the hose. I can feel her sense of relief. She turns back around to face me, pressing her wet body tightly against mine.

She whispers in a low and sexy voice. "You know what happens to naughty girls, don't you?"

"I suppose they need to be punished," I reply, trying to keep a straight face.

"Correct. Now follow me," she commands, taking hold of my right hand, before leading me towards the drying room. Once inside she stands looking at me in a very longing way.

I gasp, as she slowly lifts my wet T-shirt, gently easing it over the top of my head. I watch her face closely. She groans lightly, as her eyes unhurriedly glance over my body. I lean forward, seductively lifting the bottom of her T-shirt, gradually guiding it up above her mouth-watering breasts, as she lifts her arms up high into the air to assist. I lever it slowly over the top of her head and drop it down by my side.

We look at each other intensely. No words are needed, as our bodies close ranks. I gasp once again, as her lips gently kiss my cheeks. I feel her hands unclip my bra and in an instant my revealing breasts are ready and waiting, for whatever she has got planned. Her hands slowly knead them, as my hands fumble in great urgency to unclasp her bra.

My breathing feels shallow, as I groan with her every move. I desperately want to feel her naked breasts rubbing and pressing against mine. My body aches with excitement and lust, as the multiple sensations down below begin to get out of control. *Her beautiful firm breasts finally touch mine and a feeling of elation shivers down my spine.*

We both gasp with delight, a special moment we have been longing for, our breasts touching for the very first time. Our hands continuously run up and down each other's backs bringing us even closer together. I've never ever felt such a dynamic and sexual wanting, as her lips and tongue make their way teasingly down my neck. I move my right hand around to the front of her stomach, my fingers gently stroking and tormenting the top of her jodhpurs. She moans once again.

My hands move upwards to cup her tender breasts. "Oh, Jazz. I love you so much," she mumbles. My tongue lightly flicks across her nipple, as my hands continue to caress her heavenly breasts, whilst she pleads with me not to stop.

"Don't you look magnificent, Emperor," we suddenly hear

Aunty's voice say.

"Oh shit," says Mia, as we quickly pull ourselves apart. "Here grab this," she says with a wink, looking hot and flustered. "Wait here."

I hold my breath, as Mia wraps a huge towel around her before heading out to face Aunty.

"He looks in great form, doesn't he?" I hear Mia say.

"What have you been up to?" I hear Aunty enquire.

I hold my breath even tighter.

"The end of that damned hosepipe flew off once again and I got completely drenched," replies Mia calmly.

"Do you know what? That has been on my to do list for ages. I promise I'll order a new part this evening," Aunty replies.

I feel the urge to giggle. *How on earth does Mia come up with these excuses so quickly?*

"If you see Jasmine, could you tell her I've left her dinner in the oven on low? I expect she's busy studying. Thank you once again for all your help and I'll see you in the morning," she says.

"My pleasure entirely," replies Mia.

I hear Aunty's boots clonking along the concrete, gradually fading into the distance, as I continue to stay as quiet as a mouse. I jump, as Mia returns with a naughty grin across her face and I let out a long, deep breath in relief.

"We really do pick our moments, don't we?" laughs Mia, as she watches me anxiously trying to put my bra and T-shirt back on with a radiant and hungry look on her face.

I walk towards her, kissing her lovingly.

"I love you so much it hurts, Jazz. I never expected to feel this way about anyone. Not only do I think about you every single moment, I long for you in my dreams too," she whispers, looking lovingly into my eyes.

"I love you too Mia." I hold her as tightly against me.

"Why don't you let me finish off here? Honestly, it won't take me long. You should hurry back over to the house and get yourself dried and changed," she says.

"Are you sure? I'll see you tomorrow though, won't I?" I reply, for some reason feeling slightly anxious.

"Of course, you will silly," she reassures me, before softly kissing me one last time. "Off you go, I promise I'll message you later. Remember, Jazz, I love you with every ounce of my heart," she says once again, gently squeezing my hand.

I reluctantly start to walk away and then stop to glance back. "I love you too," I mouth to her with a smile, as I watch her blow me a kiss, which I pretend to catch.

Chapter 18

"Well? What is your answer to the question I asked you last night, you know before your Uncle rudely interrupted us? I'm patiently waiting" smiles Aunty, sipping her red wine.

"And I'm still waiting for you to enlighten me on your second rendezvous with the gorgeous, Ruby," I grin back, lifting my gin and tonic up towards her in a toast.

"Ok young lady, so why don't we make a deal? You answer my question honestly which I've noticed you've been trying to avoid and then I may reveal my second encounter with Ruby and the very naughty Nicole," she replies, staring directly at me.

"Nicole? Aunty, oh my God. Did you have a threesome?" I ask, as my mouth sits wide open not quite believing what I just heard. *Go Aunty.*

"Well, Jasmine. Have you anyone special in your life at present I should know about?" she asks me questioningly.

"It's a bit confusing," I mumble.

"Take your time," she replies softly, before taking a sip of her wine.

"I honestly don't know where to start."

"My motto is, it's always a good idea to start right at the very beginning," she says with a grin.

I avoid any eye contact. "I've only felt, you know, those special feelings that you hear so many people like yourself talk about on a couple of occasions. To be honest, I have always been more interested in my studies and more importantly, Breeze."

"Go on," she encourages.

"Last year, I saw a close girlfriend of mine standing naked in the shower, please do not push me for any names, as I'm not ready to tell you. Some of the feelings you described you had for Ruby, are very similar to the way I felt about her that day. I had palpitations, electric shocks running throughout my body. My hands were trembling, but worst of all, I felt so guilty for even having these naughty thoughts," I babble, looking down at the floor.

"Why do you think you felt guilty?" asks Aunty, in a soft voice.

"I don't know, but even more confusing was the very first day I saw my tutor, Mr Sharp. I had precisely the same feelings rushing through me then, especially when I saw his bulging package," I say, feeling slightly warm in the face.

She lets out a soft giggle. "Jasmine, I apologise, I didn't mean to laugh, it was just the way you said it," she says apologetically.

"I'm certainly not a prude by any means, and believe it or not, I've even been out on a few dates with one or two boys. Had the odd kiss here and there too, but nothing more," I reply in defence.

"Then why do you think you feel guilty? Is it because you have the same feelings and emotions for men as well as women? If so, there is nothing wrong with that at all. Trust me you are a normal, hot-blooded woman just like your Aunt," she says, as she starts to laugh.

Her laugh is incredibly infectious. I take a sip of my drink and cannot stop myself from joining in with her laughter.

"That's better," she says, as she watches me intently. "It's completely normal to have those type of thoughts at your age, especially with your hormones flying around completely out of control. Just look at what I got up to, and you are slightly older than I was back then," she says.

"But why do I feel so guilty for having these thoughts about both men and women?" I demand.

"These days, magazines and newspapers are full to the brim with photos of hunky males and stunning female models. Men wearing hugging boxer shorts, teasing you with their packages as you call them, and women flaunting themselves in bikinis which aren't really worth wearing. We all see these images every time we turn on the television, let alone splattered across social media. Talk about being in your face twenty-four seven, so to speak. No wonder, you have mixed feelings."

"Actually, you're right. I'd never thought about it like that. Some of my girlfriends go on and on about Mr Sharp's crown jewels. I guess I just joined in with their banter," I reply, feeling thoughtful.

"When the right partner finally comes along, whether male or female, trust me, Jasmine, you'll know," she says, with a warm smile.

"What if I think I have already met the right person? What do I do?" I ask, as a hot flush gradually rises into my cheeks.

"My advice would be, to enjoy every moment you can share with this very lucky person. Make sure you follow your heart and stop worrying about what everyone else is going to think or say. Your family and friends, who love you dearly, only want what is best for you and more importantly for you to be happy. I will guarantee you now, whoever you choose, whether male or female, your family and friends will welcome them into their lives with open arms. It is now time, from this moment on, to stop beating yourself up and immediately dispel those inner guilty thoughts. Make sure you listen and take note of my wise old words," she replies with a grin.

Suddenly, I feel as though that huge weight which has been dragging me down for so long, has finally lifted. My mind feels clear and focused. My guilty sins have been forgiven at last. "Thank you, Aunty. I can't tell you how desperate I've been wanting to talk to someone about how I 've been feeling, but I couldn't summon up the courage to approach the subject. I felt so silly for not being able to control my own feelings," I reply with a grin.

"Do I know this special person, by any chance?" she asks, with a glint in her eye.

"Stop teasing me, Aunty. Once I'm ready, you'll be the first to know. Now, talking about revealing, isn't it time you told me all about your threesome? I need to know every single detail before Uncle comes home at the weekend," I reply cheekily.

"Oh yes, your Uncle," she says despondently. "Don't get me wrong, I did, I mean I do love him, but I also enjoy having my own space and freedom, so I can do what I want when I want. I should be thankful we don't have to live together full-time, as I'd feel like a prisoner. I certainly couldn't put up with any man telling me what I can and can't do," she grins.

"But you are still only thirty-four years old, and only been married eight years. You spend so much time apart, don't you miss him?"

"I suppose, I miss having a cuddle on a cold winter's evening, and I used to think he had a funny sense of humour. The couple of days we manage to spend together every few weeks, is enough for me," she grins at me with a naughty wink.

"What about children? Do you and Uncle plan to have any?" I ask.

"No, Jasmine. Sadly, we found out very early on, your Uncle

has a very low sperm count. Apparently, his little fish don't swim as well as they used to, so the chances of ever conceiving are very slim. We have always said, if it happens and I do fall pregnant, then it's meant to be. To be honest, the older I get, the more contented I feel living the way we are, without any children. I'm lucky to have you in my life, and even though you are my niece, I do regard you more like a sister," she replies warmly.

"The thought of little fish swimming around inside my body, makes me feel queasy," I tell her, with a look of disgust on my face.

Aunty is laughing so much, her glass suddenly tips to the right and she accidently spills some red wine onto her beautiful cream silk blouse. "Oh, damn it, just look at the wine I've now wasted," she says in between her giggles.

"You aren't at all worried about your blouse then?"

"No way. Let me just dash to my bedroom, grab a fresh top, dab a splash of white vinegar onto the stain, and quickly put it on a hot wash. It'll be as good as new in no time. Do me a favour whilst I sort this out will you? Please top up my glass," she requests, before hurriedly disappearing off down the hallway.

Chapter 19

'Counting down the hours until I see you is driving me to despair. My lips long to press firmly against yours, just where they belong. Missing you xxx,' Mia's text reads.

"That's better," says Aunty, as she sits back down in her comfy armchair, smiling at the glass of red wine sitting well within her reach.

"That was quick," I reply with a huge smile.

Mia's words race through my head. I cannot wait to hold her close to me, to feel her lips and body entwining with mine. I take a sip of my recently topped up drink and try hard to focus back on Aunty.

"Well?" I ask.

"Ah yes, the lovely Nicole and Ruby. This might blow your socks off," she grins back.

"I haven't got any on, so don't worry," I grin.

"I suppose it was around eight in the evening, when I stood once again outside the front door to Ruby's house. I seriously had no idea what I was letting myself in for, but after the earth-shattering experience, the night before, I knew I wanted and longed for a repeat performance, although I still wasn't quite sure how Nicole was going to fit into any part of this," she says, before taking a sip of wine.

"You must have gone ahead then?"

"Oh yes. I took a deep breath before ringing the doorbell, as I stood shuffling around on my feet feeling pretty-damned nervous to be honest, but as soon as Ruby opened the door, I was once again completely under her spell."

Her smile and the way she looked at me, made my legs turn to jelly. She stood looking me up and down, taking in my short tight skirt, my long slender legs, my breasts bulging teasingly out of my blouse. She took hold of my hand, and slowly led me inside. My eyes glanced all around the lounge, coming to an immediate halt, the moment I saw a truly striking lady, sitting quietly on the sofa. I remember her magical smile, as her eyes hungrily looked me up and down.

"Nicole, I would like to introduce you to our beautiful Trudy," Ruby said, guiding me across to where Nicole was sitting.

I blushed, as Nicole immediately stood up and warmly took hold of my left hand with hers. Honestly, it was like ten thousand volts of electricity somehow shooting throughout every single part of me. I was on fire, as she invitingly patted the vacant space on the sofa next to where she'd been sitting. I quickly obliged, still unable to take my eyes off her. Her black leather skirt was short enough to reveal the red hold up lacey stockings, which ran all the way down to her matching red shoes trimmed with a swirly black pattern. Her huge round breasts, burst through her black leather waistcoat, as her matching bra struggled to hold them upright, sending a prickle all the way down my spine. Her emerald eyes eventually met mine and we smiled at each other in a very knowing way. Ruby kindly handed me a glass of champagne and the three of us clinked each other's glasses, as we toasted, "Here's to a wonderful evening." The three of us sat chatting by the warm glow of the fire. I felt so at ease, as I listened to how Nicole and Ruby had first met," continues Aunty, as she takes a deep breath and another gulp of wine.

Feeling the sudden urge to take a large sip of my gin and tonic, I reply, "This all sounds like something out of a steamy novel. Honestly, you should write it all down and publish it under a pen name."

"Ruby and Nicole had met at a swingers party the year before, and they had instantly connected in more ways than one. Even though Nicole was still single at the time, the two of them continued to see each other regularly outside of the group. Nicole told me with a huge sexy smile, she had never been into men, so her and Ruby only met when Gerald was working away. He was aware of the relationship between his wife and Nicole and believe it or not, he was the one who initially encouraged it. Evidently, he had numerous other women hidden away who kept him more than satisfied when he worked away, so he didn't mind his wife enjoying some fun too. When he arrived home at the weekends, they would tell each other in very graphic detail about their recent sexual conquests. Apparently, this really turned them on and kept their love and lust for each other alive," she continues.

"Oh my God. You are kidding, right? There is no way I would be able to cope if my partner wanted to share me with someone else. It would crucify me," I blurt out.

"Trust me. There are many people hooked on sex out there who feel sharing is caring," laughs Aunty, as she stares at the look on my face.

"I recall, Ruby was wearing long black leather boots all the way up to her thighs, skimpy leather shorts revealing her perfectly shaped buttocks and a black bodice with cross bow fastenings, which were tied loosely enough to enable her heavenly breasts to peak through. We laughed at such random and stupid things, as we merrily tucked into our second bottle of sparkling champers."

"Who fancies a little nibble," Ruby asked, looking firstly at Nicole and then towards me.

I grinned, as I slowly and seductively looked from one to the other.

"I have a fabulous idea, ladies. How about I grab us another bottle of champers, so we can pop upstairs and continue our conversation there?" Ruby suggested, raising her eyebrows with a grin towards Nicole.

I felt excited, as Nicole nodded back in agreement. They both turned to me with an inquisitive look, and I smiled. Nicole gently took my right hand, and I followed her slowly towards the staircase. I tried hard to steady my trembling hand, as I noticed the champagne swirling around in my glass. Not only was my heart beating like the clappers, but every single part of my body craved the urgent need to feel both of their bodies naked on mine. Ruby silently followed closely behind, with another bottle of chilled champagne.

I stood patiently at the door, as Nicole reluctantly let go of my hand to swing it open. With my mouth wide open, I looked around this amazing and entrancing bedroom. It was enormous. A huge round bed sat proudly in the centre of the room. Battery operated candles glowed warmly all around.

"Two stunning mirrored walls immediately caught my attention, as they glistened to the left and the right under the low seductive flickering of the flames," she continues, taking another large gulp of her wine.

"Wow, wow, wow. What an interesting and entertaining adult film this could make," is all I can manage to respond.

Aunty laughs at my comment, before clearing her throat to continue.

Soft music played all around from tiny white speakers neatly embedded high above inside the ceiling. Ruby and Nicole had both turned to smile at me, continuing to watch my reaction, as I took in our new and surreal surroundings. I knew at that precise moment I was in for a unique and unusual experience. I wasn't worried in the slightest, in fact the thought of what could lie ahead thoroughly excited me. I glanced at the black leather sofa running the full length of one wall, as Nicole gently took my hand once again and as the two of us giggled, we headed directly towards the sofa.

I vaguely heard Ruby closing the door, but my mind was totally focused elsewhere. I was filled with roaring passion. Numerous naughty thoughts continuously raced through my head, as I pondered with a grin, the encounter the three of us were about to embark on. An experience I knew I would never ever forget, and I was determined to enjoy and treasure every single second of it. I seriously could not believe I was alone with not only one, but two of the most stunningly sexy ladies I had ever seen in the whole of my life. As I sat down onto the sofa, Nicole slowly took the glass from my hand and placed it on a nearby table alongside hers. She slowly lent forward, her luscious long blonde hair falling softly towards my face, her emerald green eyes looking deeply inside mine, as her hot red lips finally caressed mine. Honestly, the passion bubbling up inside me was like a ticking time bomb, patiently waiting for the right moment to explode," she sighs, before taking another gulp of wine.

"What an awesome experience, and a bloody bizarre, but

incredible one too," I blurt out, as I now feel the need to take a rather large gulp of my drink.

"Oh yes, those have to be the most wonderful moments of my youth," grins Aunty.

"Well come on, don't keep me in suspense. What on earth happened next?" I ask, sitting upright and alert.

As Nicole continued to lean over, slowly driving me crazy, I caught a glimpse of Ruby standing closely behind her. Her body was rocking gently against Nicole's, as Ruby's hands fed their way through under her arms fondling her beautiful breasts which were right in front of my face. As Nicole moved her lips to caress my neck, I gasped and held my head back, feeling a soft tender hand leisurely glide up and down my right leg teasingly towards my crotch. Ruby knew exactly how much the pair of them were turning me on. She gently whispered, how much she needed and wanted me, and how incredibly sexy I was. She teased me, informing me, it was now her turn to pay me some undivided attention. I watched spellbound, whilst she gently removed her hands from Nicole's breasts, and slowly sat down next to me, as Nicole took one step backwards. Ruby's lips were hungry for me and mine for her.

Once again, I felt a delightful soft hand slide seductively and slowly upwards under my skirt and then back down my legs. Silky smooth fingernails circled pleasantly around the strap to my briefs. My breathing was shallow, and I felt aroused on so many levels. Trust me it was hard to concentrate on any one thing, as there was so much going on. The atmosphere was electric. Three hot sexy females yearning for each other in such an unimaginable and unique way.

"Is it warm in here, or is it just me?" Aunty says, with a warm glow across her cheeks.

"It's very hot in here," I confess, taking another large sip of my gin and tonic.

"Blimey. Just look at the time," announces Aunty, as she glances at her watch.

"Ten past ten already. Oh Aunty, you can't stop there, that would be torturous. I need to know what happened next," I plead.

"Don't you worry, Jasmine, I have plenty more still to tell you. Don't forget, our little session lasted much longer than a marathon. In fact, I didn't arrive back home until fifty hours later. To be honest, I'm completely done in and my bed is desperately calling me. I have an early lesson booked in at seven tomorrow morning," she replies.

I can feel my mouth drop open in disbelief. "Oh Lordy. I feel totally gobsmacked, but I'm thoroughly enjoying your story. How about the same time, same place tomorrow evening then?" I ask with a grin.

"It's a date," she says, slowly getting up to heads towards the kitchen with her empty glass.

My mind is in turmoil. I thought mine and Mia's encounters to date were naughty, but on second thoughts, they are totally mild, and innocent compared to Aunty's. Maybe it's time for me up the ante. I toss and turn in bed, finding it impossible to clear my mind of the strong intense wanting I feel for Mia.

Chapter 20

"Breeze, what on earth is happening to me?" I ask him softly, as he happily chomps away on the juicy orange carrot I offer.

This morning, I'd woken up completely dripping with sweat. I can't even remember a single thing about the dream I'd had, although I know it must have been pretty erotic for me to wake up in this very worrying state.

I wrap my arms tightly around his silky neck. He gently places his head lightly over my right shoulder. I take a deep breath, inhaling his beautiful smell. "I'm not sure yet what our plans are today, my boy. It all depends on what Aunty's hectic schedule is like, but I'll try to find some time to spend with you. Maybe we could go out for a ride with Mia and Ebony later?" I whisper to him. *What could be a better start to the day than this?*

"Good morning, sexy girlfriend," I suddenly hear Mia's voice say.

My stomach instantly performs a somersault and I immediately turn to look at her. Her head is leaning on her hands over the top bar of the five-bar galvanised gate with a huge grin across her face. I try to wriggle free from Breeze's headlock, gently kissing him on his muzzle before slowly walking across to, Mia. Her gorgeous smile is enough to take my breath away. I glance around to check the coast is clear. Leaning forward, I cup her chin firmly in my right hand, my lips hungrily greeting hers.

"I've missed you so much," she whispers lovingly into my ear.

"Oh, Mia, I can't stop thinking about you. I cannot tell you how desperate I'm to feel your hot, naked body pushing firmly against mine," I groan.

She looks lovingly into my eyes. "I know, my love, and I feel the same way, too. Don't forget, good things come to those that wait."

"Come on, babe, let's nip and get some coffee inside us and see what your Aunty's got planned for us today," she says, kindly opening the gate for me.

We walk towards the house, our strides in perfect timing. Our hands gently brush against each other, causing a rippling effect to run across my skin. The fluttering sensations stir, deep down below and there is nothing I can do to stop them.

We soon come to a halt in the porchway of the house

"Oh, Mia. This is driving me crazy. When can we, you know?" I plead with her.

"When the time is right. Trust me," she whispers, her lips lightly brushing mine.

We enter the kitchen to hear Aunty's cheerful voice say, "Now, there the two of you are. The kettles just boiled so please help yourselves."

"And what may I ask is on our agenda today?" asks Mia, taking charge of making the coffee.

"Yet another busy day for us all, I'm afraid," she sighs, staring blankly down at the scribbled writing in her diary.

"Is there anything we can do to help?" I ask, feeling sorry for her. The huge daily workload she tries hard to juggle must cause her constant headaches and worry.

"How much time have you got?" she asks, half laughing.

"As much time as you need, isn't that right, Jazz?" answers Mia, placing a mug of coffee in front of me, with a smile that makes me tingle.

"Of course, that's right," I reply, my thoughts completely elsewhere. Momentarily, I take in every single inch of Mia's slender body. "I can't wait," I accidently say out aloud.

I vaguely hear Mia giggle, just as Aunty replies, "I must say, you're very keen to help your old Aunty, but you didn't come here to work your backside off every single day, Jasmine. You are supposed to be enjoying a well-deserved break. You know, chilling out and cracking on with your studying."

Mia's tongue slowly circles the edges of her luscious lips. My cheeks feel warm and flustered.

"Oh, please, please stop," I groan to myself. I feel breathless and I cannot take my eyes off her, but once again and to my utter embarrassment, the words have already left my lips.

"Stop what?" asks Aunty, looking up from her diary, with her glasses perched neatly on the end of her nose.

"Er, stop feeling bad, that's what I said. I'm more than happy to help out, you know I enjoy every single moment I spend here, so please stop worrying," I say. I quickly glance over at Mia. She has turned to face the other way, her shoulders quickly move up and down, no doubt with silent laughter.

"What did I do to deserve such a wonderful and caring niece as you?" Aunty replies in a softly spoken voice.

"I haven't got a clue. I guess, you just got lucky," I grin.

"Oh, by the way. Did you manage to get your entries in for the show jumping classes on Saturday? I keep meaning to ask," Aunty says.

"We certainly did. I've entered the ninety-five centimetre to one metre, and Mia's entered the eighty centimetres intermediate class. We'll probably go for a little warm up over the clear round course too," I reply.

Looking fully composed at last, Mia finally turns around. "But what if I make a complete idiot of myself in front of everyone?" she asks, looking worried.

"The two most important things to remember are taking part and having fun. If either of you are lucky enough to win or even get placed, then that, of course, is always a bonus. By the way, I've been thinking about this coming Saturday. As I will be out most of the evening with your Uncle, how would the two of you like to have the place all to yourselves? Maybe a movie night, or just a girl's night in? I doubt we will be back before midnight at the earliest. I've decided to get a taxi there and back so we can both have a few drinks, although I cannot guarantee what state the pair of us will be in when we eventually arrive home. In fact, even better. Why don't you stay the night, Mia? It would make me feel a lot less guilty knowing Jasmine has company on her final evening," says Aunty, looking at me, then to Mia and then back at me again.

"What a wonderful idea. I would love to. I'm sure the two of us can find plenty of things to keep us occupied, can't we, Jazz?" Mia says, with a very naughty grin.

"Great, that's all sorted then," replies Aunty, pushing up her glasses before continuing to study her diary.

I feel hot and flustered. So many thoughts are racing through my mind. Mia and I will be spending our very first night together. *How awesome is this?* Naughty images flash through my mind, as I struggle to concentrate on anything else. '*Oh, dear Lordy,*' I sigh, feeling mortified once again, hearing my words have been spoken out loudly once again.

"Sorry, I missed that," says Aunty, who thankfully still has her head stuck face down in her diary.

My cheeks quickly turn to a beetroot colour. "I said, I doubt we'll get bored." I reply quickly.

"I totally agree. I'm sure you can find plenty of fun things to keep you entertained," Aunty says.

I nearly choke on my coffee. As quickly as I can, I jump off my chair and walk in the opposite direction. All I can hear is Mia's muffled laughter. I know for sure, if I turn to look at Mia right now, I'll completely lose the plot and Aunty will then want to know what the bloody hell is going on between the pair of us. I take in long deep breaths until I feel the heat slowly subside from my cheeks.

"I think I've managed to work out a plan. See what you think of this. Jasmine, if you could ride Caper around the village, Mia can then lead out Spirit closely by your side. Thirty minutes would be ample. Patch and Warrior could do with a twenty-minute lunge, but, Jasmine, could you please take charge of Warrior; be warned, he can be a right little devil sometimes. Be on your guard and be careful he doesn't take a chunk out of you. Yoda and Hazel could also do with a quick bath, as today is their day off, so a little bit of pampering will do them both the world of good. If you both fancy another thirty minutes of dressage, I could fit you in, if you can make it around four o'clock. Oh, and that reminds me, the parts we desperately need for the hosepipe should arrive at some point today. Mia, it will save you looking like you have just arrived back from a pool party. How does this all sound?" she asks, before letting out a long deep breath.

I remember back to our bath time antics yesterday. Mia's erect nipples, her beautiful breasts, my hands caressing her soft silky skin.

"I think it all sounds doable. Jazz?" Mia asks, bringing me quickly out of my daydream.

"Of course, anything to help," I mumble.

"We'd better get cracking then hadn't we, Jazz?" Mia says, her eyes burning with desire.

"Yes. Of course. Let's get to it," I grin.

We head down the hallway towards the back door. "Have fun, stay safe and thank you," calls out Aunty.

We head off chatting in the direction of the yard.

"Oh, Jazz, I don't know how I managed to keep a straight face back there," Mia says.

"I can't believe we have the house to all ourselves Saturday evening. How awesome will this be?" I reply, taking hold of her right hand before gently pulling her towards the feed room.

Thankfully, the coast is clear, not a single soul in sight. Slowly closing the door behind us, I momentarily release Mia's hand, as I drag one of the plastic feed bins across the floor, placing firmly against the closed door. I turn to look at Mia, who has a cheeky grin across her face, and within seconds her sweet lips hungrily taste mine.

I moan in sheer pleasure, as her tongue slowly circles around mine. Her slender fingers run lightly through my long blonde hair, pushing her body closely against mine. My hands leisurely wander downwards to the bottom of her T-shirt, slowly easing it upwards. Her hot breath blows softly across my cheeks. She groans at the touch of my hands gliding tenderly up and down her soft and tender back.

"Oh, Jazz, I love you so much," she mumbles, her tongue moving across to circle the inside of my right ear.

This gentle teasing from her tongue is driving me crazy. The uncontrollable ripples, deep down below flow wildly, just as her hands sneak naughtily under my bra. "I love you, too, Mia." The feelings running throughout every single part of my body right at this present moment, are driving me completely to despair. "Please don't stop," I mutter.

Her tongue slowly flickers against my right nipple.

I gasp and hold my breath. Her playful tongue moves slowly

across to awaken my left nipple, completely taking my breath away. I close my eyes. I honestly don't know how much longer I can resist these magical spasms surging insanely, deep down below.

Mia instantly pulls away, standing still with one finger to her lip.

I quickly panic. I can hear voices coming from not too far away. Oh my God, someone is trying to open the door.

"Hello. Is anybody there?" calls out Nick's chirpy voice.

"Hold on for just two seconds, Nick. I'm just finishing clearing up the odd bits of food from behind the feed bins" Mia quickly calls back.

"No hurry at all, Mia. I really appreciate you doing this. This is yet another job I've been meaning to get around to doing all week, but like a lot of things on my to-do list, I always somehow seem to run out of time. I'll gladly leave you to finish it off. It's time for me to have a quick brew anyway. See you later," he calls out.

I continue to hold my breath. Nick merrily chats away to Charlotte and I finally release my breath, as their voices eventually fade away into the distance.

"What another close escape," Mia giggles. She immediately turns to kiss me tenderly, my heart still pounding at the thought of Nick catching us in the act.

"Roll on Saturday night," I whisper, my tongue eagerly searching for hers.

She reluctantly pulls her lips away. "You do realise, we now have an extra job to add to our already busy schedule, don't you?" Mia asks.

I look at her, feeling slightly confused.

"We've now got to clean out the blinking feed room," she laughs.

"Oh, bloody hell," I respond in desperation.

She watches me fumble, trying to tuck my firm hard breasts

back into my bra. "Let's get to it, sexy girlfriend," she sighs.

I feel my face glow bright red.

She continues in a very seductive voice, "Jazz. Now that is what I call such a waste. Your succulent and mouth-watering breasts should not be hidden away inside your damned bra. Their rightful place is where my hands and tongue have constant access, to give them everything they yearn for and deserve. I need them pressing firmly against mine."

Pull yourself together Jazz. Not long to wait now, that is if you can last it out. Let's see how strong your will power really is, shall we? My legs turn completely to jelly at this thought.

Chapter 21

Mia jumps quickly onto one of the feed bins; her hands brushing crazily through her upside-down hair.

Trying not to laugh, I ask, "What on earth is the matter?"

"A bloody huge tarantula. Surely you saw it run at great speed across the floor right in front of me?" she cries out.

"Oh, Mia, don't be so silly. Tarantulas don't live in the UK. In fact, the only related species is called a purse web spider. It was probably just a hungry house spider who's just popped out to find something to eat," I tell her, stifling my giggles.

"I don't bloody care what it's called. I'm not moving until I know it's gone," she says nervously.

"Ok, ok, calm down. Why don't you just stay where you are until I've cleared the rest of this mess up? I'll then let you know when it's safe for you to come down," I reply, suddenly feeling sorry for initially laughing. She really does look scared.

"Thank you," she mutters.

"You can thank me later," I grin. I glance over to see she fortunately has a tiny little smile on her face. "Right, are you ready?"

I ask her, holding my hand out to take hers.

As her hand grasps mine tightly, sudden bolts of electricity take me completely unaware. I look up into Mia's eyes and I immediately know she felt them too. *What is happening between us?*

Mia quickly jumps down off the bin landing safely by my side. "Wow, Jazz. Did you feel that, too?" she asks.

Before I even have time to reply, her shining green eyes look deeply into mine, sending a wondrous hot tremor all the way down my spine, before her lips secure their rightful place on mine.

"Bloody hell. I forgot all about that huge tarantula. Come on, Jazz. Hurry up. I need to get out of here, pronto!" she says, hurriedly releasing her lips from mine. Her quivering hands urgently find mine. Gripping them tightly, she quickly drags me out of the tack room and into the sizzling glorious sunshine.

Thankfully, her heavy breathing begins to return to normal. "Oh, Mia, I honestly didn't know how scared you were of spiders."

"I've always been terrified of them, ever since I was little. Probably because Mum always turned hysterical at any sight of one," she shares.

"Hey, everyone has some sort of phobia, so don't worry about it. I promise, I won't allow one to get anywhere near you whilst I'm by your side. Are you feeling better now and ready to make a start on our to do list?"

"Of course, I'm ready. Thank you for being so understanding and caring. I'm lucky to have you in my life," she says with a loving smile.

"I'll just nip off and get Caper tacked up. I should be ready meet you at the front of the yard in around fifteen minutes."

"Missing you already," she replies, before turning around to head off in the opposite direction.

"Don't me such a numpty," I tell Caper, as he dances around the mounting block, making the process of me getting on, totally impossible.

"Do you need a hand?" calls out Charlotte's cheerful voice, heading directly towards me.

"Yes, please. He's full of himself," I reply.

She firmly takes hold of the reins, before standing in front of him. "He hasn't been ridden since the beginning of last week, due to an infected wound on his hind leg. He has finished the course of antibiotics and the swelling has finally subsided. Probably why he is feeling a bit fresh," she says.

"Steady, boy," I tell him, sitting lightly on his back. Standing at only fourteen hands, he feels minute compared to Breeze. I quickly tighten his girth, adjust my stirrups, and thank Charlotte for her help before making my way to meet Mia.

I sit deep and still in the saddle, my hands lightly on the reins, as this fabulous chestnut Arab prances and shuffles around, feeling agitated, but powerful beneath me. "Hey boy, relax a little," I tell him, gently stroking his neck. He calms down for a slight second, but then starts to jiggle around again, letting out a huge bellowing whinny which vibrates all the way through his entire body, as soon as he spots Spirit.

Spirit obligingly whinnies back. The smile Mia gives me as soon as she sees me, instantly melts my heart.

We head out down the quiet country lanes. Caper is still skipping around whilst Spirit, the gentle giant, walks calmly on my inside. I can't see Mia at all. She is totally blocked from my view due to Spirit's huge and bulky body.

"Is Caper settling down yet?" Mia's asks.

I bob quietly up and down in the saddle, trying hard to get Caper to relax. "To be honest, he feels like he's ready to explode at any moment," I call back. A beautiful grey squirrel decides to scurry across the lane ahead and Caper darts sharply to the right. Good old Spirit doesn't even blink an eyelid. "You are such a scaredy cat," I tell him, with a smile, gently stroking his foamy, sweaty neck.

"Is it time for us to turn around and head back home yet?" Mia calls out.

"Sounds like a plan," I call back, as I ask Caper to halt whilst Mia turns around with Spirit. Suddenly Caper is standing tall on his hind legs. I quickly lean forward, letting out a long deep breath. Thankfully, his two front legs finally land back safely on the ground.

"Are you ok?" Mia asks, looking concerned.

"Don't you worry, I'm used to horses rearing. Breeze was a right little sod for walking around on his hind legs when I first started riding him. He even went over backwards twice with me still clinging onto him, but, thankfully, I managed to escape without even a scratch and so did he," I reply.

"Bloody hell, Jazz. Don't you ever get frightened?" she asks, looking shocked.

"Never. The adrenaline completely takes over. If I fall off, I just get straight back on and think nothing of it."

"You are amazing, although you do scare the heck out of me with some of your stories," she replies.

We head up the drive towards the yard.

"I'm going to have to hose Caper down. Just look at the state of him," I tell her.

She stops and turns to look at him. "He looks like a froth ball," she replies with a grin.

"Would you mind meeting me at the bathing area once you have turned out Spirit? I could probably do with a hand to wash down this little rascal," I ask.

"I'll see you there shortly," she smiles, before leading Spirit off in the opposite direction.

Caper immediately starts to dance around again, whinnying furiously, taking a strong hold, as he tries to bolt after Spirit. I sit quietly in the saddle, and politely ask him to stand. He argues with me, rearing up once again, getting himself in a frenzy. I quickly slide off and pull the reins over his head and I laugh at the expression suddenly on his face. I think he's surprised to see me standing next to him. "I believe some light lunging before riding you in future would do you the world of good, don't you? It'll give you a chance to get some of that pent up frustration out of you," I tell him, leading him across to the yard. Once I remove his saddle, he immediately calms down.

Mia holds him, whilst the nice cold water washes away the foamy sweat.

"I wonder if he could be suffering with a back problem. He seemed constantly agitated and not at all happy when I was riding him, but as soon as I removed his saddle, he instantly stopped fidgeting around and began to relax," I say.

"Turn off the hose for a second and let me have a feel of his back," Mia says.

I quickly do as she asks before swapping places with her. I watch mesmerised. Her slender fingers firmly massage the length of Caper's spine, with me wishing all the time it was my body she was working on. Caper goes from standing calmly to suddenly rearing up. I grasp the reins firmly. "Whoa boy," I tell him.

"I think he's a pulled muscle just to the right of T12, where the back of his saddle sits. That would explain his erratic behaviour," Mia informs me, with a smile.

"Wow, when did you learn all this?" I ask her, feeling proud and impressed with her knowledge.

"On my training," she replies with a wink.

"You know you can always practice on any part of my body whenever you want to," I tell her, with a cheeky grin.

Her tongue slowly rolls around the outside of her lips. "Who knows? Maybe I will take you up on your very kind offer," she replies.

"Oh, Mia, the thought of your hands exploring every single part of my body, and, I mean every single part, would be such a pleasurable experience," I reply, feeling hot and flushed.

"Ok, so which one of you would like their dream to come true?" enquires Aunty, suddenly appearing from around the corner.

"M-m-m me. I was just saying, if I'm lucky enough to get chosen for the *Olympic Team*, it would be a dream come true," I mumble, not daring to look at her.

"Jasmine, I totally agree. I cannot tell you how proud I am of everything you've already achieved, but you're right, it would be a dream come true for us all," she grins. "Oh, how was Caper?"

I quickly explain to Aunty all about Mia's findings.

"Just here," Mia says, gently touching his tender spot.

Caper instantly rears up in discomfort.

"I had no idea you would cover this type of knowledge on your course. I must say, I'm very impressed, Mia. I'll give Gareth a call and ask him to pop over as soon as possible," she says, who looks to be glowing from Aunty's recent compliment.

"Shall we put Caper back in his stable for now?" I ask.

"Yes, please. If I don't bump into you again, I'll see you both in the school at four pm sharp," she replies, before turning and hurriedly dashing back towards the yard.

I turn to lead Caper away. "Come on lad. Let's get you settled in your stable." Quickly stopping, I let out a gasp. Mia's hands press firmly against my buttocks, slowly massaging them in a very sexual manner. My legs instantly turn into jelly.

"They feel in good shape to me," I hear her say. Her hot breath blows gently across the right side of my neck. Goosebumps suddenly sizzle and prickle across the top of my tender skin.

"Oh, Nurse Mia. I think I've pulled a muscle, deep down below. Would you be kind enough to check it out for me?" I whisper.

Mia's unexpected laughter makes both me and Caper jump.

I turn to face her. "Is that a no then?" I ask, with a sulky look across my face.

"Good try, Jazz, but you just need to hang on for a little while longer. If you can manage to keep your legs firmly crossed and behave yourself until Saturday evening, how would you like me to carefully check out every single inch of your gorgeous body to confirm it's in good working order, before we proceed to our explosive finale?" she replies. She raises her index finger, seductively tracing the outline of my lips.

"Oh my God. Yes please." I gasp in delight. Her sparkling green eyes stare deeply into mine. I can see the passion and longing from deep within them. Her magical touch is causing mini earthquakes, deep down below. Her lips eventually touch mine, but part quickly, as Caper starts to fidget.

"I'm sorry for keeping you hanging around boy. Come on, let's get you back safely to your stable," I tell him, with a slight tremble to my voice. I slowly lead Caper back to the main yard. Those luscious and sensual feelings race frantically around inside.

"Missing you already, babe. I'll pop and get Yoda in from the field. See you back here shortly," Mia calls.

Roll on Saturday night. Let the long-awaited fireworks commence.

Chapter 22

"Hi there, Yoda. Now look at you, don't you resemble a bundle of cuteness," I tell him, gently stroking his gorgeous bay neck. He only stands at just over eleven hands. A gorgeous little Dartmoor who is a big favourite amongst the beginners.

Mia glances over his neck to smile, her right hand lightly brushing mine. Tiny little jolts make their journey up my arm.

"Yoda looks so weeny after spending time with, Spirit," she laughs. The water from the end of the hosepipe gently flows across his little back.

"Shall I grab the shampoo?" I enquire.

"Yes, please, although I do think after your feeble attempt last time, it might be safer for me to apply it," she replies, with a cheeky grin.

"How rude. If I remember rightly, my bubbles were the culprit for getting us both drenched. Just think back to what happened afterwards," I tell her, starting to feel turned on at the thought.

"How could I forget?" she answers, with a low sexy tone to her voice. Her hand suddenly flicks the end of the hosepipe in my direction. "Whoops, sorry," she continues, with a straight face.

I glare at her. The water travels down my neck, trickling slowly in between my breasts, whilst Mia looks at me in a questioning way. I watch the naughty grin appear across her beautiful face. "If you carry on behaving like this young lady, you do realise this could be a punishable offence?" I reply.

"I'm sorry, I didn't mean to. My hand jumped all on its own," she says, trying to look sorrowful.

"I'm afraid I don't believe you. Any further misbehaviour of this kind will be immediately added to my naughty list. I'll then tot up the final tally before deciding on the severity of your punishment," I say, my body quivering in anticipation.

"I'm trembling in my boots," she cheekily says. Her tongue spirals around her lips before purposely flicking another splash of water directly over my chest.

"So, it really does look like you want to be punished then, doesn't it?" I feel the coldness of the water touching my erect and tingling nipples.

"How's it going?" asks Charlotte, appearing out of nowhere.

"Great thank you," replies Mia, slowly dropping the hosepipe onto the ground, before hurriedly picking up the bottle of shampoo.

"Looks like I've arrived just in time," grins Charlotte, looking up and down my wet T-shirt.

I hope your bloody nipples aren't still standing on end.

"Brilliant," grins Mia.

She continues to massage the shampoo gently into Yoda, who seems oblivious to the goings on around him. He seems happy and content munching on his full to bursting hay net.

"Would it save you some time if I nip off and catch Hazel? She can sometimes be a naughty little madam trying to be caught" Charlotte enquires.

"That would be a great help, if you sure you don't mind," I

reply with a smile.

"My pleasure. I'll leave the new thread and nozzle just here. I hope it fits. See you shortly," she says, before placing the two items onto the floor, then scurrying off in the direction of one of the many fields.

I glance at Mia and the two of us laugh. I look down to see my nipples pointing firmly in her direction.

"Very, very nice," she informs me. Her tongue starts to tease me naughtily once again.

I pick up the hosepipe and scraper. "I think we ought to get back to the task in hand, don't you? Trust me, I'll take great pleasure in dishing out your punishment later." I get stuck in, trying to remove all the bubbles.

"Here she is," says Charlotte, just as I am about to turn the tap off.

I look across at Hazel, who is a delightful, but unusual looking Shetland pony. Palomino in colour, with one eye black and the other one dark sea blue. She must stand at only around eight hands and could easily walk underneath Breeze's belly. *What a fabulous little and large pair they would make.*

"Shall we swap over? I don't mind walking Yoda around until he's dry so you can crack on with little Hazel here. I do, by chance, happen to have a spare twenty minutes," says Charlotte.

"That would be such a help, Charlotte. We still have Patch and Warrior to lunge and groom before our lesson at four," Mia replies gratefully.

Hazel stretches her little head attempting to reach for the hay net but is finding it impossible.

We laugh at her sulky face. Mia unties the string and lowers it down, much to Hazel's delight.

"Isn't she just adorable?" Mia asks. Bending over towards me, leaning across Hazel's back, gently massaging the shampoo across her back.

"Very adorable indeed," I reply cheekily. I quickly kneel down to get a better view of Mia's wondrous and succulent breasts, as they sit invitingly in front of my eyes. Stretching out my arms, I cup both hands softly around them, giving them a generous squeeze, before allowing my tongue to wander freely over her delicate, smooth skin. The urgings down below immediately awaken. I pull the right cup of her bra down slowly to reveal one very hard, awaiting nipple. My tongue immediately diverts, naughtily teasing the edge of her nipple before my mouth caresses it tenderly, my teeth gently holding on and then letting go.

"Oh, bloody hell, Jazz. What the heck are you doing to me? Anyone could walk around the corner and catch us at any second. You can't resist missing a single opportunity to turn me on, can you?" she gasps, although she doesn't attempt to pull away.

"You want me to stop?" I ask.

"Not really, but maybe for just fifteen minutes or so until we've finished off little Hazel here and then I would be more than happy for you to continue with your naughty seduction techniques," she answers, with a cheeky grin and a flushed face.

"Deal," I tell her.

She tucks her gorgeous right breast safely out of my reach, and I let out a loud disappointed sigh. She laughs and grabs a handful of bubbles, placing them softly onto the end of my nose.

"You do realise, this now gives you three marks in total on your naughty list?" I tell her, flicking off the bubbles from my nose, my eyes still staring deeply into hers.

"Bring it on, girlfriend," she replies. Her lips seductively suck the tip of her right index finger.

Oh Lordy. Take deep breaths, Jazz.

"Would you be so kind as to turn the tap on for me please?" she asks, in a low sexy voice.

"Unlike the poor tap, I'm already very turned on." I try to ignore the pumping sensations before doing as she asks.

"Bloody hell," she screams out.

I rush towards her, but quickly come to a standstill when I see she is completely drenched from top to bottom.

"Bloody, bloody nozzle. Turn off that blinking tap, Jazz," she shouts out loudly.

I struggle to contain my laughter. "Maybe this is payback time for not letting me finish what I started earlier," I tell her once I am able to speak.

"Are you just going to stand there and laugh? Or are you going to help?" she asks, with her hands firmly on her hips.

I quickly head back to the tap, ensuring it's turned off tightly before walking back to Mia.

Hazel doesn't seem at all bothered with the happenings around her, she just continues to happily munch on her hay.

I slowly look Mia up and down, and a quiver of excitement runs down my spine. Her hard nipples shine through her wet T-shirt, her jodhpurs cling tightly to her body, her stunning black hair hangs sodden around her beautiful face. I head towards her with a naughty look on my face.

"Don't even think about it," she says sternly.

"How rude of you, Mia. What kind of thoughts did you think were running through my mind then? I was only coming to fix the hosepipe by replacing that nuisance of a thread and nozzle," I tell her, tongue in cheek.

She begins to laugh.

I slowly kneel down on all fours trying to reach for the end of the hosepipe. My right arm stretches between her long slender legs, and my left hand cannot resist delicately stroking the inside of her thigh.

"Are you wet all over, Mia?" I whisper softly, finally managing to retrieve the hosepipe.

Her lips urgently and intensely kiss mine. "I certainly am now," she whispers.

"Wow," I groan.

"Not long to wait now, my darling. I'm counting down the hours, minutes and even the seconds," she says, her eyes looking lovingly into mine.

"Me, too, Mia. I cannot wait to sample and treasure every single moment. Why don't I finish fixing the hosepipe and rinse off Hazel? You should nip and get changed into some dry clothes. I would love to offer to help, but we still have quite a lot of work to get through," I suggest with a smile.

"Only if you don't mind," she says, her lips lightly brushing mine.

"No problem. I'll get Patch ready for his lunging session and meet you at the ring when you are ready," I reply.

I watch her turn to head off in the direction of the house.

"Good boy. Now walking," I instruct Patch. His stunning long and thick feathers sweep the sand magically into the air. He is a perfect example of a true Gypsy Vanner. The beautiful black and white patches scattered artistically across his thick set build, his long white mane flowing all the way down to his chest plus his silky white tail with a few erratic black hairs entwined within, ripples gloriously in the warm afternoon sunlight.

"Wow, just wow," I hear Mia's voice say.

"Doesn't he look impressive?" I call back with a grin.

"Can I have a go?" she asks.

"Be my guest," I reply.

I watch her angelic figure slowly walk towards me. Her black sleeveless blouse hangs loosely over the top of her figure-hugging black jodhpurs, her long black hair tied back to the left in a loose fetching ponytail, her skull cap swinging in perfect rhythm to her stride gently swaying to and frow in her right hand. "Patch. I do have to say you look truly incredible," she tells him, gently stroking his beautifully conditioned neck, before securing the chin strap to her skull cap.

"I've already given him ten minutes going clockwise, so maybe you can do the same anti clockwise?" I smile.

"For some reason, my brain always seems to get confused going anti clockwise," she says, sounding unsure.

"Don't worry, Mia. I'll stay closely by your side and give you some pointers if I feel you need any," I tell her calmly.

"That's it. Well done. Now, slowly let him have a little more rein and gently flick the lunge whip behind him, asking him to move forward," I instruct.

"Bugger," she says, fumbling, the lunge whip dropping down onto the sand.

"Hey, don't you worry. Honestly, you are doing really well," I encourage, quickly bending down to retrieve the whip. "Look, try holding the lunge whip slightly higher," I tell her.

I slowly put my arms around her beautiful slender waist, guiding her right arm into the correct position. I feel her body tremble at my unexpected touch. "That's it, well done. Now gently flick the whip just behind him and click him on. Perfect," I tell her. My body moves slowly against hers, as her feet shuffle anti clockwise in the sand.

"And trotting," she tells Patch. He instantly responds.

Even though I can't see her face, I know she's smiling. I can smell her body scent, as my body slowly turns around with hers and it's driving me crazy. The ten minutes are finally up. "See, you can do it," I tell her proudly.

"You give me so much confidence, Jazz. I feel like I can achieve anything with you by my side." She turns to face me, her lips brushing mine.

I look at her tenderly, the eternal love I feel for her races throughout my veins.

"Shall I take Patch back to his stable, give him a quick groom and check his feet, whilst you get Warrior ready?" she asks, with a huge grin across her face.

"Sounds like a great plan to me. I can't believe it's nearly twenty-five to three already. See you back here shortly," I tell her with a loving smile. I watch enthralled, as she leads Patch out of the schooling ring. My eyes wander, drifting down to her sexy buttocks. They manoeuvre from side to side, my hands eager to squeeze them. She sadly fades away into the far distance and I sigh longingly.

Chapter 23

I lead Warrior out of the field, towards the yard so I can give him a quick check over. "I hear you can be a bit of a rebel," I tell him. He keeps one eye on me, slowly licking his lips, arching his strong neck whilst dancing to my right. I tie him up securely, ensuring his teeth cannot reach any part of my body, before quickly checking all four hooves. Putting on my body protector, and then swapping his head collar for the cavesson, I attach the lunge line and head off back towards the ring. The second I turn to bolt the gate behind us, I feel his teeth take a ferocious nip at my back.

"I see, young man. So, you are going to try and test my patience, are you?" I ask him, feeling thankful for the safety of my body protector.

The white of his right eye glares at me. He snorts and stamps his front foreleg in temper.

I swiftly get him moving around the ring, not daring to take my eyes off him, slowly moving my right hand downwards to pick up the lunge whip.

He may only be fourteen hands, but this strong-willed New

Forest pony, certainly has plenty of attitude. He canters around the ring in an uncontrolled manner, his hind legs kicking fiercely out, trying as hard as he can to head directly towards me. I flick my whip and smile. He begrudgingly moves himself outwards to the perimeter of the ring and I patiently wait for his temper to subside. Unfortunately, he isn't showing any signs of slowing down, repeatedly snorting in anger.

"Do you need a hand?" I hear Mia's voice calling.

"No. Please stay where you are. It's not safe for you to come in here," I shout back, not daring to take my eye off this crazy pony. After another five minutes or so, he thankfully starts to listen to me, and I eventually manage to bring him back to a halt. I drop the whip and slowly walk towards him, reeling in the lunge line, his black stomach heaving in and out with his recent exertions. I clip the end of the line to the ring on the offside of the cavesson. "Good boy," I tell him calmly. I lead him back towards the centre of the ring, stupidly taking my eye off him for a split second. The shock of his teeth bearing deeply and painfully through the flesh at the top of my right arm takes me completely by surprise. "Bloody hell." Thankfully, my squealing makes him jump backwards, and within seconds I am back in control, sending him firmly away to the outer of the ring.

"Bloody hell, Jazz. Are you ok?" I hear Mia shout.

"I'm fine," I call back. The painful throbs and stinging in my right arm, causes me to take in a sudden gasp of air. "And walking," I finally command, the ten minutes thankfully coming to an end.

Warrior looks completely worn out, just like I feel. Foam is completely lathered around his neck and underneath his belly. He's going to need a good old wash down, that's for sure.

Mia kindly opens the gate with a concerned look on her face. "What a little sod. Are you sure you are ok?" she asks.

"Just a little sore," I tell, not daring to allow my eyes to glance down at the top of my arm. I know only too well he's broken the skin. The droplets of warm blood slowly trickling down my arm gives the game away.

"You're bleeding!" she gasps, suddenly noticing the red blood seeping through the light blue sleeve of my blouse.

I keep a very close eye on Warrior. "I'm sure it's not that bad."

"Let me go and grab the first aid kit," Mia says.

I watch her run towards the tack room.

"Are you ok?" asks Charlotte, walking towards me, looking at my blood-stained blouse.

"I'm fine. My fault entirely. I was stupid enough to take my eyes off him for a split second," I reply.

She immediately takes hold of the lunge line. "Here let me take him from you, so Mia can get that checked over," she informs me.

I nod thankfully. Charlotte leads Warrior towards the bathing area and before I know it, Mia's standing right in front of me.

"Come on, let's walk to the house, so I can take a proper look and get your arm cleaned up," she says.

I slowly do as she asks, and it isn't long before I'm sitting comfortably at the kitchen table. I smile, watching my beautiful sexy nurse pour boiling water from the kettle into a ceramic bowl. She occasionally looks over to check on me, and I'm thankful when she places a hot mug of coffee in front of me.

She eventually sits down on the chair opposite. "Right, my gorgeous girlfriend. Let's see what damage has been done."

I gasp in delight, as she gently starts to undo the buttons on the front of my blouse. Watching her slowly undress me, is turning me on.

"Now, Miss. I'll have no naughty suggestions from you, thank you. I need you to stay still whilst I get on and do my job," she says firmly. "Stand up for a moment, Jazz."

I stand as still as I can. Mia removes my left arm out of the sleeve, then walks behind me. Slowly wrapping her arms around my chest, she gently tries to ease my blouse off from over the wound. "Damn it. I'm sorry, Jazz, but it looks like I'm going to have to cut off your sleeve. Unfortunately, some of the blood has already dried and is stuck firmly against the material. I promise I'll buy you a new one," she says. I watch her head towards one of the kitchen drawers to pull out an enormous pair of scissors. "Sit back down," she instructs. As she carefully cuts through the material, I observe the concentration across her face. "Now stay as still as you can. This may hurt, so, be brave," she continues softly.

I feel a pulling sensation against my skin, and the tingles commence once again not only in my arm, but also, deep down below. "Ouch," I moan. I'm finding it hard to control my urgings with her being so close, let alone behave myself. The only item I'm left wearing on the top half of my body is my bra, and I can feel my erect nipples waiting longingly for Mia's tongue to caress them. Each time her arm brushes lightly against my breast, the throbbing, deep down below becomes even more intense. The smell of antiseptic travels slowly up my nose.

"Why don't you take a sip of your coffee, whilst I just clean this up? You know what? You're going to have one heck of a bruise there, that's for sure."

"Oh, but, nurse Mia, I'm sure Warrior bit me in other areas, too. Maybe you ought to check me all over just to be on the safe side," I say, seductively.

"Behave yourself," she says, unable to resist a little laugh. The warm water trickles over my skin and I jump slightly, as she gently cleans up my wound. "Nearly done. I'll just pop on some antiseptic cream, cover the wound with a swab and then lightly bandage it up. I'll check on it later on before I go home. Once the wound has started to close, I can then start to apply the good old arnica cream to help with the bruising. How are you feeling?" her voice soft and caring.

"I'm sure a long passionate kiss followed by some TLC, would help me feel so much better," I reply cheekily.

Her delicious red lips spring into action, pressing intensely against mine. I push my body towards her, my tongue searches deeply for hers. I gasp. Her index finger traces teasingly around the outskirts of my bra. I hold my breath. Her loving kissing and caressing causing some major reactions from, deep down below. I sigh, as her lips caress the length of my neck. "Oh, Mia, that is making me feel so much better. Please don't stop."

She glances at her watch in slight panic. "I need to stop and finish dressing your wound, Jazz. Don't forget we have a lesson very soon. Are you going to feel up to riding?"

"I'm certainly not going to miss our lesson for anything," I tell her softly.

"Bloody hell, Jazz. It is twenty past three already. You know your Aunty hates anyone being late. We had better get our backsides moving," she sighs.

"One more kiss," I plead.

She looks deeply into my eyes, then looks down to my succulent breasts, her lips gently kissing each of them in turn.

My body is on fire and craving for her touch. I don't want her to stop.

"Come here. Let me finish dressing that wound of yours and then you should go and grab a new top to wear. I'll nip off and catch Breeze for you to give you a head start and meet you at the yard when you're ready," she continues, carefully placing a cotton swab over my wound, before neatly bandaging it up. "See you shortly," she says, before kissing my lips quickly and thcn disappearing quickly out through the kitchen door.

I sit for a moment waiting for the throbbing not only in my arm, but deep down below to ease. Picking up two paracetamol tablets, I quickly wash them down with a cold glass of water, before racing to my bedroom, to pull out a clean denim blouse from the wardrobe, which I struggle to pull over the thick bandage. I could have chosen a simple T-shirt, but the thought of Mia having to unbutton my blouse once again, will be well worth the hassle and pain of putting this on. I dash as fast as I can across to the yard, glancing at my watch to see we only have fifteen minutes to get to the school on time.

I'm thankful to see Breeze waiting patiently for me in an empty stall. As soon as he sees me, he whinnies happily, and my heart soars with internal love for him. Mia has kindly placed his saddle and bridle outside the stable door. I look at him suddenly realising he has been groomed too. I quickly check his hooves and am thrilled to see they have also been picked out. I can't wait to thank Mia for getting Breeze ready for me when I get her all alone later.

I struggle to lift my saddle onto his back, due to the constant ache in my right arm, but I grit my teeth determined to do this without asking for help. I let out a huge sigh of relief once his saddle and bridle are finally on, gently kissing him on his soft warm muzzle before leading him across to the mounting block. With my body protector on and my skull cap firmly in place, I raise my right leg over the saddle. I land lightly into my seat, before my feet slowly search for the stirrup irons. Sitting here on my boy, has made the throbbing pain disappear in an instant. I gently urge him forward. "Come on boy. Let's go and have some fun," I tell him.

Mia is ready and waiting outside the school, glancing down anxiously at her watch; her beautiful face looking slightly hot and bothered. The smile she gives me when I arrive at her side is priceless. The love she feels for me is noticeable in her stunning green eyes, as they gaze deeply into mine.

Roll on Saturday night.

Aunty suddenly appears.

"Are you ok, Jasmine? I heard on the grapevine, that little devil Warrior, managed to take a chunk out of you," Aunty says, looking directly towards me.

"I'm fine, thank you. All thanks to Mia for acting so quickly. Having a trainee paramedic on site is very useful indeed," I reply, turning to grin at Mia.

I watch Mia's cheeks start to turn beetroot in colour. "Well done, Mia," Aunty grins.

"Right. You both know the drill by now, so come on, off you both go. Time to get your mounts warmed up," she instructs.

I happily follow Ebony and Mia, as we work through our paces of the various warm-up stages. Breeze feels truly wonderful and strong beneath me. My view ahead is second to none, Mia's captivating bottom moving sexily back and forth in the saddle. *What more could a girl ask for?*

"Wonderful work," beams Aunty. "Now today, I want you to master the rein back. I know you and Breeze can already do this without thinking Jasmine, but I thought it would be great for Mia and Ebony to learn it, too. Anyway, it is always good to refresh old and learned moves when we get the chance to. Is this ok with you both?"

She continues looking from Mia and back to me. We both nod in agreement.

"Good. Now I want you both to dismount," she instructs.

Mia slowly eases her sexy body from out of her saddle.

I cannot take my eyes off her.

"You too, Jasmine," Aunty says firmly.

I quickly focus back on what I'm supposed to be doing and glance across at Mia, to see she is laughing.

"Good. Now, the thing I love about rein back, is that it's easy to teach from the ground. Plus, you never know when this aid could be a godsend in a certain situation. For example, reversing out of an area where you are completely confined and have no way of moving forward. Jasmine, could you please demonstrate with Breeze?" she asks me.

I gently touch Breeze's chest. "Back," I command. He immediately responds, happily doing as I ask.

"Good. Now, Mia, please try this with Ebony," she continues.

I watch closely. Mia places her slender hand on Ebony's chest and mutters the word "back," but unfortunately there is no movement at all from her beautiful black mare.

"Here," says Aunty, walking over to the two of them. "Press slightly firmly just here and say back as though you mean it," she instructs her.

Ebony instantly takes a step backwards. Mia's face looks completely astonished as to how quickly Ebony responded to Aunty's voice and touch. Aunty rein-backs her mare twice more. "Wow," she grins.

"Your turn now," Aunty says.

Mia now looks confident. She places her hand firmly against Ebony's gleaming chest, asking her to go back in an authoritative voice. Ebony takes a step backwards and the glee on Mia's face, is priceless.

Aunty gently pats her on the back of her body protector.

"Well done," I call out.

"Now let's try it with you both mounted."

Aunty offers her right arm out to give Mia a leg up.

I smile dreamily. Mia's beautiful backside points in my direction before Aunty springs her high up into the saddle, before striding across to me. Within seconds, I'm safely back in the saddle.

"Ok, Jasmine. Please show Mia how to perform the rein back mounted," Aunty says.

I stroke Breeze softly on his neck, before gently sliding my legs an inch behind his girth, sitting lightly in my saddle, ensuring my body is upright. "Back," I ask him. I close my fingers softly around the reins. Breeze responds beautifully and takes a step backwards, with all four legs standing squarely.

"Fantastic," Aunty beams.

Mia applauds with a big grin on her face.

"Right, Mia. Your turn," Aunty commands. She firmly moves Mia's legs into the correct position to give her some guidance. "Now sit up straight and close your fingers whilst commanding the word back."

I watch with a huge grin across on my face. Ebony steps back and Mia's face turns into a picture of delight.

"Well done, Mia," beams Aunty. "You can continue to practice this with Ebony every so often, but it's important not to do too many; it can cause stress to your horses' back and joints. Don't forget, practice makes perfect. Now, ladies, I must dash. I have another lesson to teach in just over thirty minutes. Please feel free to enjoy another twenty minutes in the school doing whatever you wish, and I'll see you later."

Mia smiles at me, and the longing I feel for her aches from deep within my soul. I ask Breeze to move closer to Ebony before slowly leaning forward to kiss her perfect red lips.

Chapter 24

Mia's eyes look lovingly into mine. "How's your arm feeling?" she asks.

"My arm feels ok, thank you, but there are some other areas of my body that desperately require the attention of my personal nurse," I whisper, my tongue searching for hers.

"Mmm," she moans in delight, as our tongues entwine eagerly.

Breeze starts to fidget, and I reluctantly pull away. "Come on, I'll give you a race to the other end of the school. Are you ready?" I ask, before urging Breeze forward.

"You cheat," I hear Mia shout.

The two of us fly to the other side of the school like a flash of lightning. I watch and smile. The two of them canter towards us. I can see Mia is grinning. As she sits deep into the saddle, with her body looking relaxed and happy. What a spectacular image the two of them make. "You took your time," I giggle.

"That is yet another mark I can add to your naughty list," she grins.

I raise one eyebrow. "You're the one who has been a lot

naughtier than me and don't forget I still need to dish out your punishment."

"And what exactly is the punishment you have planned?" she asks, leaning towards me, her tongue licking naughtily around her lips.

"You'll have to wait and see now, won't you? Don't worry, I have a wicked idea as to how you can say sorry for your naughty behaviour," I reply, with a mischievous grin.

Her sexy playful smile causes the warm embers which are already flickering around inside me to suddenly flare up, reaching a climax in an explosion of fire. I feel hot and flushed. I visualise Mia's wet, naked, body rocking gently against mine and the blood rushes directly up to my cheeks

"Jazz. Are you ok?" she asks, looking slightly concerned.

"I'm more than ok. I promise," I grin back.

"We only have fifteen minutes left, so we need make the most of it," she announces, turning Ebony around and asking her to trot to the other side of the school.

We head off in hot pursuit. "Come on, Breeze, let's go and catch them," I tell him in excitement.

Mia glances around to see us cantering towards her at great speed and urges Ebony to go faster. The four of us chase each other around the outside of the school having the time of our lives. Out of the corner of my eye, I see Aunty appear at the entrance and quickly ease Breeze down to a trot.

"It looks like the two of you have had a whale of a time," she laughs.

"We have," grins Mia, turning to look at me.

"I'm sorry to spoil your fun, but I do have a lesson to teach in five minutes," she announces.

"No worries at all and thank you for letting us use the school. We have had an amazing time. I'll redress Jazz's arm before I head off home, and I'll see you first thing in the morning as usual," Mia smiles.

My heart starts to beat rapidly at the thought of Mia touching me tenderly once again. It also sounds like Aunty won't be in the house, so Mia and I will have it all to ourselves. Certain areas of my body begin to ignite at the thought of the two of us all alone. I sit smiling to myself.

"Drinks at eight as usual?" I vaguely hear Aunty ask.

"Oh, yes. I'm looking forward to it," I reply, my thoughts jumping back across to Ruby and Nicole.

We say our goodbyes to Aunty and head back to the yard.

"I'll come and find you once I've settled Ebony down for the night, Jazz," Mia informs me.

I begin to untack Breeze. "That was great fun, wasn't it, my boy?" I ask him. Trying to lift the saddle from off his back, causes a dull and heavy ache at the top of my right arm. Feeling frustrated, I take the weight of the saddle with my left arm. I reach up to take Breeze's bridle off, the pain once again causing me to stop and take a deep breath. *Must be the bruising, Jazz*. Feeling highly frustrated, I manage to groom Breeze by holding the body brush firmly in my left hand. Taking a lot longer than it normally would, I eventually manage to pick out his hooves and the two of us head back towards the field. Blossom puts her head up high into the air greeting Breeze with a huge welcoming whinny. He dances around, whilst I struggle to open the gate. Once safely through, I quickly release his head collar and watch the two of them race around the field as though they haven't seen each other in months. I stretch high to hang Breeze's head collar up onto the hook in the tack room.

"There you are, sexy girlfriend," whispers Mia suddenly, leaning over my left shoulder.

"Bloody hell, Mia, you made me jump," I half scream.

"Sorry," she replies, not looking it one little bit.

"You will be," I tell her, with a naughty smile.

"Right then, Jazz. Let's get back to the house, so I can check over that arm of yours," she smiles.

My right hand purposely brushes past her left buttock. "Yes, nurse Mia."

She turns with both eyebrows raised. "Follow me," she orders, flicking her long black hair over her shoulder before heading out of the tack room.

I follow her back to the house. My pulse races rapidly. Oh, the way she walks, her sexy buttocks seductively moving from side to side, is causing me to feel very hot, deep down below for the umpteenth time today.

"Right. Just sit down there for a moment whilst I get myself organised," she says.

I watch her wash her hands thoroughly, before heading back towards me.

"Ok," she says softly. "Let me have a look."

Her hands gently unbutton my blouse causing goosebumps to magically appear. I take a deep breath and find it hard to keep my sexual urges under control.

"Stand up for me, Jazz," she asks.

I do as she requests, although my legs feel slightly weak and wobbly.

"Ok. I want you to try and pull your arm out of the sleeve, but do it very slowly," she says.

I try to raise my right arm, but grimace at the sudden pain.

"Oh, babe, it looks like that hurts. Hold on for one second, and I'll try another way. Ok, now take your left arm out first and I will try to pull your other sleeve down."

My arm falls out of the left sleeve easily. Mia walks behind me, bringing the rest of the hanging blouse with her to my right. She gently peels the other sleeve down carefully over my right arm. I gasp. Her undressing me like this, is turning me on and I'm finding it hard not to fling myself at her. I stand feeling horny in only my jodhpurs and bra. Mia looks at me in a hungry way, her fingers gently caressing each side of my neck. I feel fit to explode, as her sizzling lips move in to kiss mine. I groan in ecstasy. Her hands run seductively up and down my naked back, my skin tingling with the pleasure of her touch.

"Oh, Jazz. I love you so much," she says, her lips moving slowly downwards towards my breasts.

"You are driving me bonkers," I manage to mumble. *The fireworks inside get ready to explode.* My hands run teasingly around the outside of her thighs, before naughtily sneaking up and underneath her T-shirt. They tenderly explore her naked skin. She gasps. I feel her tummy flutter under my gentle touch. Her tongue flickers urgently against my erect right nipple. The temperature is rising dramatically. I move my hands back up to her head letting them run lovingly through her hair, before pushing myself harder against her firm succulent breasts.

A phone beeping from somewhere close by, makes us both jump causing our steamy and sensual session to come to an unexpected and abrupt end. "Oh, bloody hell, Jazz. That's my bloody phone. I'm so sorry," groans Mia. Her hands reluctantly leave the warmth of my back in desperate search of her phone. I take long deep calming breaths, begrudgingly taking a step back from Mia.

"Hi, Mum. Yes, I'm fine, thank you. Out of breath? Oh yes, I suppose I am. I've just run all the way from the yard to the house to grab a pair of scissors. A loaf of bread. No problem. I'll pick one up on the way home. Ok, see you soon," Mia says, her face looking flushed and stunningly gorgeous.

We look at the state of each other and laugh out loud.

"Bloody hell. All for the sake of a loaf of sodding bread," Mia sighs, the look on her face makes me laugh even louder. "I'm so sorry, babe."

"Don't worry. It's not your fault," I whisper, before my lips press gently against hers.

Her head slowly looks down to the beads of sweat lightly dotted across my breasts.

"Looks like we've got ourselves into a right old sizzling state, eh?" she grins.

I look lovingly into her vibrant green eyes. "I want you now more than anything. I never thought it could be possible to feel such an intense longing for another human being."

"Not long to wait now, my love. Come on, I think we need to get ourselves quickly straightened up, so I can finish treating that wound of yours. Not very professional of me to leave a job only half done, now is it?" she laughs.

"I suppose I should take half the blame for side-tracking you," I grin.

"Why, thank you, sweet girlfriend," she replies, with a smile that melts my heart. She finishes applying the soft crepe bandage.

"I desperately need a shower, Mia. My poor body has been thoroughly and endlessly teased by you all day long," I tell her with a naughty grin.

"There's nothing stopping you having a shower, Jazz, but I don't want your wound getting wet. Hold on, let me find some cling film to cover the top of the bandage and then you can take it off as soon as you've finished showering. Hopefully, by tomorrow the flesh where the teeth marks are should have healed over. We can then remove the pad and bandage and let the good old fresh air do its job. I'll take a look and decide for sure in the morning. It might be an idea to wear a stretchy vest top for now, too," she says, eventually finishing off wrapping the four layers of cling film firmly around my arm.

"Oh, Mia, I don't want you to go. Wouldn't it be safer if you stayed to help me shower? You know, just in case my wound hurts or gets wet," I tell her, with a pathetic look across my face.

Her instant burst of laughter takes me completely by surprise. "Jazz. You do make me laugh, but fortunately for you, you only have a minor cut, so I don't think that actually warrants a live-in nurse," she says, in between her laughter.

"Was worth a try though, don't you agree?"

"Oh, yes. You get a ten out of ten for trying," she says, just as her lips tenderly touch mine.

"Are you sure I don't need supervising?" I plea once more.

"You are a naughty, but sexy little minx, Jazz. Now, can you please try to behave yourself? I'll text you later this evening to make sure you've survived your shower," she answers, before giving me one last kiss and a gentle tap on my bottom before heading out through the door.

I stand thoughtfully letting out a loud frustrated sigh just as the door slams shut. I bend over to pick up my blouse from off the floor, before carefully reassembling the first aid kit. Placing the scissors safely back where they belong, I head off in the direction of the bathroom.

Chapter 25

Aunty finally sits down onto her favourite chair with a glass of red in hand. "What a long, but rewarding day," she sighs.

"I totally agree. To be honest, I haven't got a clue where the day has gone, it's completely flown by."

"Is it next Tuesday that you return to college?" Aunty asks, taking a large sip of her well-deserved wine.

"It certainly is, and I'm going to miss you all so much. How on earth am I going to cope without listening to your nightly bedtime stories?"

"It's a good job you won't be here next week, what with your Uncle hanging around for a few days. Somehow, I'll need to focus and concentrate on adapting my thoughts back to a so-called, heterosexual relationship," she laughs out loud.

"Stop it. You are making my ribs hurt from laughing so much. Isn't it time to get back to Ruby and Nicole?" I ask, grinning.

"Where did we get too?" she asks, looking thoughtful.

"The three of you were upstairs in the bedroom, all flirting and getting rather hot," I reply, waiting eagerly for her to continue.

"Oh yes, of course. Ok, here comes the next episode then. Ruby had been the first one to speak."

"All of a sudden, it's feeling awfully hot and steamy in here, so who fancies removing a layer of clothing?"

Her wet and hot lips reluctantly left mine. I remember feeling slightly shocked.

Well, before I could stop the words leaving my mouth, I suddenly blurted out, "Wouldn't it really fun to spice things up even more. What if we were to play a little Striptease game, say with some dice? How about, whoever shakes the highest number, gets to remove an item of clothing of their choice from one of the losers?"

"Now, you're talking, Trudy, that is what I call a genius idea," Nicole replied with a huge grin across her face.

"Top up the drinks then my lovelies, and I'll just pop downstairs to see if I can find a pair of dice. This is going to be so much fun," Ruby giggled.

Her eyes sparkled and her beautiful smile caused my body to pulsate in areas I hadn't even known existed. Nicole topped up our glasses, yet another bottle nicely polished off, whilst we gazed thoughtfully into each other's eyes, slowly sipping our drinks.

I couldn't resist Nicole any longer, and just as Ruby arrived back, my lips were hungrily exploring the top of her breastbone, my hands moving slowly around the outside of her huge firm breasts. She groaned. Her fingers deeply entwined themselves around my hair pulling me in closer. I heard Ruby's sexy voice coming from behind me. Her hands began to slide eagerly up and down my sides, and her tongue teasing the inside my ear was enough to drive me wild.

"She hesitantly pulled away, breathing deeply, before eventually standing up. Nicole and I turned to look at her, a huge smile covered her hot flushed face, as," Aunty says, pausing momentarily to top up her wine.

"This is such an incredible saga. Doesn't it bring those warm loving feelings back to life, telling me all this? Do you regret marrying Uncle when you remember those wondrous and precious moments you spent with Ruby and Nicole?" I ask, suddenly feeling sorry for her. The pure joy which spreads across her face, as she reveals her secrets and soul to me, make me wonder if she now regrets not choosing a different path.

"Oh, Jasmine. Of course, it does. It's hard to stop all those feelings and emotions from reeling back, although if I'm being completely honest, it's made me feel extremely happy reminiscing about all those secret but memorable times. As for your Uncle, well no I don't regret marrying him, but who knows? If we ever decide to split up, I'll be the first in the queue to push my trolley around Sainsburys in search of my ideal woman or alternatively I could ask you to set me up a profile on one of those dating apps," she laughs, with a naughty grin.

I laugh loudly, picturing Aunty with a beautiful sexy lady sitting perfectly in her shopping trolley in a packed-out Supermarket, casually approaching the checkout counter.

"Who won the first dice game?" I ask, struggling to control my laughter.

"Trust me. We all won in the end."

Ruby, was the first to throw, getting an unbeatable score of twelve. Nicole sat back watching, her face full of wanting, as Ruby slowly undid the buttons to my blouse. She then took her time to kiss every single section of my flesh where my blouse had once been. The throbbing aches and the boiling hot passion I felt were hard to fight. I took long deep breaths in a bid to control my urgings, patiently waiting for my turn to throw the dice. Luckily, I won the next throw.

Nicole's eyes looked pleadingly into mine, and without any hesitation at all, I sexily walked towards her. Her tongue circled the top of her champagne glass seducing me. Very slowly, I knelt down in front of her, and teasingly peeled down her silky stockings one by one. My lips moving tenderly across every single part of her long slender legs. My fingers lightly ran up and down the inside of her inner thigh. She moaned with deep pleasure. How I managed to have so much self-control, is beyond me!

I'm delighted to tell you I also won the next throw. Honestly, I was on a roll. This time I turned to face Ruby. The smile she gave me caused goosebumps to appear throughout every single centimetre of my body, whilst Nicole watched on. I carefully untied the laces on her top, gently lifting it over her head, before tossing it carelessly down to the ground. Her breasts looked heavenly, just as I'd remembered them from the evening before. I was tempted to unclip her bra there and then, but that would have been classed as cheating, so I took my time nuzzling my face softly against her breasts, my tongue circling all around. It turned me on to hear her satisfying moans. My lips continued to explore the base of her neck, her breasts pushing firmly against mine, my hands running up and down her naked back. Her soft moaning continued. Suddenly, I felt Nicole's hot breath against the back of my neck, her sexy hot body rocking slowly against mine. Her breathing becoming shallow, before she eventually pulled away pleading to us, it was now her turn to throw the dice. Ruby and I laughed at the sulky look on Nicole's face.

The energy surrounding us was electrifying; our breathing was heavy. I suppose you could almost call it panting. I took a moment to compose myself, sipping on the cold champagne, as we all threw the dice once again. Nicole was delighted to have won this time, and with no hesitation at all, she headed straight towards me. My body ached with anticipation. Her stunning eyes met mine and I felt *completely hypnotised. I lost all self-control, as her right hand seductively unfastening the zip to the back of my skirt. I felt it drop to the floor, and standing only in my bra and briefs, the intensity between us got stronger by the second. Nicole continued to drive me crazy from the front. Her teeth gently nibbling and biting my skin. I threw my head back not quite knowing how much longer I could last, especially when I felt Ruby's hands roll up and down the back of my legs stopping teasingly just under my crotch.*

"You feel so hot," she mumbled, her lips travelling seductively around my backside.

This was a truly sensational experience. Two erotic and highly sexed ladies turning me into putty right before their eyes.

"Your throw, Ruby,' Nicole, finally said, the two of them reluctantly stopping.

I stood captivated trying to catch my breath, closely watching the dice roll across the table to decide whose turn it would be next. Ruby was thrilled to have won. I held my breath, trying hard to fight my urges. Watching her sexily remove Nicole's black leather waistcoat resulted in certain areas of my body losing their control. This was all proving too hard for me cope, watching the waistcoat tumble down onto the floor to join our other items of clothing. The beauty of Nicole's body standing before me in a black thong and sexy laced bra completely took my breath away. I blinked slowly, licking my lips, and not being able to resist a moment longer, I walked boldly across to them both.

"You two are driving me wild," I whispered, kissing Nicole in a magical and passionately way.

"Ditto," Ruby muttered from behind me, her lips caressing my shoulders, her hands hungrily roaming around my back.

I felt the clasp to my bra being unclipped. Ruby's hands slowly guided the straps down my arms and over my hands, pushing herself even closer to me. Her hands stretched forward, reaching hurriedly to touch Nicole's back to unclip her bra. I let out a groan of delight. Nicole's gorgeous breasts finally firmly against mine. I remember moaning with pleasure. Ruby's ravishing naked breasts pressed firmly against my back and I thought I was about to explode. I had never felt anything so sensual in the whole of my life and to say I was completely turned on is an understatement. The passion and temperature continued to rise completely out of control. The three of us kissed with hunger, the pure desire driving us crazy, as we continued to explore every single part of each other's bodies. Ruby was the first one to reluctantly pull away, closely followed by Nicole. I stood trembling with passion. I was putty in their hands and they knew it. At precisely the same time, each of them gently took hold of one of my hands and led me slowly towards the bed. My heart was pounding, I felt dizzy and light-headed with the intense love and sexual emotions I was experiencing. They unhurriedly guided me across to the bed, no words were spoken. It felt like I was walking on air. Nicole, and Ruby panted breathlessly, possibly due the thought of what lied ahead.

"You go first, my darling," Nicole said to me in a loving warm voice. I scrambled awkwardly onto the huge round bed.

I was completely taken aback when the bed started to wobble. I felt slightly giddy and knew for sure it wasn't the champagne. The bed gently swayed with my every move and Nicole and Ruby laughed at my shocked face. I seriously thought I was floating in heaven.

"You like my waterbed then, do you, Trudy?" Ruby, asked, with a naughty, yet sparkling look in her eyes.

I bobbed up and down in front of their eyes, whilst they continued to laugh at my surprised expression. My breasts swung to the rhythm of each bounce, before I eventually managed to scramble across to the centre of the bed, thankfully landing flat out on my back.

I laughed along with them, as I slowly got used to the

undulations of the bed. Ruby dressed in only her briefs quickly joined me on the left side and Nicole in her black revealing thong to the right. The bed slowly rocked and swayed with their every move. The feeling of them both lying almost naked either side of me, set every single pulse in my body racing rapidly. I felt their lips and hands caress and explore my hot wanting body. I lay wriggling with desire. They continued to drive me towards a place I could have never imagined existed.

"With perfect timing, the two of them worked in tandem, gently removing my briefs down to my ankles and I am afraid to say Jasmine, this is where the story must stop. So, just like last time, I shall leave the rest of this encounter entirely to your own imagination," she finishes, raising her glass up to her hot blushing cheeks.

"Bloody hell," is all I can manage to say.

"I bet you're truly shocked by my naughty behaviour, aren't you?" Aunty asks, not daring to look at me.

"To be honest. No, I am not. Your stories are not only full of passion, love and enjoyment, but are intriguing, heart-warming and such a joy to listen to. I never knew what a naughty little minx you are, under that goody-two-shoes face of yours," I reply, when my mouth eventually allows me to speak.

"Really? Are you sure you're ok with me bearing my soul to you?" Aunty asks, with a warm smile back on her face.

"Oh yes, of course I am. Blimey Aunty, even though it was such a long time ago, it's unbelievable to think you remember every single moment, just like it was yesterday," I say, before taking a very much needed sip of my drink.

"You're right. Those precious memories will always stay with me, forever close to my heart and no-one can ever take them away," she says, with a faraway look.

"All of us make beautiful memories every single day and we should feel lucky to be able to treasure them for the rest of our lives. Did you see either, Nicole or Ruby after this raunchy session?" I ask.

"Oh, Jasmine. Trust me, our antics didn't finish there. Don't forget, we spent over fifty hours together. This is what happened in just the first few hours of our adventure. There is plenty more to follow, believe me," she grins, looking at my surprised expression.

"That could be the title of your book. A dicey fifty hours," I grin.

Aunty howls with laughter.

"I'll never be able to look at a pair of dice in the same way from now on," I tell her, in a serious sounding voice.

She laughs loudly and splutters on her drink once again. "Isn't it time for you to go to bed, before I throw this bloody wine over you?" she says, trying to control her laughter.

"No not yet. Please tell me one more chapter," I ask her, with a begging look.

"But it's almost a quarter to ten," she replies.

"Still early then, isn't it?" I grin, crossing my fingers in anticipation.

"Oh, why not? Go on then, one more episode, but before I continue, I think you should top up my wine," she grins, angling the crystal glass towards me.

Chapter 26

"I remember waking up, not quite understanding where I was. I stretched my arms high up into the air whilst yawning, when the bed started to move suddenly beneath me, and the memories of the night before came flooding back. What an unforgettable and life changing experience it had been. I looked around, but there was no sign of Nicole or Ruby. I quickly threw off the bed sheet, my naked body awkwardly manoeuvring to the edge of the bed. A piece of paper sitting on the nearby cabinet caught my eye and I reached over to take a peep. It read, *'Good morning, my darling, I hope you slept well. Feel free to jump in the shower. I have left some fresh towels and a dressing gown waiting for you in the bathroom. Pop down for breakfast when you are ready. See you soon gorgeous, Ruby x.'* I smiled warmly and headed off in the direction of the bathroom," she says.

"What a thoughtful and caring wake up note."

"Anyway, as I showered, I could smell Ruby and Nicole over every single inch of me. I reluctantly washed their sexual odour away with the sweet-scented shower gel, feeling slightly sad. Deep inside, I was hoping and praying there would be a lot more fun to come and it wouldn't be too long before I had the pleasure of their ravishing naked bodies wriggling against mine once again," she continues.

"And was there?" I ask, feeling intrigued.

"Oh yes, lots more to come. I made my way downstairs, feeling totally refreshed and on top of the world, wearing this beautiful white Egyptian dressing gown with just my underwear underneath. As I entered the kitchen, I came to a sudden stop, standing with my mouth wide open. I could not believe what I was seeing. Ruby and Nicole were merrily chatting away in the kitchen, dressed in French maid outfits," she giggles.

"Bloody hell. What on earth were the two of them up to?" I ask fascinated.

Ruby and Nicole looked across at me laughing at the surprised and shocked expression across my face.

"Good morning my darling," Ruby said, walking towards me, her soft lips tenderly brushing mine.

Nicole soon came to join us, gently squeezing my buttocks before kissing me softly on the back of my neck.

My skin quivered with the touch of their lips and that sexual longing I tried hard to contain began to resurface all over again.

"Good morning," I whispered; my legs starting to feel weak.

"Let's get a few shots of caffeine inside you and you'll soon be as good as new. We need you to be on top form and totally revitalised for the fabulous day ahead," Ruby winked.

I followed the two of them back into the kitchen, still not quite understanding the meaning of their dress code. The two of them looked so damned sexy. Ruby wore a red fitted corset with her beautiful breasts bulging out, a revealing leather mini skirt to match and long black hold up stockings with red lace around the top, running gallantly down to a pair of four-inch-high heeled shoes. I looked closely at Nicole, and she too looked ravishing in a black leather corset, her succulent breasts bursting at the seams, a mini skirt to match, and black hold up stockings running all the way to what must have been at least five-inch-high heel shoes.

I blinked continuously, whilst pinching myself, totally convinced I was in the middle of a dream.

Their hair was neatly tied back. Nicole wore a black leather choker with little diamond studs around her neck. A stunning ruby necklace fitted tightly around Ruby's slender and elegant neck.

Honestly, they both looked not only stunning, but hot and sexy, too," she says, with a wicked glint in her eyes.

I sipped on my coffee whilst they explained just exactly what they were about to get up to, and I nearly ended up choking, as they revealed what lie ahead.

"Can you see that screen up there?" Ruby asked, pointing up towards the wall. I looked up and nodded.

"Well, believe it or not, that is in fact a camera streaming live straight across to my iPhone."

I was still confused.

"We love to buy nice clothes, go for spa days and eat at the finest restaurants, so Ruby and I decided to come up with a little business idea which instantly took off in a very big way and the money just kept rolling on in," laughed Nicole.

"There are a lot of men and women out there who have many unusual and sexual fetishes. We simply act them out and get paid well in return," grinned Ruby. I was speechless.

"We go live in ten minutes, so let me grab you another coffee. If you want to, why not sit on the sofa, and watch the pair of us in action? No laughing though," continued Ruby, before leaning forward to kiss me affectionally once again.

"Honestly, the whole situation seemed so surreal and bizarre, but the following hour turned out to be one of the funniest and most entertaining things I have ever witnessed," laughs Aunty, as she picks up her half empty glass.

"What did they actually do?" I ask, totally engrossed in her story.

"Oh, Jasmine. Where do I start?"

"I watched intrigued. Ruby put on some wireless ear plugs, whilst Nicole busily placed numerous cleaning materials on top of the nearby table. Included amongst the items was a feather duster, some wooden pegs, pink rubber gloves, a rubber toilet plunger and strangely enough a box of cornflakes. Oh, and a hoover stood closely by."

I picture the whole scene, before desperately needing another large sip of my drink. I cannot help myself and laugh out loud.

Ruby then called out, "Five, four, three, two, one, and action. Nicole, we are now going live. Good morning, Mr Benson, and what can myself and my sexy assistant, Nicole, do for you today?" she said in a very seductive voice. "No problem, that will cost twenty pounds," she replied whilst pausing for a few seconds.

"Payment received," Nicole confirmed with a wink and a very naughty smile, giving the thumbs up to Ruby.

I watched speechless, as Ruby dropped a handful of cornflakes onto the centre of the kitchen floor.

"Bend over and pick them up, now," she commanded to Nicole, pointing downwards.

I held my breath, leaning slightly forward, just in time to see Nicole slowly get down on all fours, her gorgeous backside pointing high up into the air directly facing the camera. The single strap of her black sexy thong was the only visual item between her bum cheeks.

"Honestly, my eyes nearly popped out of my head," giggles Aunty.

I try hard to stop the laughter that has been threatening, but it is impossible.

"Trust me. It gets even funnier."

"Yes, Mr Benson. I'll tell her to hurry up. You are completely right, and yes, I totally agree with you, if she doesn't speed up, of course she deserves to be punished. Don't you worry, I'm more than happy to tickle her backside with my feather duster, but that will cost you an extra tenner," Ruby continued, as Nicole put a thumb up to her.

"Payment received Mr Benson, thank you. Nicole, you have been very naughty," Ruby said, placing the long thin heel of her right shoe firmly onto Nicole's back. She slowly waved the multicoloured feather duster around looking directly up at the camera, revealing her stunning inner thigh.

"I'm so sorry. Please forgive me," Nicole pleaded, whilst Ruby lightly flicked the feather duster across her magnificent bum cheeks," Aunty says, in between her laughs.

"Oh my God! That is hilarious," I reply, my ribs aching from the nonstop laughter.

"By this time, I had placed the throw over the top of my head trying to drown out my laughter. I also felt guilty for finding it such a big turn on in a funny sort of way. Anyway, the whole session was due to last for just over an hour, but one of the funniest requests came from a Mr Shackle. This is what happened next."

"Mr Shackle, how lovely to see you again and what can myself and the luscious Nicole do for you this time?" Ruby asked looking directly up at the camera, her index finger slowly rubbing inside her

inner lip.

"Really? Well, as you are probably aware, a request of this calibre is going to cost you at least one hundred pounds."

As soon as I heard this, I decided to come out of hiding from under the throw. I was desperate to know what on earth was going to happen next.

Nicole put her thumb up to Ruby, once again confirming payment had been received. She then turned to smile at me giving me another naughty wink. I was finding it hard to control the sexual urges churning around deep inside, watching these two sexy beauties in full action.

"Nicole. Please do as Mr Shackle asks and fill up the sink with warm water, making sure you create lots of wonderful and magical bubbles," Ruby requested.

She stood behind Nicole at the sink, pressing her body firmly against hers.

"Nicole. Now please stand over there and give Mr Shackle one of your special smiles," she then commanded. Nicole stood posing, pouting her lips, with her hands firmly on her hips, as Ruby walked towards her with a double handful of bubbles.

"Mr Shackle has asked me, on his behalf, of course, if I would be kind enough to give your wonderful breasts a pleasurable bubbling massage. Nicole, please could you undo your waist coat and take it nice and slow," Ruby seductively whispered.

Their performance was not only intriguing, but also breath taking and so bloody entertaining to watch. Nicole immediately did as she was asked, eventually allowing her waistcoat to drop down onto the floor. She looked up at the camera teasingly with just one finger running across her succulent red lips, before it disappeared seductively into her mouth.

"I hope you are enjoying yourself, Mr Shackle," Nicole said sexily, after teasingly removing her finger.

I held my breath as Ruby walked across to Nicole, sexily wriggling her hips before standing directly in front of her. They stood at a sideways angle, which I assumed was for the benefit of the camera. I remember letting out another gasp. Ruby slowly massaged a large handful of bubbles seductively around Nicole's mouth-watering breasts. I yearned to join in the fun. It felt sensual and erotic.

"Yes, Mr Shackle. As always, your wish is my command. You are completely right. It is now Nicole's turn to massage my big Mamma's as you call them," Ruby said.

Honestly, by this time, I was so desperate to laugh out loudly. I haven't got a clue how Ruby, and Nicole managed to keep straight faces. I observed Nicole closely. She walked in a very sexy, but sultry manner towards the sink, whilst Ruby slowly undid the laces to her stunning silk corset, before teasingly easing it over her shoulders, allowing it to rest firmly on her waist. Her beautiful red bra full to bursting with her so-called big Mamma's, patiently waited for the handful of bubbles to arrive," Aunty says. The tears roll down her face, and she glances across at me.

"Unbelievable. I cannot believe how much they got paid for doing this. I wonder how much we could earn?" I reply. The tears beginning to stream down my face.

"Trust me. It got more bizarre by the second."

Nicole continued to massage Ruby's big Mamma's and very stupidly I suddenly came up with what I thought was an amazing idea. As quietly as I could, I slowly got up from the sofa and walked across to the table. I immediately found what I was looking for, a pen and a piece of paper.

I hurriedly scribbled down, 'Why not ask Mr Shackle if he would like to watch the two of you massage baby oil slowly and seductively into my virgin chest. Tell him, I'm your personal shopper, and for something as special as this, it'll cost him an extra two hundred pounds.'

I then carefully slid the note across the breakfast bar. Ruby watched my every move, looking slightly intrigued.

"Nicole, Mr Shackle, would like to see even more bubbles, although sadly his time is almost up," Ruby announced, slowly heading across to read my note.

Her eyes glistened and the naughty grin on her face made my heart melt with desire. The passion and longing I felt for the two of them had been smouldering away deeply inside, so much so, I felt ready to explode again.

"Mr Shackle. As you are probably aware, you only have ten seconds left. We were wondering if you would like to consider an extra special treat which has been just added to our agenda? This is a one-off performance. I can assure you now, it's something you may never get to see, ever again," Ruby drooled.

"You see, my gorgeous personal shopper Danielle is here at present sorting out my drawers. I hasten to add, she is also a very young virgin. How would you like to see myself and the irresistible Nicole massage baby oil all around Danielle's naked breasts, for five minutes, right in front of your eyes? It would obviously cost an extra two hundred pounds, but please don't take too long in giving me your answer, as we do have plenty of other callers patiently waiting in the queue who I know would be thrilled to be offered the opportunity to see this once in a lifetime performance," Ruby tells him.

My heart instantly started to pound loudly. I hadn't a clue what the heck had come over me. Why had I suggested such a ridiculous idea? I felt anxious, and suddenly shy. I held my breath, and watched feeling horrified, as Nicole suddenly put her thumb up with a huge grin spread across her face.

"Now you are talking," Ruby said, turning to walk sexily towards me, gently taking hold of my hand.

"I completely blanked out my nerves and any initial concerns, when Ruby kissed me passionately, slowly undoing the belt to my dressing gown. Her breasts pushed against mine and we were lost momentarily, in a world of our own," she smiles.

"Oh my God. Tell me you didn't do it?" I gasp, not quite believing what I'd just heard.

"Oh, yes, I did it. To be honest, it was such an incredible and sensual experience. I even forgot all about Mr Shackle watching. I was totally engrossed in the indescribable pleasure and attention Ruby and Nicole's tender hands were paying me. Let me tell you now, it was truly remarkable. I would have been more than happy to pay two hundred pounds out of my own pocket to experience those moments all over again. I mean, who would be crazy enough not to take up the opportunity of having two gorgeous sexy ladies tenderly massage handfuls of baby oil into your breasts?' she laughs.

The tears continue to run down her cheeks once again. "Oh my God. Go Aunty. I mean, bloody hell, you earned two hundred pounds in just under five minutes. Bring it on," I cry out, taking a very large sip of my gin and tonic.

"By the end of that hour, can you believe there was six hundred and twenty pounds sitting in the kitty? Trust me, that was a huge amount of money back then," she grins.

"We are both in the wrong bloody business, aren't we? I hope it didn't all end there?" I ask. *What a dark horse Aunty is.*

"God no. Remember, we had fifty hours in total and by the way, young lady, it's way past our bedtime. I can continue the saga tomorrow evening," she says, in between her laughter.

"I suppose you're right," I reply, swilling down what is left of my gin. "See you in the morning then, oh and by the way, sweet dreams," I continue in a cheeky voice. I lay tossing and turning. My mind running through the day's events. *Only three full days left with Mia.*

Chapter 27

Groaning out loudly, I attempt to roll over. My bed feels completely different, hard but fluffy. I open my eyes, but quickly close them again. The brightness from the streaming sun, blinding me by surprise. I attempt a second time, eventually managing to glance down at my watch. *What the heck are you doing on the bloody floor, Jazz?*

Very slowly, I drag myself up, immediately noticing my right arm feels heavy and achy. *Why on earth is my duvet lying on the floor across the other side of the bedroom with my pillow sitting beside it?* I sit on the edge of the bed trying to get my bearings. My dreams are getting out of control. One memorable part comes flooding back to me. A warm knowing smile emerges across my face. I let out a long and satisfying sigh. Mia and I had been lying in a deep straw bed within a disused stable out in the middle of nowhere. Our love making was hot and passionate. We rolled around in the mountain of golden straw, the moonlight magically flooding in through the cracks in the old wooden stable. I laugh to myself when it suddenly occurs to me, I must have rolled out of the bed.

As quickly as I can, I make my bed, before heading across to the bathroom for a well needed morning shower. Wrapping a plastic bag around the bandage for protection, I think how miraculous it is for it still to be intact. Staring at the multicoloured bruising which seems to have appeared out of nowhere, running from my shoulder down to my elbow, shocks me momentarily. I close my eyes, trying to focus on something other than the constant throbbing in my arm. Mia's beautiful smile stares back at me, as the soft sponge flows lightly across my breasts. My nipples instantly stand to attention. Slowly, but purposely, I move the sponge downwards and playfully just beyond my belly button. The sponge proceeds to slide mischievously between my legs, gliding around to that tender and special area right in the centre. A wonderful ongoing fluttering sensation takes me completely by surprise. Letting out a satisfied moan, I take a deep breath, as the pulsating, deep down below slowly disappears. *What on earth just happened?*

These new and sexual feelings I'm experiencing are beyond heavenly. They are hard to control, and I honestly don't understand what they mean. The worrying part is, that they seem to be getting stronger by the day. *Not long to wait now. Only two days left until you and Mia can share for real those magical moments you've both been longing for.* Suddenly, the pulsating throbbing way down below, decides to reappear from out of nowhere. This confuses me. It has happened completely out of the blue. *Bloody hell, Jazz. You need to get a grip and pull yourself together NOW.*

I walk down the pathway deep in thought. The beautiful fresh air, the gentle breeze whirling around my face, with the sun shining warmly all around, miraculously cleanse my troublesome thoughts. I take a long deep breath, feeling grateful. "Good morning, my lad. How are you on this wonderful and glorious Thursday morning?" I ask Breeze. I lovingly wrap my arms around him, wincing slightly at the dull ache running through my right arm.

Breeze nickers a little whinny in response. The vibrations from his wonderful morning welcome, sweep effortlessly across my back.

"I love it when you talk to me in your own special way, Breeze. I'm the luckiest person in the whole wide world to have you as my best friend," I whisper to him. Our tender moment is interrupted. Blossom's soft muzzle rummages through the pockets of my jodhpurs in search of treats. "Ah, now that fooled you, Blossom, didn't it? Look, I have hidden your treat firmly away in a place where you will never find it. Guess where it is? Look, it's safely down my top," I laugh.

A surprised look emerges in her eyes, as she suddenly watches the carrot appear out of thin air. Breeze gives me a very sullen look.

"Please don't look like that, I have one for you, too. Right, my lovelies. I need to dash off now, but I'll see you both very soon," I tell them. Slowly, I look around wondering where on earth Mia is. Glancing down at my watch, I see it isn't even quarter to seven yet.

Time for a nice mug of hot coffee.

"Hey there, sexy girlfriend, I was just about to come and find you. How's your arm feeling today?" Mia's soft voice greets me.

I walk towards her feeling in a trance. She takes me into her arms, kissing me eagerly against my awaiting lips, in the most passionate way so far. "Mia, you are driving me insane," I whisper.

Her lips slowly move down to my neck. "Not long now, Jazz. I'm counting down the hours until the two of us can finally become one," she murmurs back, her breathing quickening by the second. "Shit," she says, before quickly pulling away and rushing across to grab hold of the kettle.

"Good morning, ladies," says Aunty, purposefully striding in before placing two carrier bags of heavy looking shopping onto the kitchen work top, with a huff and a puff.

"Why on earth have you been out shopping so early? I could have done that for you," I say.

I try to act as normally as I possibly can.

"I thought I'd get it done and out of the way. Surprise, surprise, I have yet another busy day ahead," she sighs.

She turns to look at me smiling, before focusing on the black, blue, red, and purple bruising running from my elbow to my shoulder, as I struggle to unpack the shopping.

"Bloody hell, Jasmine. Now, that is what I call a whopper and a half," says Aunty, still staring at my arm.

"Let me take a look, Jazz," Mia says, walking quickly towards me after seeing the concern on Aunty's face.

"It only aches and feels a bit heavy. Nothing to worry about," I tell Mia.

She slowly unravels the bandage. "Phew, such a relief to see. The aching is only the bruising coming out, Jazz. Let me have a quick look at that wound," she informs me, gently pulling off the cotton pad. "Magnificent. Just as I'd hoped. It has healed fantastically overnight. Now just sit tight, whilst I try to locate the arnica cream."

I struggle to control myself.

Mia's fingers gently massage the cream seductively up and down my arm. That reoccurring fluttering continues, deep down below. Turning my head, I quickly try to focus on Aunty who is oblivious to anything going on around her, as she concentrates on putting the shopping away.

"There we are. You are all done, Jazz. Don't worry, I'll keep a very close eye on your arm," she says with a grin. Her fingers naughtily brushing purposely over my breasts.

The fluttering gets stronger by the second. I try to clear my mind and focus on anything else other than, Mia. "So, what are the plans for today?" I ask Aunty.

I watch Mia's stunning body lean forward over the sink. Her sexy bum cheeks wobble in rhythm with her vigorous hand washing.

"Well, yet another busy day on the agenda today," sighs Aunty.

"Is there anything we can do to help?" asks Mia, walking back towards us, her beautiful breasts bouncing up and down with every step she takes.

Very nice indeed. Surprisingly, the words seemed to have shot out loudly from my mouth. Thankfully, there is no reaction from Aunty. A hot flush slowly rises to my cheeks.

"Well, I've been thinking. Seeing as you've both have helped me out all week, how would the two of you like to try out the cross-country course this morning? You deserve to take a break from the regular daily chores. I think it would do you the world of good to get out there and enjoy yourselves. Joanne and Lorna will be helping me this morning, and I also have Nick and Charlotte, so I think between us, we can manage everything just fine. Luckily, Lorna is covering my lessons on Sunday, I thought it was better to be on the safe side, in case I have a hangover to deal with. By the way, if you could both possibly spare a couple of hours around one thirty this afternoon, I could really do with your help. Would that be ok?" she asks.

Mia and I look at each other nodding at Aunty with a grin.

"Actually, I've asked Nick and Charlotte to bed down the last empty stable we have available. You know, the one right at the end of block two. This afternoon, we have an exciting new livery arriving, scheduled for around two o'clock," Aunty announces, with a big smile on her face.

"Really? Who, is it? Do we know them?" Mia asks.

"Oh yes, I'm sure you both do. The horse is an unbroken four-year old gelding, standing at sixteen three hands. His pedigree is truly outstanding. Some of his relatives include winners of Group one races on the flat, top class races over jumps, including three Cheltenham winners and his dam is the famous international eventer *The Sky's the Limit,"* she replies.

For some reason, the name rings a bell and my brain hurriedly searches for the information I desperately need to find. "Oh my God.

The Sky's the Limit? I followed every second of her career. If I remember rightly, she was ridden and owned by the talented and gorgeous Lucia Charlton. *Wow, wow, wow.* Lucia was my teenage idol. In fact, she was the one who inspired me to concentrate and focus on the riding techniques I use today. I even had a poster of her stuck on my bedroom wall. Oh my God," I reply. I can see Mia looking at me, with one eyebrow raised, and a confused expression across her face.

"I followed her career with great interest, too. You probably already know that she retired last year, wanting to concentrate more on the breeding side of things," Aunty replies. A dreamy look covers Aunty's face and I begin to feel slightly curious.

I've only ever seen that faraway look on her face, when she's been telling me one of her naughty stories. I wonder what on earth this could be about.

"Does Lucia own the four-year old who is arriving today? If so, why is she putting him in livery here when she obviously has her own stud?" Mia asks, still looking puzzled.

"A very good question, Mia. Yes, she does own him. Lucia has recently been going through a very messy divorce. It's been all over the papers, and the local news. I am surprised you haven't heard all about it. She has always been quite well known for having the odd fling here and there, but she finally pushed her luck and got caught out red-handed last year by her stunning French wife, Maddison, who was supposed to be in New York with her Sister. Maddison arrived home a few days early, only to find Lucia dressed in a slinky black leather outfit, waving around a riding whip, whilst their twenty-six-year-old Spanish head groom lay helplessly naked whilst handcuffed to their gold-plated headboard. Apparently, the groom, Izabella, was covered in whipped cream, chocolate sauce and not forgetting two large strawberries sitting on the end of each nipple. There is no way, Lucia could wriggle out of this one. When

Maddison caught them, Lucia's face was covered in chocolate and whipped cream too," Aunty replies.

"Oh my God," I blurt out. I feel completely shocked to hear this recent news about the naughty and disgraceful behaviour of my idol.

Mia struggles hard to contain herself, her laughter getting louder by the second.

Suddenly, I, too, see the funny side. I picture the scene once again. Two juicy red strawberries sitting nicely on top of Izabella's firm nipples. I can't help but join in with Mia's infectious laughter and it isn't long, before Aunty finds she cannot resist any longer either.

"We shouldn't laugh ladies," Aunty says, trying hard to compose herself.

This sets Mia and I off all over again. The three of us struggle to wipe away the tears of laughter.

Chapter 28

"Right. I need you both to be serious. Autumn Wonder will be staying here until Lucia has completed on the purchase of her new Stud, which should happen in the next two to four weeks. Sadly, Maddison's solicitors forced the sale of their other stud, which is due to complete tomorrow. Lucia and Maddison had originally bought the property together and Izabella wanted her money back as soon as possible. It was too much of a financial risk for Lucia to buy Maddison out. It was too big a project for her on her own. The stud, I recently found out, sold for just over three million pounds. Lucia has been fortunate enough to find a smaller stud, which she's managed to buy outright. Her plans are to modernise and expand it. It's also going to take time to rebuild her professional reputation. Lucia is said to be one of the most exciting breeders to recently arrive on the scene. She owns a fabulous variety of top-class youngsters, who all have huge potential. Thankfully, she's managed to secure temporary places for her other seventeen horses but found herself desperately needing somewhere safe to keep, Autumn Wonder. Even though he isn't yet broken, his current sale value stands at around two hundred and fifty thousand pounds. Lucia's new stud is only located fifteen miles from here. Apparently, she found me online, gave me a call yesterday afternoon, and the rest is history," Aunty continues.

"Wow," is all I can manage to say. Mia and I stare at each other with a naughty grin. "How old is Lucia?" I ask, feeling intrigued. "I would think off the top of my head, probably in her late-thirties," Aunty replies. That faraway look flashes across her face once again.

"We'd better get cracking then, Jazz. I can't wait to try out the cross-country course," Mia announces. She glances at me, her eyes looking longingly into mine.

"By the way. No one else can know, Autumn Wonder is staying here. It needs to be our little secret. Of course, I'll tell Nick and Charlotte, but there'll only be the five of us who know the truth. I've also assured, Lucia, I'll personally be in sole charge of his daily care. Lucia has grown a huge fan following over the years and we certainly don't want any of her groupies hanging around here in the hope that they can catch a glimpse of their idol. Understand?" Aunty announces, in a very serious way.

"How exciting," grins Mia.

"Mia, would you mind if I catch up with you a bit later, say around ten o'clock? I just want to give Mum a quick call and fit in an hour's revision whilst we have a bit of free time." I ask, with a warm loving smile.

"No problem at all, Jazz. I'll see you over at the yard when you're ready. Anyway, I need to clean my tack. I could do yours too if you'd like me to?" she smiles warmly. Her beautiful emerald eyes penetrate through mine, causing the flutters to suddenly reboot.

My tongue slowly licks the outer of my lips. I reply sexily, "That would be a tremendous help. I promise I'll find a way to thank you later." Feeling shocked at my words, my hands immediately cover my face in horror. Turning slowly around, I worriedly wait for

Aunty's reaction, but she is oblivious to anything going on around her and I sigh with relief. She looks to be deep in a world of her own.

Mia is laughing, as she turns to head off towards the door. She suddenly stops and smiles. Her lips silently mouth the words, *I love you.*

I stand for a moment and take in a deep breath before turning around to face Aunty. "Aunty, what on earth's the matter? I know for certain something is troubling you. Please tell me. Maybe I can help?"

"Oh, Jasmine. I still have so much to tell you, you know about the rest of those fifty hours," she says, completely avoiding my eyes.

"But what has that got to do with anything?" I ask softly.

"Well, the part we haven't got to yet is when Nicole, Ruby, and I popped out for a celebration lunch that afternoon, courtesy of our little earnings," she sighs.

"What happened?" I ask.

"There was a gorgeous lady in the restaurant. She had been sitting all alone at a table opposite. She kept glancing over, smiling occasionally at our hysterical laughter. We felt sorry for her, and eventually asked if she'd like to join the three of us. She gratefully and readily accepted, quickly fitting in perfectly into our merry little group. Honestly, she was breath taking. Long auburn wavy hair, green entrancing eyes, a beautiful body, and her lips; Oh my God, those lips were something else. Straight away the two of us shared an unbelievable strong sexual chemistry. The four of us flirted outrageously with each other, downing four bottles of champagne in total. Lucia and I soon realised we had so much in common, our love of horses being the main one," Aunty continues, before taking a long deep breath.

"Are you are trying to tell me that you ended up having a foursome? If so, why is that a problem?" I reply, with a soft gentle tone to my voice.

Aunty slowly looks up into my eyes, with tears threatening. "Jasmine, it was Lucia. The fourth lady was called, Lucia," she finally says.

I am totally confused and seem to have completely lost the plot. "*Lucia Charlton*," she repeats.

It takes a moment for her words to sink in. "Oh my God. You mean *theeee,* Lucia Charlton? Bloody hell. Oh my God." I blurt out.

Aunty slowly nods her head confirming any doubts I had. "What the bloody hell am I going to do, Jasmine?" she asks me, sounding desperate and distressed.

"When did you last see her?" I ask, still unable to completely digest this recent information.

"Why not make me a strong coffee, and I can then fill you in," she says with a sigh.

I rush across the kitchen to boil the kettle, with my head still reeling. *Did Aunty really sleep with my idol? The woman I occasionally lay in bed fantasising about. 'Oh Lordy',* I think to myself, still feeling dazed. I place the hot mug of coffee down onto the table. "There you go Aunty," I tell her softly. I sit opposite, patiently waiting for her to continue.

"I won't go into it all now, as I have a lesson to teach in half an hour. I'll fill you in with the rest this evening. I haven't seen Lucia for over fourteen years. That very first day we met, feels like it happened only yesterday. It has all come flooding back sending my emotions haywire. Only two weeks after our initial meeting, Lucia headed off to Australia, and that is where her career as one of the top three-day eventers really started. We kept in touch for a while, but the texts soon began to fizzle out. I continued to follow her career. She progressed at a great speed and I was proud of everything she achieved. She always had such a determined and fiery spirit, probably due to her red hair, and I mean all over," she continues, with a naughty grin.

"I wonder what she's going to say when she sees you." I am still trying to take this all in.

"She doesn't even know it's me yet. Don't forget, all those years ago my surname was Jacobs, not Baker," she continues.

"Oh Lordy," I mutter.

"Exactly. I really haven't a clue what I'm going to feel or how I'll react when I see her once again," says Aunty.

"Not long now then, Aunty. I can't wait to hear the whole story about what antics the four of you got up to after your meal," I reply. Suddenly, I'm really looking forward to our catch up this evening.

"Trust me. I've so much more to tell you," she replies, with that wistful faraway smile.

"What would you like Mia and I to do when Lucia arrives?" I ask.

"I don't know. Maybe you can keep a close eye on Autumn Wonder for me, whilst Lucia and I sort out the paperwork for the insurance etc? The local security firm will be here at ten this morning to fit a CCTV camera in his stable. It'll run through to my phone so I can keep an eye on him twenty-four seven, all paid for by, Lucia, of course," she informs me.

Suddenly, I cannot help laughing out loud.

"What's so funny?" Aunty asks, looking confused.

"Just when you mentioned the camera feed to your phone. It reminded me of the set up in Ruby's kitchen."

Aunty suddenly joins in with my laughter and I notice she has that naughty twinkle back in her eyes.

"Oh, Jasmine, trust me. There is so much more to tell you about the happenings that went on in Ruby's kitchen, including some very outrageous behaviour the next morning. Mr Shackle will never see anything like that again in his lifetime, I can tell you that for sure. Four sexy women in front of the camera, literally blew his mind," she laughs.

"You mean, Lucia joined in, too?" I ask.

"Don't forget the fifty hours," she giggles.

"Now this just gets better and better. Seriously, you need to turn this into a book. It could be a worldwide best seller," I tell her.

"I'm not sure about that, but I'm glad you are enjoying my tales. I need to get ready for my lesson now. Please promise me again, you will not mention any of this to anyone?" she says, looking slightly sheepish.

"I promise. Cross my heart," I reply sincerely.

"Maybe we could meet back here around one? Having you around will help to settle my nerves," she continues.

"Of course. Please try not to worry. I believe, sometimes things happen for a reason. We shall just have to wait and see. See you back here at one," I confirm.

Chapter 29

My head is still whirling, as I walk across the field to catch Breeze. He slowly lifts his head, nickers a welcome, and walks directly towards me. Blossom looks up quickly, but soon puts her head back down to continue grazing under the warm morning sunshine. "Hey, boy. Wow, what a crazy morning I've had already. I would love to tell you all about it, but I'm sworn to secrecy. Do you fancy having a crack at the cross-country course today?" I ask him. He slowly sniffs my right arm, before lowering his head down into the headcollar.

I can't believe he's helping me out like this. He must sense that I have an achy arm. *How amazing is this?* We walk slowly across to the yard, and I cannot stop thinking about, Lucia and Aunty. *How are they going to react seeing each other again after all this time?*

Breeze suddenly lifts his head up high whinnying across the other side of the yard to Ebony and my thoughts vanish into thin air.

"Hey, handsome," Mia grins. She slowly and tenderly strokes Breeze's golden neck. I watch her hand gently move up and down his neck, wishing her hands were caressing every inch of my body.

Mia must be a mind reader. Her hypnotic eyes immediately fixate on mine. A warm smile covers her beautiful face. Her lips lean forward to delicately brush mine. My tongue hurriedly searches for hers. The fluttering deep down below, begins to cause chaos.

"Excuse me, love," a male voice suddenly calls out from over the other side of the yard.

Mia is the first one to pull away. "How can I help you?" she asks.

I feel slightly embarrassed, not knowing if he had witnessed the pair of us kissing.

"I'm from, Benson's security. Here to see a Trudy Baker. I'm fifteen minutes early though," he replies, with a smile.

"Hey, Mia, maybe I should deal with this. Aunty is busy teaching a lesson. Would you mind keeping an eye on Breeze for me? I shouldn't be too long," I ask her.

"Of course, not problem at all." Her hand purposely brushes against the inside of my thigh, instantly sending a tingly sensation to add onto the already chaotic sensations, deep down below.

I head across to the security man, taking a deep breath, trying hard to compose myself.

"Hi there. I'm Trudy's niece, Jasmine. Aunty is tied up at present, but I'm more than happy to show you the stable where the camera needs to be fitted, if it would help?" I tell him, with a smile.

"Nice to meet you, Jasmine" he says, holding out his right hand to shake mine.

"Likewise," I reply.

His rough hairy hand touches mine. "Who did you get on the wrong side of?" he asks, looking down at my right arm.

"A horse," I reply.

"Well, I hope I won't bump into him," he replies, nervously looking around.

I point my right arm in the opposite direction, "No need to worry. He's safely locked away in that rickety old dungeon way over there," I reply, with a smirk.

His eyes stare into mine looking horrified.

"Only joking," I tell him laughing.

A huge grin suddenly appears across his bearded face. "Blimey lassie, you nearly had me there," he says.

"Come on, follow me," I tell him.

"Wow, what a lovely set up your Aunt has here. My seven-year-old daughter is absolutely crazy about ponies. She has hundreds of pony posters covering her bedroom walls and spends hours pretending the sweeping brush is her pony, galloping crazily around the house on her invisible mount," he says, with a warm smile.

"You should think about booking her in for some lessons. Aunty has a weekly beginner's class. She would love it," I reply.

"I'm sure she would. She'd be in her element. Maybe, I'll have a chat with your Aunt when I see her," he says.

"Well. This is the stable where the camera needs to be fitted. I'm sure Aunty will be here shortly. Is there anything I can get you? A tea or coffee maybe?" I ask.

"No, lassie. Honestly, I'm fine, thank you. I'll just pop back to the van to grab my equipment and then I can get cracking," he says.

"Ok. I'll leave you to it then," I reply, before turning to make my way back to the main yard.

Mia is bending over to grab the end of Ebony's girth. I stand for a second to admire her gorgeous buttocks. I check all around to make sure the coast is clear, before creeping quietly towards her. She's busy tightening up Ebony's girth. The temptation is too much, and I can't resist running my hands slowly and softly up and down her slender sides.

Mia initially jumps at my touch, but very slowly her body

begins to relax. Her hands take hold of mine guiding them upwards to her breasts. I gently kiss the side of her neck, my hands lovingly massaging her breasts, my fingers teasing her hard erect nipples from underneath her vest stop, my body pressing firmly against hers. "Oh, Jazz," she whispers.

I continue to flick my tongue slowly around her neck. Hot pulsating throbbing sensations instantly appear, deep down below. Her soft mutterings of pleasure turn me on by the second.

"Excuse me, lassie. I'm sorry to interrupt again, but could you possibly tell me where the toilets are please?" I suddenly hear the security man ask.

I slowly turn around to see him standing with a grin, and the colour immediately drains from my face. I clear my throat before awkwardly replying. "Just follow the signs to block one and you'll see the toilets are right at the end," I manage to say.

Mia hasn't moved an inch. Resembling a statue, her body appears to be completely rigid.

"Thank you, lassie," he calls back, before turning around to head in the opposite direction.

"Bloody hell, Jazz," gasps Mia. "Do you think he saw us?"

"So, what if he did? He shouldn't be so bloody nosey then, should he?" I reply.

She slowly turns around to grin at me. "Girlfriend, shall we ride?" she asks, with a naughty look on her face.

"Oh, yes, please, bring it on. I'm ready for the ride of a lifetime," I tell her, with a mischievous grin. Once again, my face feels hot and flushed. That moist feeling flowing between my legs has returned. I'm thankful to be wearing black jodhpurs for a change, instead of my usual cream ones. *What is happening to me?* I walk towards Breeze who is standing contently with one hind leg resting. His eyes are half closed, as he relaxes in the warmth of the glorious sunshine. I'm surprised to see that he's all tacked up and ready to go. He even has his brushing boots on too, to protect his legs from the solid jumps ahead. Bless Mia, she must have got Breeze ready for me, whilst I was busy dealing with the security man. *'I will find a pleasurable way to thank her later,'* I grin to myself. I head to the tack room to grab my body protector and hat.

"Are you ready then?" Mia asks.

I sit comfortably in my saddle, double checking my girth. "Let's do this," I reply, not daring to look at her in case those incredible sensations come back with a vengeance. We ride side by side down towards the start of the cross-country course.

"Is Trudy ok?" Mia asks, with a concerned look.

"She's fine Mia. To be honest, I think she's been working way too hard. I know she is desperately trying to keep on top of things before Uncle arrives home," I reply, gently stroking Breeze's neck.

"It probably isn't my place to say anything, but, no, Jazz. Please forget what I just said," Mia says, turning her head to look the other way.

"Hey, what on earth is wrong, Mia?" I enquire softly.

"Nothing," she replies.

"Come on. I know you only too well. If there is something you think I should know, then please tell me. I promise it won't go any further. Trust me, I'm the best at keeping secrets," I tell her.

"Ok. But please, this must stay just between the two of us," she quietly says.

"I promise," I reply, starting to feel slightly anxious.

"It may be nothing to worry about, Jazz, but the last time your Uncle came home, there seemed to be a lot of friction and tension between them," she confesses.

"How do you mean?"

"One morning, I headed towards the front door as usual, but suddenly stopped when I heard raised voices coming from inside the house. I didn't mean to eavesdrop, Jazz, I promise," she says, looking serious.

"Hey, don't you worry. I've eavesdropped many a time, trust me."

"I heard your Aunt yelling at him. I can't remember the correct words, but it was something like, *'I thought I could forgive you with time, William, but I'm not sure if I ever can. The trust we once had has been destroyed and our wedding vows broken into thousands of tiny pieces. You are just one of those men who cannot learn to keep their bloody dicks in their trousers. I am sorry, but I still need more time.'*

Your Uncle had replied something like, 'But Trudy, I don't know how many times I have told you how sorry I am. Please forgive me. I promise, it will never happen again. It was all just a terrible, terrible mistake.'

That's all I heard. I rang the doorbell instead of walking in like I usually do. William glanced and nodded at me before striding off towards the office, slamming the door firmly behind him. Your Aunt tried hard to behave normally, but she did look very troubled. William left the very next day and I haven't seen him since. I have been keeping a close eye on Trudy though and she seems to be coping ok," Mia blurts out, without pausing for breath.

I bring Breeze to an immediate halt, standing looking at Mia with my mouth wide open. My brain tries to process this new information. The only thing I can blurt out is, "Bloody hell."

"I'm sorry, Jazz. I shouldn't have told you," Mia says. Her eyes look down towards the ground avoiding looking at me.

"I'm glad you did, Mia and thank you for trusting me. What a scumbag he is," I reply.

I place my right hand tenderly around her left one and can feel the anger bubbling up inside me, as I try hard to stay calm and focused. *'Poor Aunty. Why on earth hasn't she told me?'* I wonder to myself.

"How long ago was this?" I question Mia.

"About five weeks. I'm not looking forward to seeing him after what I heard last time," Mia says sadly.

"Mia, I could never forgive you if you ever cheated on me. It would break my heart into a million tiny pieces," I tell her, looking deeply and longingly into her mesmerising eyes.

"I would never do that to you, Jazz. I know for sure that you are not only my true love, but my soul mate, too. My body, heart and soul are totally committed to you, and only you. I want us to still be in love after sixty years, sitting happily, swaying away in our old wooden rocking chairs," she replies, with a laugh.

I picture the two of us in our eighties rocking away in our chairs, looking out onto a glorious field full of rescued horses and cannot help the laughter from erupting. "I love you with every ounce of my heart, Mia. Now, shall we go and have some fun?" I ask, determined to shut everything else out of my mind.

Chapter 30

We lead our mounts in hand around the cross-country course. "Just look at this view," Mia says. We tenderly hold hands as though we haven't got a care in the world.

"Breath-taking," I reply.

"I don't want to jump that one either," Mia says, pointing at a solidly built jump, but slightly sitting at an angle, standing roughly around three foot high.

"Hey, you only need to jump the ones you feel comfortable with. There isn't any pressure for you to do anything you don't want to," I tell her softly.

"Are you going to jump them all?" she asks me, looking slightly concerned and anxious.

"I am," I reply, confidently.

"You know this Lucia woman who is bringing her horse over later? Well, did you have the hots for her?" she suddenly asks me.

I feel my cheeks slowly turning red. "I would be lying to you if I said no. Yes, I admit I had the hots for her. Lucia's photo was on my bedroom wall, but I had other pictures of male riders there too. I suppose, I would call it a crush rather than anything else. Trust me when I tell you, Mia, you are the only one for me," I answer, in a serious manner.

"But what if those feelings you felt for her, suddenly resurface this afternoon when you see her in real life?" she asks, sounding worried.

I stop and stand to face her, cupping her chin gently in my right hand. "Mia, you are the most beautiful woman in the whole universe. I can promise you now, I only have eyes for you. You're not only my true love, but you are my everything; don't you ever forget this," I reply softly, before pressing my lips hungrily against hers. Our kiss seems to last a lifetime, full of passion, wanting and needing. Eventually, we reluctantly pull away. The beautiful smile lighting up her face, the way her eyes look intensely into mine, is the only confirmation I need to show how much she loves me, and I feel completely the same. No words are needed. We are totally united.

Feeling flustered and rather damp, deep down below, I offer Mia a leg up, but she completely refuses, glancing across at my badly bruised arm. "Let me leg you up, Jazz. I can easily mount Ebony by climbing on top of that jump over there," she grins, looking back to her normal happy self.

"If you insist," I reply gratefully. I lift my left leg readily, her right arm firmly under my shinbone thrusts me high up and into the saddle. "Why thank you, girlfriend. I shall repay you in kind later," I tell her wickedly.

I watch with a loving smile, as she leads Ebony across towards the solid jump. Within seconds she's safely mounted too, and I think to myself how lucky I am to have her in my life. I immediately stop myself from thinking any naughty thoughts, knowing only too well how important it is to have my full concentration and focus only on the cross-country course ahead.

Mia and Ebony walk directly towards me. "How many jumps

are there in total?" she asks.

"Sixteen," I reply, with a grin.

"Ok, well that makes it just eleven for me and Ebony, Jazz. There are five out there, I'm definitely not going to attempt," she replies.

"Eleven would be a huge achievement for you both. How about we start warming up?" I ask.

"Good idea. I'll follow you. I love to see your cute little ass bouncing up and down in the saddle. It makes me feel wet and warm downstairs," she confesses.

I can't help but giggle at her words. "I'm counting down the hours until my hands and tongue can explore your, downstairs area," I tell her, with a naughty wink.

"Jazz, what are you trying to do to me?" she moans, before quickly standing up in her stirrups leaning forward, looking as though she is trying to take the pressure off her nether regions.

So, Mia is experiencing precisely the same feelings, as me? Well, well, well, now that is some awesome news to hear. Get yourself prepared for Saturday night Jazz, as it looks like the fireworks will finally be exploding.

"You ok?" she calls.

"I'm more than fine," I reply, asking Breeze to walk forward. Breeze trots fluently beneath me for a good five minutes, before I ask him to move into a collected canter along the endless stretch of beautiful green grass. Taking a deep breath, I inhale the freshness of the country air all around me. "I bet you are looking forward to this my boy, aren't you? We're going to have so much fun, fun, fun," I tell him. I put my thumb up to Mia with a grin, lining Breeze up, asking him to stand calmly for a couple of minutes at the start of the course. With his ears pricked forward and his eyes bulging with anticipation, he does as I ask. "Off we go boy," I tell him, giving him a gentle squeeze. We canter towards the first jump. He clears it as though there is nothing there, and we head slightly uphill towards the next jump.

I keep my hands low and my breathing relaxed, as jump two comes into view. It looks to be twelve black tyres threaded through a sturdy pole with a wooden log sitting at least a foot above them. I can feel our rhythm and stride is perfect. Leaning forward, I let the power of Breeze's body fly over the obstacle effortlessly. We follow the wooden sign imprinted with a white painted arrow guiding us in the right direction for jump three. A brush fenced hurdle sits before us. We canter eagerly towards it, sailing over, appearing as though we have miraculously sprouted wings. My adrenaline is pumping through my veins, the grin on my face sits permanent, as I quickly glance over my right shoulder to check on Mia and Ebony. They look to be cantering towards the hurdle, and thankfully, still in one piece. I turn my concentration back on the job ahead. The course seems to descend steeply down a hill. Leaning back in my saddle, I bring Breeze back to a trot. He fights me for a split second before responding to my cue. At the bottom of the hill, I can just about see the next jump is another tyre one with a huge log sitting across the top. As the ground suddenly levels, I urge Breeze into a canter. One stride, two stride, three strides and we are over easily.

"Good boy. Nice jump," I tell him, with a pat down his warm golden neck. A long stretch of luscious green grass stands invitingly ahead. I decide to urge Breeze into a full-blown gallop. He happily responds, swallowing up the ground hungrily with every stride he takes. This exhilarating experience of being out in the open countryside, flying along at a great speed, is second to none. The two of us joined together completely as one. I begrudgingly ask him to slow down, as we head towards jump five. Timed to perfection, we clear it with ease. Jump six clear, jump seven we simply sail over. We veer to the right, and head towards the majestic woodland awaiting us in the near distance.

As we enter the darkness of the mystical woodland, the temperature drops dramatically, the surrounding magnificent trees completely blocking out any daylight. Three heavy logs stacked on top of each other unexpectedly appear out of nowhere, but I needn't worry, Breeze has everything under control. He clears it easily. I'm elated, cantering along the track beneath us, the soft soil flying up high through the air all around, before disappearing completely out of sight. Jump nine is approaching very quickly. A few rotten straw bales sit two high across the width of the track. Breeze takes off at least two feet before them, and I grin as the whole of his body stretches from top to tail, lifting us effortlessly into the air, clearing them with at least another two foot to spare. We follow the winding path and suddenly the strong brightly lit rays from the sunshine take me completely by surprise, the darkness of the woods quickly disappearing behind us. I'm thankful to feel the warmth of the sun, once again embracing us.

No one in their right mind could miss jump eleven. A three-foot wooden gate painted an illuminous yellow and a vibrant red colour, whilst triangular shaped flags sit either side, blowing softly around in the warm summer breeze. For a moment, I feel Breeze slightly hesitate. I quickly take charge and urge him forward. Within seconds, we glide through the air soaring over the gate with inches to spare.

We head towards the water jump. "Good boy. Well done," I tell him encouragingly.

The strong colourful rays of glorious sunshine glisten brightly on the rippling water, just behind the heavy tree trunk which sits boldly in front. I lean forward. Breeze thrusts his beautiful body up high and over the trunk, flying like a bird to clear the three feet of rippling water, and not a splash to be heard. "That was bloody awesome," I congratulate him, with a huge grin across my face.

We clear jump thirteen and fourteen without any trouble at all, and head slightly left towards the final two jumps on the home turn. A narrow fence, sitting in the middle of nowhere and probably only three foot wide with wooden wings either side, awaits us. The gap doesn't look big enough for the pair of us to fit through, but as we get closer, I'm confident we can do this. I focus on keeping Breeze straight and centred. We approach the testing obstacle at great speed. I gasp as my muscular and brave boy sails over the jump to perfection. I bellow a *yippee* in relief. We head towards the final jump, a simple steeplechase which turns out to be a piece of cake. Landing safely, I thrust my left arm high up into the air in triumph.

I'm slightly out of breath, as I ease him down to a trot, then a walk before coming to a standstill. "Oh my God Breeze, wasn't that just awesome?"

The sound of Breeze's flanks heaving in time with my breathlessness brings a big grin to my face.

I have been so focused on our jumping, somehow, I'd completely forgotten about Mia.

I look out into the distance and can just about make out the outline of a horse and rider. They are still in one piece, which is a big relief. I slowly dismount Breeze, elated once my feet are firmly back down on the soft green grass. I loosen his girth and lift the reins gently over the top of his head. Wrapping my arms around his sweaty silk neck, I gently kiss him and tell him how very proud I am of him. He snorts in response. I release my arms just in time to see Mia and Ebony fly over the last jump.

Her face is a delight to see. She slowly eases Ebony down to a walk. Her beautiful cheeks glow with happiness on their recent achievement and her smile, oh that smile is enough to turn my legs to jelly. "We managed to jump ten in the end, Jazz. How awesome is that?" she grins. Her breathing sounds slightly heavy, as I watch her sexy body slide down from out of the saddle.

"That is truly awesome, Mia. You should be very proud of yourself and Ebony." I'm unable to take my eyes off her beautiful backside. The desire inside me, already scrambling around, especially deep down below, heightens.

Mia removes her skull cap, before running her hands gently through her dark flowing hair. She seductively unfastens the Velcro fastenings on her body protector, slowly easing it up and over her head to reveal her round firm breasts hidden away under her thin blue vest top. I am in a trance, as she slowly leads Ebony towards me and Breeze; her eyes focused firmly on mine.

A pleasurable tingle runs up and down my spine. She leans forward, and her lips tenderly touch mine.

She eventually looks up and smiles, before slowly unclipping the chin strap to my skull cap, lifting it gently off my head, before bending down to place it safely on the ground. I gasp, as she releases the Velcro straps on my body protector, removing that, too.

I begin to feel hot and turned on. Her hands delicately slide underneath my vest stop. "Oh, Mia," I whisper. "Your touch is making me tremble from head to toe."

"My aim is to delight and pleasure every single inch of you. I want to take you to a place you have never been before," she replies, in a soft voice, slowly unclipping my bra.

My hands run lightly through her long dark hair. "You're doing a wonderful job so far." With my eyes closed cherishing this wonderful moment, I feel Mia lifting my vest top upwards. Her hands gently cup my breasts; I let out a moan of ecstasy whilst her tongue flickers teasingly over my swollen right nipple.

It isn't the only thing that feels swollen. The flickers and tremors get underway with great force once again, deep down below. I pull her head closer against my chest before my hands wander down towards her buttocks. My fingertips teasingly circle around the soft fabric to her jodhpurs. She lets out a little satisfied moan. Her smooth fingernails run softly up and down my back, and I sigh with contentment. My trembling right fingers sneak slowly and naughtily inside the waistband of her jodhpurs.

"Bloody hell, Jazz," she groans. Her mouth and tongue playfully tease my nipple.

A bolt of electricity shoots upwards from, deep down below and I hold my breath whilst I revel in this magical feeling. "Mia, I don't think I can hang on much longer," I mutter.

"Not long now, my love," she mumbles, slowly pulling away.

"Oh, Mia. Please don't stop," I beg.

"I have to, Jazz. As much as I want to make love to you this very second, this is not the right time or place. Remember, we need to get back before your poster girl arrives," she says, with a naughty grin on her face. She looks cheekily into my eyes.

"You are not going to let me forget about Lucia, are you?" I reply, with a laugh.

"Nope," she smiles, turning to remove the end of Ebony's reins, she had safely hooked through her right arm.

"I cannot believe you are jealous of someone neither of us have even met."

"Well, I am. It has taken me all my life to find you. There's no way I'm going to let any other woman try to take you away from me," she says, sounding determined.

"Wow, get you, Mia. Did you know, you really turn me on when you get all hot and possessive?" I tease.

"You haven't seen anything yet." she says with a wink.

Those thumping pulsations deep down below dance wildly around.

She watches me fasten up my body protector and my chin strap. "Come here and let me give you a leg up," she says.

I bend my left leg ready, my left hand holding the reins at the top of the saddle, my right one holding onto the back.

"Are you ready?" she enquires.

I wait patiently for her arm to lift under my left shin bone, but instead I feel her hand run up between my inner right leg gently rubbing the area in between my legs. I nearly fall to the ground. A huge surge of desire instantly erupts, deep down below. "Bloody hell!" I gasp, trying hard to catch my breath. I lean against Breeze's strong body feeling breathless and weak.

Mia laughs at my reaction. "You like?" she asks softly.

I turn to face her, my tongue urgently searching for hers. I'm desperate for Mia to make love to me now. I have never wanted anything so badly in the whole of my life.

"Whoa, now steady on my horny girlfriend," she grins, reluctantly pulling away. "I'll take that as a yes then. You liked it."

"Roll on Saturday night. It can't arrive soon enough for me," I smile, looking longingly into her eyes.

"I promise, I'll give you a proper leg up this time," she laughs, before thrusting me back into my saddle.

I gently lean forward to wrap my arms tightly around his neck. "Oh Breeze, what the heck is happening to me?" He snorts loudly in response. *I wonder if that was a snort of disgust at our naughty behaviour?*

Chapter 31

We ride slowly back to the yard. My mind is in turmoil. I think about what Mia told me about Aunty earlier and let out a deep sigh.

"Are you ok?" Mia asks, her hand slowly touching mine, as we ride side by side.

"Just thinking about Aunty, Mia."

"I'm sure that they'll eventually work it out between them," she replies.

"I'm not too sure about that. I know Aunty only too well and she's not one for forgiving easily, trust me. I remember her once telling me, how a good friend of hers at secondary school had tried to steal a boy away from her who she was supposed to be seeing. She caught them kissing behind the school bins and never spoke to either of them ever again and believe it or not, she was only thirteen at the time. Aunty never forgets betrayal," I reply.

"God help your Uncle then, that's all I can say," Mia says, looking thoughtful.

"Once we get back and have untacked etc, would you mind if I have a private half hour with Aunty at the house before Lucia arrives?"

"Of course, Jazz. You aren't going to mention anything to her about what I told you earlier, are you?" she asks, looking anxious for a second.

"Don't be silly, Mia. When I make a promise to keep a secret, that is exactly what I do. Lucia isn't due to arrive until two pm, so why not come up to the house at one thirty and Aunty can then tell us what she wants us to do?" I reply, gently squeezing her hand. The reassuring smile she gives me, makes me feel positive that everything will work out for the best and I let out a sigh of relief.

I gently wash down Breeze's girth area. "What a star you were today. I am so proud of you," I tell him. He turns to look at me with his stunning blue eyes, proceeding to rest his heavy head over my left shoulder. "Oh, Breeze. Whatever did I do to deserve you?" I drop the sponge and wrap my arms tightly around his warm satin neck. I slowly take a deep breath to inhale the magical scent from his warm body, smiling as I gently exhale. This is the best medicine I could ask for, what with all the events going on at present. Breeze never fails to make everything seem better and much less complicated. I release his lead rope. "Time to get you back to Blossom, my boy. I have a very interesting afternoon ahead, and I'd better get a wriggle on," I tell him.

We take our time walking back to the field, my head spinning with the goings on between Aunty and Uncle. *Will Aunty tell me about Uncle's affair?* I lean over the gate watching Breeze and Blossom trotting in the warm midday sunshine, trying hard to clear my head, before turning thoughtfully up the path towards the house.

I walk into an empty kitchen. "Hey Aunty, I'm back," I call out. There is no response at all. *I wonder where she could be.* I glance at my watch to see it is five past one. Aunty is never late. Switching the kettle on to boil, I'm still deep in thought, when the sudden smell of a light scented perfume begins to waft up my nostrils. Quickly turning around, I stand looking at Aunty with my mouth ajar.

"I'm gasping for a cuppa," Aunty says, in a matter-of-fact way.

I watch her dash around tidying up the paperwork on the kitchen table. I have never ever seen her look so smart. I take in her black hugging jodhpurs, defining every inch of her curvy body. Her long black riding boots, shine like diamonds. Her recently straightened long black hair adorns over her tight-fitting white blouse. Shiny gold buttons sit all the way down the centre and on each of the turned back sleeve cuffs. The top two buttons are casually undone, revealing an eye-catching glimpse of her hugely formed breasts.

Oh Lordy. I try to concentrate on making the coffee. *What on earth is Aunty up to?* I walk across with her coffee and she smiles at me gratefully. "Are you ok?" I ask her softly. It must be years since I've seen her wear make-up. Her bright red lipstick highlights her full lips to perfection. The black mascara makes her eyes look dark and sexy. The soft pink blusher defines her cheekbones beautifully and her stunning gold jewellery adds the finishing touch. I glance down to her left hand, to see her wedding ring is missing. Only a diamond studded horseshoe ring sits proudly on the third finger of her right hand. I'm completely taken aback with how gorgeous she looks. *No wonder Ruby, Nicole and Lucia found it hard to keep their hands off her.* "You look absolutely stunning," I tell her, pulling out a chair to sit opposite.

"I wanted to make a good impression. Lucia is paying me well to look after Autumn Wonder," she grins.

"Is that all though?" I ask, with a cheeky grin.

"I haven't a clue what you mean," she replies, avoiding any eye contact, before suddenly looking up with a huge smile across her face. Her naughty wink makes me laugh out loud.

"But you are a happily married woman," I tell her, feeling shocked.

"I used to be," she sighs.

"What do you mean?" I ask her softly.

"I wasn't going to mention anything to you. I didn't want to spoil your visit, Jasmine." A sad look spreads across her face. "What on earth's the matter?" I urgently ask.

She glances at her watch, before looking back at me. "Here goes then. Confession time, once again. Your Uncle had an affair with one of his work colleagues in New York. I only found out by accident a couple of months ago. He'd been acting strangely on his previous visit, and to be honest, he showed all the tell-tale signs of someone trying to hide something. For example, sending long text messages regularly, always keeping his phone at an angle so I couldn't see the screen. He'd then place it safely away into his trouser pocket rather than leaving it lying around like he usually did. Late at night when he thought I was asleep, he would sneak out to have secret conversations at the bottom of the garden, whereas before he would always make any calls from the office. I would stand and watch him from our bedroom window, as he laughed down the phone. He started acting cold and distant towards me. Don't get me wrong, he would always peck me lightly on the cheek in the morning and again in the evening, but as far as anything else goes, well that all went out of the window the year before last," she confides, before taking a sip of her coffee.

"I seriously hadn't got a clue. Does Mum know?"

"Yes, she does. She's been a great support to me, always on the end of the phone to listen," she replies.

"How on earth did you find out about the affair?" I ask.

"Now there's a story to tell. William was in the shower one evening when his phone rang. I tried calling him, but he didn't respond, so I went ahead and answered it. The screen flashed up with the name, Jack. A woman's voice on the other end spoke softly in a sexy American accent. I'll never forget her words."

'Hi darling, have you told her about us yet? How did she take it? 'When are you coming home?' she'd said.

I remember standing in shock thinking she must have dialled a wrong number.

'Who is this?' I'd asked.

Suddenly, the line went deadly silent, and she hung up quickly. I sat on the edge of the bed staring down at his phone for what felt like hours. A few minutes later, a message flagged up on the screen.

'Call me, William. I'm desperately missing hearing your voice, love you, honey bun, Jax kiss, kiss, kiss.' I was totally gobsmacked and was still sitting on the edge of the bed when he eventually came back from his shower."

I looked at him questioningly before holding up his phone directly in front of him.

'Who the heck is Jax?' I asked, trying to stay as calm as I possibly could. He avoided any eye contact with me, continuing to look down at the floor obviously trying to give himself some thinking time.

'Well?' I asked again.

'Trudy, what the bloody hell are you talking about?" he mumbled.

'William, don't you dare lie to me,' I replied, starting to feel angry.

'Jax is just a work colleague, that's all,' he said.

I watched his fingers start to twitch. I calmly reread the text message out loud to him, as I watched him walk awkwardly around the bedroom.

'You weren't going to bloody tell me, were you?' I demanded.

Walking towards me, he slowly knelt down in front of me.

'I'm sorry, Trudy. Honestly. It meant nothing. I promise,' he pleaded.

I immediately stood up and redialled Jax's phone number, putting it onto loud-speaker mode.

'What the hell do you think you are doing?' he demanded, trying to snatch the phone from out of my hands.

'William is that you? I am missing you so much. Our home doesn't feel the same without you, especially our bed,' the American voice said, just before your Uncle managed to pull the phone away from me, immediately ending the call.

"I watched him squirm for a while and then I casually walked out of the bedroom slamming the door behind me. To cut a long story short, he eventually confessed that the affair had been going on for around eleven months, and apparently, he'd kept meaning to end it, but could never find the right time. Anyway, he promised to end the affair straight away and begged me to forgive him, asking me to give him one last chance. To be honest, I couldn't get my head around the whole situation and asked him to leave immediately. I needed time on my own to think. He came back around four weeks ago, just for the weekend, but the atmosphere between us was awkward and frosty. Even though he swore to me that he had ended the affair, to be honest, I didn't believe him. I also know deep down in my heart I could never ever forgive him for cheating. He has begged continuously for me to give him one last chance for him to explain his side of the story, hence his visit scheduled for this weekend. To be honest, Jasmine, I couldn't care less if I never see him again," she confesses, finishing the last drop of her coffee.

"What an absolute knob," I say out loudly, feeling upset and betrayed by what he has put my Aunty through.

"I'm sure Mia knows something's wrong and to be honest I don't mind if you tell her what has happened, although make sure she keeps it to herself for now. It will save me a job having to explain it all over again. I did feel sorry for her last time he was here; you could have cut the atmosphere with a knife," she replies.

"Of course, I'll tell her for you. She'll probably be as shocked as I am," I reply.

"To be honest, I'm not looking forward to seeing him on Saturday evening," she confesses.

"But why the fancy restaurant then?" I query.

"I'm guessing what he has in mind, is if he gets me into a five-star restaurant for a romantic candle lit meal, and a few alcoholic drinks to get me tipsy, we'll be able to magically rekindle all those old loving feelings we used to share for each other. Well, if he thinks that's going to work, he's going be very disappointed. I'm only going along for the free food and booze, as he's already paid in advance," she laughs.

It's good to hear her laugh again and I join in, too. "Good for you, Aunty," I tell her with a smile.

She glances at her watch again, just as her phone alerts, an incoming new message. "Lucia is only fifteen minutes away. Oh, bloody hell, Jasmine, I'm starting to feel butterflies in my stomach at the thought of seeing her again, after all this time," she confesses.

"Take deep breaths. I'm sure it will all be fine. To be honest, I cannot wait to hear the rest of your story this evening. Pity it isn't time for a gin and tonic now. I don't know about you, but I feel like I could do with one," I reply, with a big grin.

"I was thinking, would you mind asking Mia to keep out of the way until Autumn Breeze is safely in his stable? I really don't want her to hear the conversation between Lucia and I, in case it gets awkward, if you know what I mean?" she continues.

"What's awkward?" Mia's smiling face asks, appearing in the doorway.

I look at her and smile lovingly. The sight of my gorgeous girl standing in her skinny vest top, both hands on her hips, her breasts in desperate need of my hands and tongue, is enough to drive me to despair. *Get a bloody grip, Jazz.*

"I was just saying to Jasmine, it might be better if we don't overcrowd the new arrival until he's completely settled in his stable, just in case he gets spooked," Aunty says.

"That's a very sensible idea. To be honest, I think I would rather sit and watch from a distance, but please be careful, Jazz, and make sure you don't reopen that wound," she says, turning to look directly at me.

"Don't you worry, I'll call you, once it's safe. Do I need to put any more cream on yet?" I ask.

"It won't hurt to rub in some more arnica cream to help with the bruising. Here, let me do it for you," she replies, heading to the cabinet to get out the cream. Mia bends over to massage some cream into my multicoloured arm. I feel the warmth gradually rise upwards into my cheeks. I close my eyes and enjoy every single second of Mia's magic touch.

I hear Aunty's chair slide, and slowly open my eyes.

"Wow Trudy, I thought there was something different about you when I walked in. You look truly stunning, just look at you. Wow," says Mia.

"How very rude, Mia! Are you trying to say, I normally look pretty rough then?" Aunty replies, in a serious voice.

"N-n-n no, of course not," Mia stutters.

Her hand suddenly comes to an abrupt halt on my arm. Her face is a real treat, as Aunty laughs out loudly, whilst Mia stands looking mortified with both hands covering her face.

"Only joking, Mia," laughs Aunty. "Come on, Jasmine, let's go and wait for this new arrival and get him settled in," she says.

Mia lets out a huge sigh of relief. Her fingers seem to fumble, as she tries to place the tiny top back onto the tube of cream.

I can't resist pinching Mia's buttocks, before I rush off to catch up with Aunty.

"Are you ok? Just remember, to take deep breaths," I say, as she squeezes my hand in thanks.

Chapter 32

Aunty strides up and down the pathway, continuously twiddling her thumbs. "Please could you just double check my security app is still working?" she asks, coming to a standstill, before handing me her phone.

I notice her trembling hands. "Of course," I reply. I tap on the app to check all is well. "It's such a cool set up. I have never seen anything like this before. You can even move the camera around just by sliding your finger on the arrows."

"Pretty state of the art, isn't it? Lucia only wants the best for Autumn Wonder. I bet Ruby would have lots of fun if she had a moving camera in her kitchen," Aunty chuckles.

It's a relief to see Aunty laughing and joking once again.

A huge silver horsebox suddenly comes into view.

"Breathe," I remind Aunty.

Eventually, it grinds to a halt. A bellowing whinny calls loudly from inside the box. The front passenger door to the cabin slowly opens. The first thing I see is a beautifully shaped bottom wrapped nicely inside a pure white pair of jodhpurs. The figure slowly climbs down. I hold my breath. A truly stunning and elegant looking lady turns around to face us both. Her long black laced riding boots fit snuggly up to her knees. My eyes slowly wander up to the black tight fitting sleeveless blouse. Her curly auburn hair sits just below her shoulders. Her ocean blue eyes and her gorgeous smile light up her face like the vision of Aphrodite. Lucia walks confidently towards us.

I hear Aunty let out a gasp.

"Hi there, I'm looking for Trudy Baker," she asks, holding out her slender right hand to Aunty.

I cannot believe my poster girl is standing right in front of me. I can tell you now, I am far from disappointed. She is truly stunning. I can now see how Aunty easily fell for her. My blood pressure rises quickly, the heat rushing uncontrollably upwards to my cheeks.

"I'm Trudy," Aunty answers, in a surprisingly calm voice. I watch closely as their hands touch. Their eyes look to be locked on each other's. A bolt of electricity seems to travel between them.

"Trudy? My Trudy? It can't be," exclaims Lucia, holding her left hand up to her mouth in disbelief.

"Yes, Lucia. It's me," Aunty replies, with a slightly shaky voice.

"Oh my God, Trudy? I never thought I would see you again," Lucia half screams, before wrapping her arms tightly around Aunty.

I watch as the two of them hold each other close after all this time apart. A single tear forms in my eye.

They reluctantly pull apart, holding onto each other's hands tightly. "Lucia. It is so good to see you. I didn't think you would remember me," Aunty says.

"How could I ever forget you? The time we spent together were the best moments of my life. Oh, Trudy, we have so much to catch up on," Lucia gasps, slowly leaning forward to tenderly kiss Aunty's left cheek.

"Oh, by the way, this is my lovely niece, Jasmine and before you get any ideas, she is far too young for you," Aunty grins, pointing a finger directly at Lucia.

"Believe me, Trudy. Those days of chasing beautiful young women around, are well and truly gone. I have learned my lesson the hard way," she smiles back, her eyes not leaving Aunty's.

Wow! Does this mean Lucia thinks I'm beautiful? I cannot believe my idol is standing here, right in front of me. Eventually, Lucia turns to focus properly on me. I watch with reddened cheeks whilst her magical blue eyes scan every part of my body in under a split second.

"Nice to meet you, Jasmine," she says, finally releasing Aunty's hand.

Taken completely by surprise, I suddenly feel her arms wrap around me before proceeding to give me a massive hug. *Oh Lordy.* The closeness of her body makes me tremble with delight. She finally let's go. "Feel free to call me, Jazz," I shakily inform her with one of my cutest smiles. I take a deep breath, trying to calm down my beating heart.

"Shall we get Autumn Wonder settled in and if you have enough time, how would you fancy a coffee?" Aunty asks her. The loving smile across her face so heart-warming to see.

"I have all the time in the world for you Trudy and I'm certainly in no rush at all. I cannot believe we will soon be sort of neighbours, too. I honestly feel like I have won the lottery, seeing you once again," she tells Aunty, firmly taking hold of both her hands.

"Jazz, would you mind asking Savannah to get Autumn Wonder ready to unload please? You'll find her in the driver's seat," she asks softly.

Oh my God, she remembered to call me, Jazz. How awesome is this? For goodness' sake, get a bloody grip, Jazz. This is just wrong. She's your Aunty's ex-lover, and have you already forgotten all about your own gorgeous, Mia? My thoughts immediately bring me back to my senses and I instantly feel guilty. "Of course, Lucia," I reply, heading off towards the horsebox.

The door to the driver's side opens and not long after, a woman who is probably in her mid-thirties jumps down to the ground.

"Hi, are you, Savannah?" I ask her, holding out my right hand in readiness.

"I sure am," she replies with a warm smile in a broad American accent.

"Pleased to meet you. I'm Trudy's niece, Jazz," I tell her, as her hand lingers on mine for slightly longer than I would normally expect.

"Lucia would like you to get Autumn Wonder ready to unload. Would you like a hand?" I smile.

"That would be great, Jazz, thank you," she replies gratefully.

I follow her closely towards the rear of the box and notice that she walks with a slight limp.

"This is one handsome horse you are about to meet. I am confident he has a huge jumping career in front of him. He can be a bit bolshy at times, but he is a giant pussy cat at heart," she says.

"I've never seen a horsebox this huge," I tell her, looking all around the silver paintwork, not a scratch to be seen anywhere.

"Pretty cool, ah? It's the state of art horsebox and can transport up to nine horses all at one time. It also has accommodation for up to six people too. I'll give you a mini tour later, if you like?" she asks, looking at my shocked face.

"Wow. I would love to." I watch her unbolt the lever to the rear ramp and cannot believe it when she presses a small red button and it immediately starts to make a noise, as it slowly starts to open.

"Pretty nifty, ah? Would you be so kind as to tell, Lucia, we're now ready to unload?" she asks me.

I nod, before walking back towards Lucia and Aunty who still seemed to be engrossed in each other. The sound of their laughter warms my heart. "Excuse me, Lucia, but Savannah is ready when you are," I tell her.

Lucia and Aunty turn to smile at me.

"Marvellous, thank you, Jazz. Come on, Trudy, I can't wait for you to meet, my boy," she grins at Aunty.

I closely follow the two of them. *What a beautiful and happy couple they make. I have never ever seen Aunty look this happy with Uncle at her side.* I glance around and suddenly spot Mia across the other side of the yard. She waves her arms around just above her head and I raise one hand back with a huge smile. *I cannot wait to get my hands and lips on her later.*

I have never seen such a stunning looking horse, apart from my Breeze that is. He stands resembling a Royal King, as his handsome looking body approaches the bottom of the ramp, his head held up high into the air, both eyes wide open and alert. I glance at his black travel rug to see it is neatly engraved with gold italic letters spelling out his name, and his travel boots of matching colour. A gold fitted plate sits proudly on the thick strap to the right of his black leather head collar also bearing his name.

"Well? What do you think?" Lucia asks Aunty with a grin.

"He looks to be in a class of his own. I cannot believe you bred him, Lucia. You must feel so proud of everything you have achieved," she replies.

"Not quite everything, but that's a story for another time; although you've probably already heard about it," laughs Lucia.

"Um, no comment," chuckles Aunty. "His stable is right at the end over there in the corner. Everything is ready and waiting for him," she continues.

"Come on, my boy" Lucia tells him, proudly walking him across the yard.

There are only a couple of horses' heads over their stable doors eager to greet him, and he loudly bellows back. His whole body shakes with the sound, as it slowly echoes around the yard.

I would say Lucia is probably around the same height as Aunty, five foot six, and I'm amazed to see Autumn Wonder's powerfully built body towers way above her shoulders. She ties the lead rope onto the bailing twine sitting on the solid metal ring. "There we go, my lad. What do you think of this then?" Lucia asks him.

I watch fixated, as Lucia bends over to take off all four travelling boots. Her gorgeous backside totally mesmerises me. *Jazz. Get a grip and bloody behave yourself.* I notice Aunty is also watching Lucia's every move with a huge grin across her face and Lucia smiles back, placing the four travel boots safely into Aunty's awaiting arms. They stand still, obviously sharing a very special moment, dreamily looking deeply into each other's eyes. *I wonder what on earth went on with the two of them. I can't wait to find out later.*

Lucia slowly removes the travel rug to reveal the striking shiny bay coat of this well-bred specimen.

"Wow. Now that is what I call a classy looking horse," says Aunty.

"You think so?" asks Lucia, with a huge grin.

"Without a doubt. Just look at his muscle tone, truly remarkable," replies Aunty.

My eyes pour over every inch of his wonderful fit looking body, a horse who could maybe become a top star in the future. His huge bay head turns to look at me. "He's outstanding," I mumble.

"Thank you, Jazz," grins Lucia. Lucia stretches her arms to reach his head collar, and then gently pats his thick glossy neck. "There we go," she tells him. He turns to place his muzzle on

Lucia's face, gently blowing breath from his nostrils straight up her nose. "He's done this ever since he was a baby," Lucia declares. Autumn Wonder continues, before turning around to face Aunty.

He does precisely the same to her, before boldly walking across to the stable door towards me. Autumn Wonder's breath blows softly up my nose.

"This is the perfect size stable for him. Light and airy too," I hear Lucia say to Aunty.

"I'm glad it meets with your approval," Aunty replies with a cheeky grin.

"If I remember rightly, Trudy, you always did meet with my approval, in more ways than one," Lucia cheekily replies.

I cannot believe how much flirting is going on around me. This is going to do Aunty the world of good having Lucia around for the next two weeks. Or is it?

"Shall we leave him to get settled in and pop to put the kettle on?" Aunty asks.

"That would be wonderful, as long as you are sure you have time?" Lucia answers.

"I always have time for you," replies Aunty with a grin, before the two of them walk towards me.

I unbolt the door and as soon as Lucia is safely out, she hands the rug and boots straight across to Savannah.

Aunty double checks that the two bolts are firmly locked, before hanging the leather head collar over the hook on the outside wall.

"I'm not sure how long I'm going to be, Savannah. Are you ok to hang around?" Lucia asks her.

"Well, I really need to go and check on Velvet Wonder, Destiny's Dream and Charming Greyson. I also promised to drop another sack of cubes across to Judy. Mystery's Dreams is apparently running low. It should probably only take me a couple of hours to get it all done, so I could get back here for around four-thirty to pick you up?" she replies.

"How does that sound to you, Trudy? Do you think you could cope with me hanging around for that amount of time?" Lucia asks Aunty, with a sparkle in her eyes.

"It's going to be hard, but I'm happy to give it a go," teases Aunty. Their eyes lock once again.

"That's settled then. I'll quickly unload Autumn Wonder's food, before I dash off to complete my tasks," smiles Savannah.

"Jasmine, would you mind showing Savannah where the feed room is? And then maybe you and Mia could come and join the two of us back at the house?" Aunty asks.

"Who is Mia?" asks Lucia.

A sudden pang of jealousy stabs straight through the middle of my heart. '*There is no way, Lucia is getting her hands anywhere near my beautiful, Mia,*' I say to myself, suddenly feeling very protective of her.

"I offered to give Jazz a quick tour of the horsebox, if that's ok with you?" Savannah asks, Lucia.

"Of course, that's ok," she replies, with a beautiful smile.

"Come on then, Jazz. Shall we get the feed unloaded and then you can introduce me to, Mia. Maybe she would like to see the inside of the horsebox, too?" she asks me.

"I'm sure she would love to. Thank you," I grin back at her.

I watch Aunty link arms with Lucia, as they head in the direction of the house. "See you later," Aunty calls.

Chapter 33

I quickly glance around looking for Mia. Spotting her instantly, I beckon her over, watching with a huge grin on my face, as she instantly walks towards me. Her beautiful smile makes my legs go weak and the fluttering, deep down below starts to churn away slowly.

"Mia, I would like you to meet, Savannah. She works for Lucia and is going to give us a quick tour of the inside of the horsebox," I tell her, with a grin.

Mia and Savannah's hands shake firmly in greeting. Another pang of jealousy shoots directly through me. Savannah continues to hold onto Mia's right hand, her eyes taking in every inch of her fabulous body.

"Shall I show you where to put Autumn Wonder's food," I say, feeling thankful my words seem to have finally encouraged Savannah to let go of Mia's hand.

"Sure, Jazz," she replies, still busy ogling Mia.

"This way then," I say sharply. Mia turns to look at me questioningly.

Mia suddenly notices Savannah's limp. "Would you like a hand?" she kindly asks her.

I immediately feel bad for the sharp manner, in which I spoke to Savannah. "I can help, too. Let me go and grab a wheelbarrow. I'll be back in a couple of minutes," I call, before heading off to track one down.

Savannah loads the three bags of food from the side of the horsebox onto the wheelbarrow, as though they are as light as a feather.

"Right," says Savannah once the food is stored safely away. "Would you still like a quick tour?"

"Yes, please," Mia and I say, almost at the same time.

I cannot believe the luxury hidden away inside this monster of a horsebox.

"It is in fact called an *Equicruiser* and is designed and built by *Mercedes*. It weighs twenty-six tonnes and has two hydraulic ramps, one at the front and the other at the back," she informs us, as we head towards the padded stalls.

"Your horses travel in such luxury. Just look, they even have flip out windows," says Mia, looking as astonished as me.

"We also have underfloor storage areas too. Look, this is where we store our tack and bags of feed away safely. Follow me, you will love this," Savannah tells us.

We walk into what looks to be a lounge. I stand with my mouth wide open. A huge forty-two-inch flat screen TV immediately catches my attention, sitting central in the wall opposite the beautiful fitted beige leather upholstery. I slowly look around taking in the spectacular LED lighting.

"We also have a satellite, HD, DVD player and even a surround sound system," says Savannah.

"This is unbelievable," says Mia, looking at me with a huge grin.

"Follow me," beckons Savannah.

We stand in the kitchen looking at the cooker and sink. "No way," I blurt out.

"Pretty smart, ah?" Savannah replies.

We look around in amazement at the next room. "A bathroom and bloody shower, too. This is like a house on wheels," gasps Mia.

"A separate toilet, too, and we haven't finished just yet," Savannah announces proudly.

"Oh my God. A double bed?" I shout out, looking at the red satin duvet cover with matching pillowcases.

For a slight second, I imagine Mia and I having all of this to ourselves. Her body lying naked hungrily waiting for me, as I gently kiss her from her lips all the way down her gorgeous and slender body. The flutters deep down below, return with a vengeance.

Mia looks across at me raising her eyebrows. *Is it possible she is thinking the same?* I notice the many designer radiators sitting proudly on the walls, before following Savannah and Mia through to the cabin.

"We have a touch screen radio, and a CCTV system so we can keep an eye on the horses at all times. Not forgetting Blue Tooth and a built in Sat Nav. Oh, and I nearly forgot to mention the heated seats," Savannah grins.

"This could be how you and Breeze may travel, once you get your place in the *Olympic team*," Mia says, sounding extremely excited at the prospect.

Savannah immediately turns to look at me. "*The Olympic Team?*" she asks me, her eyes bulging.

"It's a long way off," I tell her, not really wanting to go into the whole story.

"I'll make sure I look out for you then," she says, with a huge grin.

I feel the blood rush up quickly into my cheeks.

"Right, ladies. I am going to have to love you and leave you, as I still have work to do," she informs us.

"Thank you so much for the tour; it has been totally mind-blowing," says Mia, with a grateful smile.

"My pleasure entirely. It sounds like we will be seeing a lot of each other," she replies, giving Mia a warm smile.

Another pang of jealousy immediately shoots through my heart. *'Not if I've got anything to do with it,'* I say to myself, pursing my lips.

Savannah shakes my hand, before taking hold of Mia's.

She holds onto Mia's hand for much longer than is necessary. Once again, the fury builds up from deep within me. *Argghhhh.*

"See you both later," she calls, limping awkwardly back to the horsebox.

We watch as the huge monster of a horsebox finally drives off into the distance.

"I wonder what happened to her leg?" Mia says.

"She fancies you," I blurt out.

"Don't be so silly, Jazz, and for your information, Savannah is not my type," she says, with a grin.

"Is that so? Please explain to me who your type is then, Mia?" I question her, cupping her chin softly in my right hand.

"Um, let me think. I guess you would just about do," she says, with a straight face.

"Would you now?" I say to her, my lips hungrily caressing hers.

"Yep. In fact, you will do just nicely," she replies.

I take her hand and gently entwine it in mine. "Come on. I bet you are dying to meet, Autumn Wonder, aren't you? I also have something I need to talk to you about before we head back to the house," I tell her.

Autumn Wonder immediately walks towards the stable door to greet us.

"Wow. Now that is what I call a talented looking prospect. He is huge!" exclaims Mia.

He lowers his head to greet her, with tiny strands of hay hanging at different angles from his mouth.

"Who knows? We may even see him on the TV in the next couple of years," I reply. Stroking his silky bay head, I look deep into his enormous black eyes, laughing to see my own reflection sitting deeply inside them.

"What did you want to talk to me about, Jazz? Is everything ok?" Mia asks.

"Let's go and sit over on that bench over there." I reply, pointing to the other side of the yard. I quickly explain to Mia all about Uncle's affair and assure her Aunty had asked me to fill her in.

"I don't believe it. I knew something was wrong, but I never imagined it could be anything this serious," Mia eventually says, looking shocked.

"All that we can do, is to be there to support, with whatever decision she makes," I reply, with a deep sigh.

"That has really thrown me. Is he still coming back here at the weekend?" she questions.

"As far as I know, but I suppose things could change in the next couple of days," I tell her. Glancing around to check the coast is clear, I can't help my lips tenderly brushing hers. She responds with no hesitation at all.

"I love you, Jazz. I never want us to split up. It would break my heart into a thousand pieces," she says, with a tear threatening.

I cup my hand softly under her chin, staring deeply into her watery eyes. "Hey, Mia, our journey has only just started. We should focus on our future and enjoy every precious moment the two of us are lucky enough to be able to spend together."

"You're right. I'm just being silly," she smiles.

"Time for you to meet the luscious, Lucia at last," I tell her with a grin, holding my right hand out to softly take hers.

Chapter 34

"So, you must be the lovely, Mia," smiles Lucia, her eyes looking all over Mia, momentarily pausing at her beautiful breasts.

"Pleased to meet you," Mia replies, her cheeks suddenly changing colour.

Lucia slowly stands up and walks sexily across the kitchen throwing her arms tightly around, Mia. Another pang of jealousy shoots painfully through my heart.

"The kettle has just boiled. Help yourselves and feel free to join us," Aunty says. Aunty is full of joy and happiness. Her eyes sparkle in the mid-afternoon sunshine. It's been a very long time since I've seen her smile like this.

Finally, Lucia takes her hands off my girlfriend. "So, Mia. What do you do?" she asks.

"I'm a trainee paramedic," she replies. I place a mug of hot coffee directly in front of Mia. She glances up at me with a thank you.

"How wonderful, Mia. None of us can manage without the valued help of all the emergency services. I, for one, admit, I have needed their help on more than one occasion," she tells Mia.

"Didn't you break your collarbone a few years ago? Oh, and not forgetting your left leg in over six places?" Aunty queries.

"Yes, I did. Seriously, that was a horrendous accident. It took me months to recover," she sighs.

"Blimey. How on earth did that happen?" I ask.

"It was the final of a three-day event in Australia, and we were way ahead on the leader board. It was my fault completely. I mistimed the width of the tricky ditch and before I knew it, my poor mare had done a complete somersault, landing down heavily on top of me. I spent just over twelve weeks recovering, metal rods, numerous nuts and bolts keeping my leg together against a solidly built frame. Thankfully, and the most important thing was that my mare managed to come out of the incident completely unscathed," she replies.

"Thank goodness for that," says Mia, looking shocked.

"Who on earth did you have an argument with?" Lucia asks me, her eyes fixated on my multicoloured arm.

"A horse, of course," I laugh.

"Jazz is hoping to qualify for a place on the *British Olympic team*," Aunty announces proudly.

"That is amazing news. Good for you, Jazz. Clearly, talent runs in the family in more ways than one. Jazz, I'll certainly follow your riding career with great interest. It's such a shame you are heading back home on Sunday, but if you have any free time, I would love to see you and your horse in action," she smiles. *What sort of action?*

"I'm not sure if you have any plans over this coming weekend, but both Mia and Jazz are jumping at a local show on Saturday morning. If you are free, maybe this could be the ideal time to see them perform," Aunty says.

"I'm free this weekend. I would be honoured to come along to watch and support you both. It would also be a good opportunity to check out the local talent, too," she tells Aunty.

"Really, Lucia?" Aunty laughs.

"I meant talented riders," Lucia replies, with a naughty wink.

"Look at him, happily munching on his hay," Aunty says to Lucia, holding her phone in front of her eyes.

"The moment I first laid eyes on Autumn Wonder, I knew he had the quality to make it to the top and that is why I have given him plenty of time to mature. He is such a gutsy horse and a fast learner," Lucia replies.

"What are your future plans for him?" I ask Lucia.

"Eventually, and I am confident enough to say, that he should make a first class, three-day eventer. He moves with such fluency and strength. His determination is second to none. You should see him in full action, he can go from walk to canter with just a verbal command," she replies.

"Don't forget, I have booked you an hour's slot at one o'clock in the school for tomorrow and then daily at two o'clock, for the rest of the time Autumn Wonder is residing here," Aunty says.

"Thank you, Trudy. I really do appreciate all your help and kindness. When I woke up this morning, I had no idea I would be seeing you again after all these years, not in my wildest dreams," Lucia says, looking at Aunty lovingly.

"I didn't have a clue that you two had even met before," blurts out Mia, sounding surprised.

"Oh, damn it. Where has the time flown? That's Savannah messaging to say she's already outside waiting for me," Lucia announces.

I watch Aunty's face change quickly to one of sadness.

"Jazz and Mia. It has been a real pleasure meeting you both today. If you are free and if you would like to, you are welcome to watch me school, Autumn Wonder tomorrow. Plus, if you have enough time, I would love to meet your horses, too," she says, reluctantly standing up to get ready to leave.

Mia and I look at each other with a grin. "We would love to, thank you," I reply, with a warm smile.

"I'll see you off, Lucia, and I'll see you girls later. I have my last lesson to teach at five," says Aunty, looking directly at Lucia.

"See you girls tomorrow," Lucia says, before heading to the front door with Aunty closely behind.

I peep through the window, and smile. The two of them look to be deep in conversation slowly walking down the pathway towards the yard.

"Where do they know each other from and how long have they known each other? It's a bit weird that Trudy didn't mention any of this when we were talking about Lucia this morning," I vaguely hear Mia say.

I hold my breath. Lucia and Aunty have suddenly come to a complete standstill. Lucia's finger slowly runs across Aunty's left cheek. Aunty wraps her hand around Lucia's. I smile. They embrace each other tightly looking to be locked away in a magical world of their own.

Feeling guilty for being nosey, I quickly turn around to focus back on, Mia.

Mia walks directly towards me looking at me in that very special way and my legs instantly turn to jelly. "I think it's about time for me to rub some more cream onto your arm, don't you, girlfriend?" she says, armed with the tube of arnica.

I feel relieved, that Mia hasn't questioned me any further on the subject of how Lucia and Aunty met. I don't want to lie to her, but it's also not my place to reveal Aunty's secret.

"Sit," she commands.

"Yes, miss," I grin. My heart is beating rapidly. The thought of Mia touching me allows those marvellous feelings, deep down below, to materialize without warning. I look at her lovingly. Those beautiful red lips reach out for mine. The special and wondrous connection we share escalates to new heights, the moment our lips finally touch. My tongue slowly searches for hers and I groan with pleasure. Her hands slowly lift my T-shirt up towards my neck, before gently pulling it over the top of my head. I watch entranced. Her beautiful slender fingers teasingly trace the outline of my bra, before reaching around to unfasten it.

She looks at me lovingly with those hypnotic eyes of hers."
"Jazz, you are so beautiful."

"I love you, too, Mia," I reply, feeling breathless from her magical touch.

I remain seated, staying completely focused on, Mia. I cannot help another gasp of delight, the second she removes her T-shirt and bra, her half naked body longingly waiting for mine. Standing up in readiness, I slowly move forward, pressing my breasts firmly against hers. The tremors deep down below, start to resurface in a way that I'm unable to explain. My hands continue to explore her smooth satin skin. Her body pushes closer against mine. The movement of her pelvis rocking slowly against mine causes an instant flutter and moist feeling to arise, deep down below.

Leaning my neck to one side, Mia slowly slides my hair out of the way, before allowing her lips to caress me as they move urgently downwards.

I moan softly. Her tongue darts teasingly against my left nipple. Flickers of excitement dance around wildly inside me. My right hand sneakily wanders downwards to her inner thigh, moving forwards and backwards softly in between her legs.

"Oh, Jazz. What are you doing to me?" she groans, her

breathing sounding shallow.

"Do you like me touching you, Mia?" I ask her, in a sexy voice.

"Oh, yes," she pleads.

I'm taken by surprise with her next move. Her right hand takes hold of mine, guiding it back into the correct place, pressing it softly against her womanly mound of Venus. "Mia, you feel so nice down there," I groan. My hand runs forwards, backwards, and from side to side. She moans out loud, pushing herself urgently with force against my hand. "You, sexy little minx," I whisper to her, before my lips desperately move downwards to her beautiful breasts.

Her pulse rate quickens the second my left hand takes a gentle hold of her left breast. My mouth hungrily finds her nipple, gently sucking and then letting go, whilst my right hand continues to work wonders, downstairs. "Jazz, you have to stop," I hear Mia's breathless voice call out.

"Oh, but, Mia, do you not like the way I'm trying to guide you to that wonderful and pleasurable place? I'm sorry," I tell her seductively.

"You will be in a minute," she whispers. Her right hand quickly moves mine away from her downstairs region.

My teeth gently nibble her right earlobe. "But, Mia, I want you right now."

"Jazz, I want our first time to be special. Not half naked in your Aunty's kitchen," she replies, reluctantly pulling away. I look at her hot and flushed face. Her succulent breasts show tiny beads of sweat which have magically emerged from deep within her soft and tender skin.

My willpower seems to be getting weaker by the day. *Can I continue to control my sexual urges? Can I hold out in readiness for that mind-blowing and life changing moment the two of us have longed for? You are doing well, Jazz. Your patience will pay off very soon. Remember, good things come to those who wait.* We look at each other and laugh at the hot and sexual state we have managed to get ourselves into. "I'm beginning to enjoy myself every time that tube of arnica appears," I tell her, with a cheeky grin.

"Oh, bloody hell. I really am sorry, Jazz. I completely forgot about your arm," she exclaims.

I walk towards her. "I think, my personal nurse needs to be punished for neglecting her patient. Do you agree?"

"Your personal nurse may have neglected your arm, but she can assure you, she has done her utmost to ensure the rest of your body is doing ok. Don't you agree?" she replies.

"Maybe," I reply, sultry.

"Jazz, now get dressed and try to behave yourself," she says.

I reluctantly pick up my T-shirt and bra from the floor. Standing two feet away from Mia, I grin naughtily, watching her struggle trying to fasten her bra. "Would you like a hand?" I ask, with a sexy smile.

"Thank you, but I think I can just about manage. You still have a naughty look across your face, Jazz. What mischievous things are you thinking now?" she asks.

"If I told you what was running through my mind right now, I don't think you would want to leave," I reply. Clipping my bra back on, before putting my T-shirt back on, I watch her closely for a reaction.

"Were you having more sexual thoughts?" she enquires, walking towards me. A naughty grin covers her flustered face, and her eyes sparkle like priceless diamonds. "Well?" she demands, slowly pushing me back down onto the wooden chair.

"Nurse, Mia. You seem to be turning me into a sex maniac. Is this behaviour normal?"

"It's completely normal to feel like this, but only when you are with me. Do you understand?" she says, with one eyebrow raised.

"Yes, Miss."

"Good. Now let me get this arm creamed up, before I leave," she continues.

The touch of her hand massaging the cool cream seductively into my skin, has an instant response from, deep down below.

"All done. I'll message you later," she says, before kissing me tenderly one last time.

Smiling to myself, I watch her walk towards the door, hesitating momentarily before turning around to blow me a kiss. *What on earth just happened between us?* The intense passion between us is close to becoming completely out of control.

Chapter 35

Aunty grins at me, before relaxing back in her armchair with a tall glass of vodka and coke in one hand.

"It's great to see you smiling once again, Aunty. You even have that naughty twinkle back in your eyes," I tell her.

"Oh, Jasmine. I cannot tell you how fabulous it was to see, Lucia today. I felt as though I was 18 all over again. Her sense of humour still makes me laugh; in fact, everything about her, truly warms my heart. I think the two of us will share some great times together when she becomes my neighbour," she replies, with that faraway look on her face.

"You could always divorce uncle and shack up with, Lucia. It would save you a trip to the supermarket in search of a sexy lady of your own."

Poor Aunty nearly chokes on her drink.

"Are you ready to tell me what happened with you and Lucia? I've been dying to find out," I ask her, sounding eager.

"You will never look at Lucia in the same way, after I tell you what the four of us got up to," she laughs.

"I'm willing to take that chance," I reply giggling.

"Which bit did we get to?" she asks.

"You were in the restaurant with Lucia, Ruby, and Nicole downing lots of champagne, sounding like you were having an awesome time."

"Oh yes," she answers, with a naughty grin.

"Well?" I question.

By seven o'clock, we were all feeling a little bit tipsy and the sexual tension between us was mounting at a tremendous speed. Honestly, we didn't stop laughing. The laughter continued to get completely out of control when Ruby told Lucia all about, Mr Shackle. Tears rolled down our faces. We noticed a few odd disapproving glares from a couple of the other diners, but we couldn't care less, in fact, it made us laugh even more. We were having a ball, simply the best time of our lives. On a few occasions, Lucia's right hand ran teasingly along the outside of my left stocking, and slowly upwards towards my thigh. I remember holding my breath, as the warm tingling began to run through my already quivering body. I gazed deeply into Lucia's angelic green eyes, with a hungry, urging look across my face. She immediately leant towards me and the moment her gorgeous hot lips touched mine, I wanted her more than I've ever wanted anything in the entirety of my life.

"Don't start without us," Ruby said, with a mischievous look across her face.

"Maybe we should make a move," Nicole suddenly announced, her tongue playfully circling her lips, unable to take her eyes off me and Lucia.

"I left my car in the car park. Do you think it would be ok to leave it here overnight?" Lucia, asked.

"Leave it with me and I'll have a word with the owner. We only

live ten minutes away, so you can pick it up in the morning," Ruby told her.

"The walk home was hilarious. The four of us linking arms, whilst the fresh air helped to quickly sober us up," Aunty says, before taking a large sip of her vodka.

"Oh my God. The four of you all back at Ruby's house. Bring it on."

Lucia was completely taken aback with the elegance of Ruby's house. Nicole was the first to grab a cold bottle of champagne from the fridge. She popped the cork and bubbles soared up and over the top of the dark green bottle. Nicole's tongue slowly and tauntingly licked the outside of the bottle. Without any warning, Ruby's soft lips began to caress the back of my neck, her hands gently squeezing my breasts, her teeth pleasantly nipping at my skin. Lucia looked across at me, her green eyes boring deeply through to my soul. Ruby was driving me insane, but I knew I wanted, Lucia more than anything. Lucia's lips finally brushed mine. I sighed in contentment; her tongue urgently searching for mine. I could feel her soft and tender hands running firmly up and down my waist. I had hungry lips caressing me to the front and back. It felt heavenly. With my eyes closed, the sexual pleasure racing throughout my body was unimaginable. I could smell champagne close by and opening one eye, I saw Nicole's hands running through Lucia's gorgeous auburn locks, her tongue flicking against her ear.

"To be honest, I didn't know whose hands were touching who," Aunty laughs.

"It sounds a bit like one of my favourite games, Twister," I tell her.

"Believe me, Jasmine, there was a lot more twisting yet to

come."

The air surrounding us was absolutely electrifying. The kissing gradually became more intense, and we were heading towards a point of no return. Ruby was the first one to pull away, followed by Nicole. Lucia was oblivious, her lips hurriedly moving downwards, one hand rubbing seductively in between my legs. I was on fire and never wanted this moment of frenzy to end.

"Who fancies a dip in the hot tub with a glass of cold champers?" I heard Ruby ask.

Lucia's hand and lips begrudgingly moved away from my excited, quivering body. She stood for a second catching her breath, looking gorgeous and ravishing. Her eyes completely fixated on mine, and a warm smile slowly appeared across her face. I could feel my heart beating like the clappers, my legs felt weak and wobbly, as electric spasms continued to flash through me.

"That was the moment, I knew I had fallen in love with her. What happened next was surreal," Aunty sighs, with a warm smile.

"I'm waiting," I tell her, taking a mouthful of my gin.

It wasn't long before the champagne was flowing for the second time that day. I could feel, Nicole's intense eyes burning straight through me. Ruby reappeared with four white Egyptian bath robes.

"Trudy, can you grab another bottle from the fridge please? Come on ladies, follow me," she instructed.

I grabbed the champagne wondering what could be awaiting us this time. We walked along a pathway made from stunning marble paving stones, towards what appeared to be a huge log cabin. Soft lights flickered gently through the windows in the late evening magical and mysterious moonlight. I could not believe the size of what Ruby called her back garden. Seriously, it was big enough to keep two large horses in. As soon as we entered the cabin, I was completely taken aback. Inside, to the right stood a magnificent looking hot tub, glossy white in colour, large enough for at least seven people. To the left, two massage tables immediately caught my eye, soft white towels pleasantly draped over them. The wall directly in front was home to a magnificent king size bed. The cream satin duvet cover stared back at me invitingly. Relaxing music played softly in the background, hidden speakers tucked away in the ceiling, just like her bedroom. Honestly, I have never seen a setting so amazing and tranquil.

Lucia's hand gently squeezed my buttocks and a tremor shot through me like a bolt.

"Time to get your clothes off ladies," Nicole announced.

I looked over at Lucia to see her eyes shining back at me like diamonds. The numerous jets began to fire up. Nicole carefully placed four glasses of champagne into the luminous drink holders dotted around the tub and then it was time to undress. Very slowly, we began to remove our own clothes, glancing at each other seductively, as the pile gradually became higher.

Lucia's eyes watched every single moment of my little strip tease, her face entranced, as I seductively peeled off my stockings. The four of us stood in only our bra and briefs and that is when the action really kicked off.

Ruby walked suggestively towards me, her stunning body once again taking my breath away. Very slowly, she turned my body around to gently unfasten my bra, the tips of her fingers continuously circling my back. Lucia gracefully made her way towards me, pausing momentarily, her eyes looking lovingly into mine. She knelt down directly in front of me, our eyes deeply connected, her fingers gently touching the outline of my briefs, before seductively and slowly peeling them down to my ankles. Her lips traced the length of my right leg, her tongue urgently flicking against my tingling skin. I gasped and held my breath, as they moved across to my inner thigh, eventually advancing to softly caress that tender area, right between my legs. For a split second, I thought I was going to pass out. Her touch, her lips, her beautiful body, her stunning auburn hair, her mesmerising green eyes, every single part of her, totally captivated me. She slowly stood up, taking my hands in hers, guiding them upwards onto her beautiful breasts. My lips lovingly fondled the top of them, my hands urgently unclipping her bra.

She moaned lightly, as it fell to the floor and finally our breasts met. I could feel her erect nipples pushing against mine, her hands gently stroking my long blonde hair, her lips teasing and nibbling my neck. I pulled away, looking into her hypnotic eyes, before slowly lowering my hands downwards to her black silky briefs. Her fingers circled the top of my head, her pelvis pushed towards me, showing me in urgency how much she wanted me. I purposely took my time to remove her briefs. I wanted to tease her, and it worked. The sexual chemistry between us was near boiling point. We were completely lost in each other and momentarily forgot all about, Ruby and Nicole, totally captivated by the intense passion between us, as we explored each other's bodies. Lucia's briefs finally fell to the floor. I glanced over at Ruby and Nicole to see the two of them already in the hot tub, their eyes glued to the events happening right in front of them. They raised a glass of champagne towards us.

Ruby, seemingly in her element, her face flushed, called over to me and Lucia with a naughty looking grin.

"Are you two red hot sexy ladies ready to join us yet?"

Lucia gently took hold of my hand, slowly leading me towards the hot tub. My legs felt weak and shaky, as I climbed down the two wooden steps. Within seconds the hot bubbling water gleefully surrounded my naked body. I watched Lucia lower herself down; I couldn't take my eyes off her.

"She is the only woman I have ever known who had waxed every single area of her body, including down, you know where," she says, pausing to take a quick drink.

Oh Lordy. Would Mia be expecting me to have a Brazilian deep down below? To be honest, I hadn't even given anything like this a single thought, that is until now. *What the heck am I going to do, about this new and awkward situation?* I giggle to myself, suddenly remembering the clippers Aunty uses regularly on the horses. *Maybe I should give them a try to see if they can work wonders on my pubic hair?*

"Are you ok?" asks Aunty, breaking my chain of thought.

"I'm fine. I was just thinking whether this could possibly be one of Mr Shackle's biggest fantasies. I wonder how much he would have been prepared to pay to see four naked women gallivanting around in a sizzling hot tub?" I grin.

"Don't you worry about, Mr Shackle. He had one heck of a treat lined up for him the following morning. Trust me," she laughs.

"Really? Go, Mr Shackle! I can't wait to hear what show the four of you put on for him. It certainly sounds like he had an amazing fifty hours, too," I reply, before joining in with her laughter.

"That's another story. One I may tell you tomorrow evening," she informs me, before quickly getting up from out of her chair.

"Where do you think you are going? You haven't finished telling me the rest of the hot tub episode yet."

"I'm just popping to get another little top up, that's all. Would you like one?"

"The way this story is going, I may well need the whole bottle," I reply, laughing.

I glance down at my phone. Another message from Mia. '*Hey sexy girlfriend. I'm busy thinking about what the two of us could be getting up to in just forty-eight hours from now. The thought of me slowly undressing you, my lips tracing every single inch of your perfect body, is making me feel very hot and wet downstairs. Love you xxx.'*

A hot flush immediately races up from the tips of my toes, all the way up to the top of my head. *'Don't you dare start getting too hot and wet downstairs without me next to you, girlfriend. Behave yourself. I'm having a serious chat with Aunty,'* I reply to her text.

Aunty soon arrives back holding her recently filled glass and a large bottle of gin.

"I was only joking," I say, tears streaming down my cheeks. We soon settle back down, and I wait eagerly for Aunty to continue.

"Back to the hot tub then," Aunty continues her story.

Well, we chatted, laughed, and enjoyed our champagne. The bubbles continued to erupt from the numerous powerful jets around us.

"What would you two say to helping out me and Nicole with our hourly session tomorrow morning? We could split the earnings between the four of us?" Ruby asked Lucia and I, completely out of the blue.

"It depends what is on your agenda. If, it has anything to do with nipple clamps or anything else that could be painful, then it's a definite no from me," I replied, looking across at Lucia.

Ruby laughed.

"Why don't you tell Lucia and Trudy what we have planned for our morning slot, Nicole?" she told her, with a naughty wink.

"Sure, why not? Ruby, for you, I was thinking, a black leather miniskirt, obviously no underwear, a seductive and revealing leather corset, the laces untied to reveal those wonderful big Mamma's of yours, fishnet stockings and four inch stilettoes." Nicole continued.

"*Big Mamma's? What on earth are Big Mamma's?*" *Lucia asked, looking confused.*

"*Your succulent breasts are a prime example,*" *Ruby pipes up, and we all started to laugh.*

"*What do you plan on the three of us wearing then, Nicole?*" *I enquired, staring across at her.*

"*Our outfits consist of short black leather dresses, left completely open at the front and long black leather boots with six-inch heels, covered in gold plated studs. Black hoods over our heads, long leather gloves with spikes on the end, strong rope in hand, not forgetting our whips and electric prod to complete the costume. We normally film sessions of this nature down in the basement. Our clients pay handsomely to watch something of this calibre. Bondage and discipline are a huge earner for us,*" *she replied.*

I sat with my mouth wide open, and Lucia instantly began to look slightly uncomfortable. Ruby and Nicole waited patiently for our reaction. I swallowed hard and was just about to speak when the two of them burst out laughing.

"*Oh, Trudy, your face was a real picture. I was only joking,*" *Nicole confessed.*

"Honestly, Jasmine, the relief that ran through my body was heavenly. I eventually saw the funny side and so did Lucia, and the laughter became infectious."

"Oh my God. What a fabulous sense of humour, Nicole had," I laugh, the tears trickling down my cheeks.

"Eventually, after the laughing subsided and Ruby had kindly topped up our glasses," Aunty continues.

I asked Nicole once again, trying to keep a straight face.

"*My darling, Lucia. Now, I think you would make one hell of a sexy nurse, and surprise, surprise, we have an outfit just your size. Trudy, how about we dress you up in a seductive police officer's uniform? Your role will require lots of bending over with your truncheon, but I'm sure you can handle this," she told me, with a grin.*

"That's more like it, but what about you and Ruby?" I replied.

"Ruby will be dressed as a plumber and I'll continue to be a dressed as a French maid. Well, are you two up for the challenge?" she asked me and Lucia.

We looked at each other and smiled, nodding in agreement across to Ruby and Nicole.

"All sorted then. Ten o'clock sharp. If it's ok with the two of you, Nicole and I need to head off to get everything ready for the morning. We have also got some very important business to deal with which cannot wait any longer. Isn't that right, my love?" she said, turning to look at Nicole, her body slowly moving to sit on top of Nicole's, her breasts rubbing across her face.

The view was spectacular, Ruby's beautiful and sexy backside pointing directly towards us. I felt, Lucia's hand glide teasingly upwards to my inner thigh. I gasped, turning quickly to face her, and our lips met hungrily. The way her hands danced around my body under the hot bubbling water was enough to drive me insane. I vaguely heard Ruby and Nicole leave.

Ruby called out something like, 'Have fun ladies. There is a cupboard full of delightful sex toys next to the bed, but looking at the two of you, I don't think you'll need any help from them.' Lucia and I were then left alone.

I have never made love in such a sensual way and certainly never in a hot tub. This was something mind-blowing and it didn't end there either. We eventually climbed out of the hot tub, slowly and seductively drying each other off. Behaving like a pair of naughty teenagers, we hurriedly made our way across to the awaiting king size bed. I cannot remember how many times we made love that evening. We had a strong sexual chemistry, something that came rushing back to me today when I saw her again.

"I woke up the next morning, the sun shining through the windows and felt like the luckiest woman in the world to have Lucia wrapped lovingly in my arms," says Aunty.

"You really fell for her big time, didn't you? Do you feel the same way about her now?" I ask, thinking how her mind must be in so much turmoil right now, what with Uncle's affair and now being reunited with Lucia.

"To be honest, I don't know, all this stuff with your Uncle is overwhelming. I will never forgive him. I've decided to tell him I want a divorce when I see him Saturday evening. With regards to Lucia, let's just say, at this present moment, I want to leave my options wide open," she replies, with a naughty grin.

"Wow. You have been thinking things through. Only you can decide what is right for you and if you do divorce Uncle, well, you are still young enough to make a fresh start. Who knows what lies ahead?"

"I'm so glad that I have you to talk to. I hope I'm not burdening you too much with all my problems?"

"Honestly, no. Definitely not. I love you and want what is best for you. I'll always be here to help and support you in any way I can."

"Right. Off, to bed with you. I love you and appreciate your kind words and support. Go on, now bugger off out of here, before you set me off with a tear or two," she laughs.

"See you in the morning. I can't wait to hear how the four of you got on. Sweet dreams," I tell her cheekily, before heading to the kitchen with my empty glass.

I lie in bed, numerous chaotic thoughts racing through my mind. I scroll excitedly down the sexy lingerie listings on *Amazon Prime*, finally clicking on a sexy red skimpy corset which catches my eye. Quickly adding it to my basket, I continue to search for some hold up stockings and a pair of sexy briefs. I giggle to myself, finding the perfect pair of red crotchless briefs. I check out my items and feel relieved to receive the email confirming that they will be delivered to Aunty's address by mid-day on Saturday. My contentment drifts me off into a deep erotic sleep.

Chapter 36

"Good morning, Jasmine. I hope you had a wonderful night's sleep," Aunty cheerfully asks me.

I'm sure she would be shocked if I told her all about the hot and raunchy dream I'd had, one that had left me dripping in sexual sweat. Although, after her most recent story, maybe not! "Not too bad thank you," I reply, my thoughts drifting back to the moment Mia's fingers had gently eased themselves inside me. You know, into that sacred place, deep down below.

"I have a lesson to teach in fifteen minutes, but I'm sure Mia will be here very soon to keep you company in my absence," she grins.

Looking her up and down, I smile, noticing the perfectly applied make up on her face. "What are your plans for today? Would you like any help?"

"If you could give me a hand with a couple of things this morning, I would appreciate it. Don't forget, Lucia will be lunging Autumn Wonder in the school at one and afterwards she is taking me for a quick bite to eat before my three o'clock lesson. I must say, I'm really looking forward to catching up with her again."

I bet you are! And I reckon, sexy Lucia, the naughty little minx, is looking forward to a quick nibble with you too.

"There you are, Jazz. I was looking for you down at the field," Mia says, suddenly appearing, the smile on her face instantly melting my heart. She continues to walk directly towards me with a naughty twinkle in her eye.

I hold my breath. *Surely Mia knows Aunty is here?* I glance across to see her busily scribbling in her diary.

"If you could take Spirit and Jackson out for a thirty-minute stroll this morning, just around the village, I can then tick this off my to do list," Aunty continues.

Mia's hand brushes against my bum cheeks. The chemistry between us is electrifying.

"We can do that, can't we, Jazz?" Mia replies, quickly turning to check on Aunty, before naughtily and firmly squeezing my buttocks.

"Sure," I reply, unable to take my eyes off Mia's breasts, defined beautifully through her figure-hugging T-shirt.

"Why don't the pair of you take a couple of hours off this afternoon and nip down to the beach? The weather forecast is for a warm and sunny day. It would do you both good to chill out before the show tomorrow. Lucia is going to give me a hand later, so you might as well take advantage and enjoy some free time," Aunty says, not looking up.

I bet she is.

"What a great idea, eh, Jazz?" Mia grins.

"You can take a couple of towels and a few nibbles with you, too."

Focusing on Mia's sexy backside wiggling across the kitchen. *I know exactly what I would like to nibble on right at this moment.*

Aunty pushes her chair back, and stands up ready to make a move, closing her diary firmly shut. "Good, that's all sorted them. Right, if I don't see you beforehand, then I'll see you both over in the school at one o'clock sharp."

I stand staring at Mia's slender body, naughty thoughts already racing through my head.

The door slams shut, and Mia's lips instantly burn furiously against mine. "I've missed you so much," she says, in between her kisses.

Our tongues dance excitedly. I pull Mia's body closer against mine. Her pelvis pushes against me, sending a raging thrill of pleasure throughout.

"Only one more sleep," she whispers, gently nibbling my earlobe.

"I think we've done well to last this long," I groan back. "I'm not sure if I can wait until tomorrow evening, Mia."

She reluctantly pulls away. "You can and you will, my love."

Taking hold of her right hand before placing it down firmly in between my warm and ready legs, I groan, "Mia, please don't stop."

"Wow, Jazz. You are feeling pretty hot down there, aren't you?" she replies sexily, her hand continuing to caress, deep down below.

"Oh, Mia," I gasp.

"Right, my horny girlfriend. You've left me no choice, but to stop, before I lose my self-control, too."

"But?" I plead.

"Behave yourself and if you can, then maybe we can continue just where we left off down at the beach later?" she says, with a cheeky smile on her face.

Smiling back, I nod in agreement, waiting patiently for the constant throbbing down below to ease.

"It might be an idea for you to rub the arnica cream on yourself this morning. I can't trust myself to touch you anymore right now," she laughs.

"Spoilsport."

"Get that coffee down you and we can then make a start on our chores."

We walk slowly towards the yard, our hands lightly brushing against each other's, causing tingling sensations that are constantly flurrying around. "I'll pop and get Spirit ready. See you back here in twenty minutes?" she says, before turning to walk in the opposite direction.

I stand and watch her stride away into the distance, letting out a huge sigh. *Not long to wait now, Jazz.*

"There you are," I tell Jackson, finally locating him at the very far end of the four-acre field. His striking leopard markings stand out easily amongst the other plain coloured horses and ponies. He lifts his head, looking slightly peeved that I've been rude enough to interrupt his grazing. "Don't worry Jax, we are only going for a little stroll around the village, nothing too strenuous," I laugh.

Within seconds, his headcollar is on and he reluctantly walks by my side towards the gate. I glance at his magnificent markings. The base colour is white with black spots beautifully flowing over the entirety of his bulky fourteen two hands frame. Jackson's nearside eye is covered by a unique circle of black hair, his white mane and long flowing tail entwined with numerous thick black stripes. He truly is stunning.

"Good, lad," I say, opening the gate, before closing it safely behind us. He behaves like a true gentleman, following me towards the yard, only occasionally glancing around. I quickly groom him from top to tail, his stripy hooves fascinating me with their unusual patterns. "Right, Jax, nearly done," I say, finishing off buckling up the throat lash on his bridle. He lets out a contented snort. Tiny beads of mucous prickle against my bare right arm, sticking against the recently applied arnica cream. I screw up my nose, just as he proceeds to do it all over again. "Come on you, Mr snotty, off we go," I tell him, pulling the reins over his head, before heading round to the front of the yard in search of Mia and Spirit.

Spirit is the first to greet us, but Jackson doesn't respond. He is so laid back, it's unbelievable.

"Isn't Jackson just stunning? I absolutely adore his markings; they are totally unique and so unusual," Mia calls out.

"I agree. He really is one of a kind." We follow Mia and Spirit, as we head towards the winding country lane. I feel lucky to have a first-class view of Mia's amorous backside. She looks so small and slender next to Spirit's giant frame.

Birds sing sweetly in the trees all around. A gentle warm breeze flows across my smiling cheeks, as the midmorning sun shines brightly high above. How relaxing and tranquil this feels. "I have never seen your Aunty smile so much. It must be lovely for her now her long lost friend is back."

If only you knew the truth. You don't know half of it!

"Yes, you're right. It is wonderful to see her so happy again. I bet she's not looking forward to seeing Uncle tomorrow evening."

She turns towards me, with one of her heart stopping smiles. "Well, I for one, am really looking forward to tomorrow evening."

My pulse rate immediately quickens at the thought of the two of us spending the whole night together.

"Is it time to turn around? You lead the way home. I want to watch your tight little ass swinging from side to side," Mia says.

Bringing Jax to a halt in readiness of turning him around to make our way home, I quietly tell him, "Close your ears Jax. Mia is just being naughty and rude."

"Very nice," Mia giggles.

I quickly exaggerate my walk allowing my hips to move sexily from side to side.

"Oh, yes, Jazz. Please keep that up all the way home. You are really turning me on."

"In what way?" I smirk.

"In every way imaginable. My hands firmly holding your sexy backside, my lips caressing the side of your neck, my tongue flickering lightly over your nipples and that's just for starters."

"Stop," I call out, the sexual emotions inside me roaring back to life once again. I hear Mia laugh out loud, and I'm grateful to see that we're nearly back at the yard. My pulse is racing, my cheeks feel hot and flushed and deep down below aches with sexual desire.

"What a gorgeous looking bunch," Lucia says, standing closely by Aunty's side.

"Jackson, the Appaloosa, is a real darling and no trouble at all. He's almost twelve, and his owner hand reared him from a foal when his mother rejected him." Aunty says.

Lucia smiles at me, taking in every single part of my body, noticeably spending a little too long on my breasts.

I know it's wrong, but the way she looks at me, for some unknown reason, causes little tremors of excitement to trickle throughout my body. I quickly look away from her enchanting green eyes, vaguely hearing her and Aunty talking away to Mia and Spirit. I seem to have drifted off into a daydream. A vision of Lucia appears, standing naked right in front of me, her wondrous round breasts, her nipples pointing towards me hard and wanting, as she slowly and seductively climbs out of the bubbling hot tub.

Bloody hell, Jazz. What is wrong with you? "This way," I tell Jax, feeling totally ashamed of myself.

"See you in the school shortly," I hear Aunty call.

Chapter 37

Mia and I sit side by side in the viewing gallery, patiently waiting for Lucia and Autumn Wonder to make their appearance.

Autumn Wonder finally enters the school. I let out a gasp and so does, Mia. My eyes take in every inch of this magnificent looking creature. His front knees rise high, as his strong, athletic body floats through the air with pure grace and elegance. He looks grand enough for a King to ride.

"What a mover," Mia gasps.

I turn to look at the concentration on her face. She looks to be in awe of this impressive gelding parading right before our eyes. Lucia seems to be in total control, leading him to the centre of the school, before unclipping the lead rope. Autumn Wonder trots proudly around the school like a top-class dressage horse. his perfect confirmation clearly showing with every move.

"I'm allowing him to enjoy a ten-minute warm up. It's important to allow him time to investigate and get used to his new surroundings," Lucia says.

His bay coat looks in immaculate condition, shining brightly in the glorious sunlight streaming in through the plate glass windows. He inquisitively investigates a pile of coloured jumps stacked away neatly in the far corner of the school. His muzzle touches one of the poles and it suddenly moves. Instantly, he turns on a sixpence, going from a walk into a gallop within a split second. His stunning long tail runs freely behind him, as he eats up the ground beneath him, speckles of tiny grains of sand flying all around. Turning once again, prancing and snorting, his nostrils flare wildly, dancing on the spot, as his muscles ripple and quiver with every single move. I hold my breath. His huge, solid body thunders powerfully towards us, his strong legs enabling him to arrive at a perfectly timed halt, just six feet away. Pricking his ears high, his princely looking wide black eyes curiously look towards Mia and I. Shaking his muscular neck, his black mane dancing, he turns once again, trotting majestically back towards Lucia.

"Liberty training is all about communication and focus between you and your horse. It builds a strong and unbreakable connection over time and there are huge benefits for you both. If you watch closely, in a second, I will demonstrate some of the handling techniques required," Lucia says.

I watch in amazement and wonder.

Autumn Breeze stands directly in front of Lucia, his head hanging low, looking calm and relaxed. She reaches out one hand, gently stroking him from the top of his ears all the way down to his soft velvety muzzle. "It's important to remember to concentrate on your breathing, as you need to feel calm and relaxed. Every single ounce of your energy feeds directly through to your horse. Any negative energy you hold, can confuse, and unsettle your horse. Deep, controlled breathing must be your number one priority. Watch closely," she calls out.

Totally enthralled in this demonstration, I lean closer.

Lucia's hand gently touches the centre of Autumn Wonder's chest. He immediately responds, taking four paces backwards, and from what I can hear, no words were even spoken.

"Did you just see that?" Mia gasps, her right hand squeezing my waist, causing an electric bolt to instantly shoot through my body.

Next, Lucia gently runs her hands all the way over Autumn Wonder's body. He doesn't move an inch. She turns to walk away from him, her body relaxed, her head down low and he immediately follows closely behind her. A completely different horse, to the wild looking one who was galloping around crazily around the school just ten minutes earlier. "Now, I'll send him out to work," she shouts, bending down to pick up the lunge whip. Her gorgeous backside aims directly towards Aunty who is watching intently from the school's closed doors. *Lucky Aunty.* With a slight flick of her whip, a good two feet behind him, Autumn Wonder immediately goes into an elegant looking trot. Even though the school is huge and oblong, he keeps to a perfect circle, roughly twenty feet away from Lucia. After five minutes or so, Lucia suddenly stops, turning her body anti clockwise and, to my utter amazement, Autumn Wonder follows suit.

"I have never seen anything as magical as this," I say.

"Unbelievable," replies Mia.

Five minutes later, Lucia comes to a halt and her horse once again mirrors her moves. She turns her body around, lowers her head and without any hesitation at all, he responds. Slowing down to a walk, he heads directly towards her, stopping just a foot away from her shoulder. I can see her smiling, as she turns towards him and gently rubs his face. Such a special and mesmerising moment to witness. All down to her body language, voice command and energy levels. "When you connect with your horse, the trust becomes mutual. The two of you can achieve anything you put your mind to. It is all about working as a team. Now, I will show you how to achieve trot to canter," she informs us. Once again, Autumn Wonder trots beautifully around in a circle. "And canter," she instructs with just a click of her tongue.

My jaw drops wide open.

He immediately responds, cantering beautifully in a perfect circle, suddenly resembling a rocking horse. His exquisite neck arches proudly whilst his powerful hind quarters push his strapping, powerful body forward. "And turn," Lucia calls out, before turning anti clockwise herself.

"Bloody hell," gasps Mia.

We watch him come to an immediate halt, unbelievably turning on a sixpence, instantly changing direction. "Now that was truly magnificent," I reply, not quite believing what my eyes have just witnessed.

"I've never seen anything like that in the whole of my life," Mia says, before firmly sitting back down.

"Body language and verbal cues are the key to free lunging. Anyone can achieve this; it just takes time, practice, and perseverance," Lucia calls, whilst asking Autumn Storm to trot, then walk, before he finally makes his way back towards her. "Well done, my boy," she congratulates him, slowly stroking his lowered head.

"Lucia, that was an outstanding performance. I have never seen anything so heart-warming and beautiful. The connection you two share is second to none. Absolutely superb," Aunty says, walking quickly across to congratulate the two of them.

"It is a precious gift when you experience a connection like this, whether it be with a horse or a human," she replies, staring deeply into Aunty's eyes, with a warm smile across her face.

"Come on, Mia. Shall we head to the front of the school and wait for them to make their way out?" I ask, not wanting her to spot the sexual chemistry obviously smouldering between, Lucia and Aunty.

Mia cheekily pinches my backside. "Not long to wait now, sexy girlfriend," she whispers softly in my ear.

A pleasurable tremor deep down below, takes me completely by surprise. Quickly coming to a complete stop, knowing we are safe from any prying eyes, I turn around to face her, gently pushing her towards the concrete wall, before pressing my lips firmly against hers.

"Oh, Jazz," groans Mia, my lips slowly moving down to her soft and slender neck, my hands urgently grasping hold of her gorgeous buttocks, firmly bringing her body closer to mine.

I feel her heart beating rapidly against my breasts. "Mia, I love you."

"I love you, too. Do you know how much you are turning me on?" she mumbles.

My lips work their way down to her chest. My hands find their way underneath her T-shirt, gently caressing her satin smooth skin. "Tell me, Mia," I whisper, feeling her body tremble at my touch.

"We need to go," she moans, searching eagerly for my lips.

"I know," I groan back.

Begrudgingly, I slowly pull my hands out from underneath her T-shirt, moving them upwards, gently taking hold of her angelic looking face. Staring deeply into her beautiful green eyes, I kiss her tenderly on her soft awaiting lips.

"I think the two of us should have a paddle in the sea later," she says, her eyes looking lovingly into mine.

"That's a bit random," I reply laughing.

"I know, Jazz. I'm trying to focus my mind on something other than my current sexual urgings," she chuckles.

"I know the feeling only too well. We'd better go and make an appearance," I tell her, before leading the way to the front of the school.

Aunty and Lucia are nowhere to be seen, so we decide to head off in the direction of Autumn Wonder's stable.

"There you are," smiles Aunty, looking at the two of us from over the top of the stable door.

"Sorry, we got slightly waylaid," I tell her, trying to avoid any eye contact.

"Jazz, Mia? Did you enjoy our little performance?" Lucia asks, her gorgeous face suddenly appearing, leaning gently over Aunty's right shoulder.

"It was truly magical," beams Mia, with a huge smile across her still flushed face.

"I totally agree. I've never seen anything so enchanting. The bond you two share is inspiring and such a pleasure to watch," I tell her, unable to take my eyes off her gorgeous auburn hair. *I wonder how Aunty feels at this precise moment, having Lucia's sexy body leaning against hers? I definitely wouldn't say no. Bloody hell, Jazz. This needs to stop now. Lucia is your Aunty's ex-lover, and you are lucky to have Mia. Don't bloody ruin it.*

"Thank you, Jazz. To be honest, I've been pondering for a while about the possibility of holding a few demonstrations sometime in the near future. I think it would inspire other horse owners, but, unfortunately, my new place hasn't got the facilities to accommodate this yet, due to the indoor school needing a total renovation," she tells us.

"You can hold them here. We have plenty of room and the gallery can seat up to fifty spectators," Aunty pipes out, tuning to grin at Lucia, who is just inches from her face.

"Let's do it, Trudy," Lucia says, as their eyes lock together, smiling like a pair of loved up teenagers.

"Sounds like a great plan to me. Mia and I are just off to the beach for a couple of hours. I hope you two enjoy your lunch and we will catch up later," I say, knowing I need to get Mia out of the way as soon as possible. I can feel the powerful electricity flowing between the pair of them and it won't be long until Mia sees it too. I haven't got a clue what is going to happen when Uncle arrives home tomorrow evening.

"That's a shame, I wanted to meet your horses," sighs Lucia, her eyes finally leaving Aunty's.

"You can see them at the show tomorrow, Lucia. I'm sure you mentioned to me earlier, that you have a couple of appointments booked in after lunch today with some of your other horses," Aunty reminds her.

"Damn it. You're right," she sighs. "What time are you planning to head off to the show tomorrow morning?"

"Around ten o'clock at the latest," Mia informs her.

"Why don't I come along for around six thirty then? Trudy and I can school Autumn Wonder first thing and afterwards I can give you a hand to get them both ready, that is, if you would like me to? It has been ages since I've prepared a horse ready for a show. Preparation is one of my favourite parts and to be honest, I really miss it, so you would be helping me too, although I totally understand if you don't need any help," says Lucia.

"We would love to take you up on your very kind offer, wouldn't we, Mia?" I reply, looking towards her, feeling immediately guilty about not being able to control the naughty thoughts I feel, every time she looks at me.

"Absolutely," Mia beams.

"That's a date then," grins Lucia.

"Have a lovely lunch, you two. Aunty, we'll see you later, and you tomorrow morning, Lucia," I smile.

"By the way. I've managed to get Lorna to cover a couple of my lessons tomorrow, so I can tag along with Lucia to cheer my two girls on," Aunty announces, with a beautiful glow across her face.

"Thanks, Aunty, that's fabulous news. It'll be awesome for us to have you both cheering us on," I tell her, with a grin.

"The gorgeous sandy beach is calling us," Mia smiles.

"Enjoy," I call over my shoulder, before following Mia back towards the house.

Chapter 38

"Are you ready then?" Mia grins at me, before pressing a circular button to start the engine.

"Oh yes," I reply, with a naughty twinkle in my eye.

"We can't be too late back though, Jazz. I promised I would cook dinner this evening, as Mum was on a late shift last night. Isn't it lovely, Lucia is going to give us a hand in the morning? I must say she and Trudy look to be getting along very well. How did they meet again?" she queries.

"Oh blimey. I can't really remember. I'm looking forward to feeling the soft sand between my toes, though," I reply, looking through the passenger window at the picturesque country lanes.

"Me, too. I hope the sea is warm enough for a paddle. I'm taking us to that lovely beach we rode across the other day. Hopefully, it will be nice and quiet again," she replies softly.

"Are you going to tell your Mum about us?" I suddenly ask.

"Of course, I am. I know Mum will be thrilled, and knowing her, she will want to know every single detail. What about you? Do you think you are ready to tell your parents yet, or is it too soon?"

"To be honest, I haven't really thought too much about it. The first person I think we should tell is, of course, Aunty. I don't like hiding anything from her, but I reckon she'll be fine," I reply confidently.

"Really? How do you know?"

"Trust me. I know," I grin back.

"Are you hiding something from me, Jazz?"

"It's not my place to say. Let's just wait and see what happens, shall we?"

"Ok, fair enough. I wonder how she is feeling about seeing William tomorrow evening. I can't believe what a complete knob he has been. He has surely got a screw loose cheating on her. She's a real catch," she sighs.

"So, you think Aunty is pretty fit then, do you?"

"She's in pretty good shape for an older woman. Anyway, you can't talk, you used to have the hots for luscious, Lucia," she teases.

Feeling a warm glow rising slowly into my cheeks, I think back to how Lucia made me feel earlier when she looked into my eyes and a sudden rush of guilt quickly follows. "Very funny. I've told you before Mia, that was just a typical teenage crush," I reply, not daring to look across at her.

"She is pretty fit though. I can see why you had a crush on her."

"I hope you're not trying to tell me that you are into older women now?" I question, feeling insecure for a moment.

"Why would I want to sample corned beef when I have steak right in front of me?" she laughs out loudly.

Her remark makes me giggle, and my right hand gently rests on her smooth left thigh. *Bloody hell, Jazz. Don't forget to dig out those horse clippers, as soon as you can.*

"Here we are," Mia informs me, indicating to the left, before pulling up in a car park surrounded with high leafy trees.

I quickly unfasten my seat belt. "I love your car. It's really nifty."

"You'll soon get used to seeing a lot more of Daisy, especially when the pair of us come to visit you," she blatantly says.

Feeling slightly confused for a second, I suddenly wonder, '*Who the bloody hell is Daisy?*' That is, until it suddenly dawns on me, she's talking about her car.

"Surely your car has a name?" she replies giggling.

"No, she doesn't."

"Well, that's a start. So, she's a female car then?"

"I hadn't actually given it any thought, Mia. If it will make you happy, I'll let you name her next time you see her. How does that sound?"

"Wicked, Jazz, thank you. I love naming cars," she says, before leaning towards me pressing her smiling lips softly against mine.

"Weirdo."

"Come on. Let's get down to the beach," she says, with a precious smile which instantly melts my heart. Carrying a ruck sack each, we head down the narrow pathway and through the stunning woodland towards the beach.

"Can you taste that?" Mia asks, suddenly coming to a standstill.

"Salt."

"Spot on. Look, Jazz."

My eyes slowly follow to where she is pointing. The soft golden sand is only a few steps away, and the sound of gentle waves crashing along the shoreline, is music to my ears.

"Follow me."

Tiny grains of soft, warm sand suddenly embrace my feet. I adore this wonderful feeling, quickly removing my sandals, allowing the golden granulated powder to run softly between my toes.

"Hurry up," Mia calls out, eagerly heading towards the awaiting blue sea.

I stand quietly for a moment, taking in our glorious surroundings. The refreshing sea breeze gently flows all around my face. The rays from the sun, shine magically onto the endless expanse of ocean. A family of four sit relaxing to my right, a small dog running excitedly towards the soft flowing waves. Smiling, I head off in hot pursuit of Mia.

"There you are," she grins, as I slowly walk towards her.

She has already laid a large picnic blanket across the carpet of sand, not too far away from the inviting looking sea.

"You have the towels," she says, with a warm smile.

Apart from the other family who are quite a bit away to our right, I am delighted to see that the rest of the beach looks completely deserted. I grin back at Mia, before hurriedly unpacking my rucksack.

Mia taps the area to her right inviting me to join her. "This is the life."

"I totally agree," I reply, handing her a cold can of lemonade, before sitting down.

"Isn't it just beautiful?" Mia asks, her head slowly looking around in awe.

Opening my can, I hold it towards hers. "Here's to tomorrow night," I tell her, my eyes running up and down her slender legs eventually landing at the top by her skimpy shorts.

"Onwards and upwards," she says, with a cheeky grin.

Our cans touch and I watch Mia closely, as she moves the can up towards her luscious waiting lips. After taking a couple of sips, she places the can down onto the sand before lying flat out on her back. Her hands gracefully take hold of the bottom of her T-shirt and I cannot take my eyes off her. I let out a gasp, as she seductively pulls up her T-shirt revealing her nicely toned stomach. My hands urgently want to caress every single inch of her, but they reluctantly hold back. I am unsure as to whether the other family can see us or not. "You ought to put some sun cream on," I tell her, unable to concentrate, my eyes mesmerised by her gorgeous body. The familiar sensations deep down below, already begin to emerge.

"Oh, Jazz. I've only just got comfy. Would you mind rubbing the cream on?" she asks, not attempting to move at all.

"Yes, Miss," I tell her softly, taking a firm hold of the sun block. I turn to lean over, and squirt the first drop onto her right cheek, making her jump. "Don't be a wuss. Just lie still." As softly as I can, my fingers gently massage the cream into the angelic skin all around her face. Her tongue mischievously rolls around the outside of her lips. "Mia. What are you trying to do to me?" I whisper into her right ear.

"What would you like me to do to you?" she murmurs back, not even opening her eyes.

"I have a very long list. But, before I tell you, would you like me to rub some cream anywhere else?"

"Yes please. My legs and stomach need your magic touch. That is, if you don't mind."

If I don't mind? I can't wait!

Shuffling across the blanket towards her feet, I take a long deep breath to try and control my sexual urgings, before slowly squirting a single line of cream along each of her naked legs. My fingers immediately get to work, gently massaging the cream around her ankle bone, before continuing to her shin, upwards to her knee, finally arriving around the inside of her thigh. She moans softly. My fingers move wilfully underneath the material of her shorts.

"Oh, Jazz," she groans, her pelvis pushing softly against my hand.

Looking around quickly, I am pleased to see that we are

completely hidden from the other family. Leaning my head forward, my lips gently touch her naked stomach. I feel a fluttering sensation beneath her skin. I allow my tongue to gently explore just above her cute little belly button, before moving upwards towards her breasts. The passion and longing inside me are getting stronger by the second. She moans and wriggles in pleasure, her hands taking hold of the back of my head, putting my face firmly against her breasts. My right hand continues to caress her left inner thigh, and she gasps out my name, as my index finger teases and circles the tender area underneath her shorts.

"Jazz, you need to stop. I'm gradually losing my self-control with you causing a complete riot, you know, downstairs," she mutters, her breathing shallow.

I lift my head up and slowly look at her beautiful glowing face. Her green mystical eyes suddenly open, staring deeply and longingly into mine. "Did that feel good, girlfriend?" I ask her.

She answers my question with her lips, hungrily and urgently kissing mine.

"Time for you to cool down, I think," I tell her, before reluctantly prising our lips apart.

"Bloody hell, Jazz. I cannot describe the effect your sensual caressing has on me. Honestly, you nearly drove me to a place of no return," she mumbles, slowly trying to sit up, her breathing still not back to normal.

"I'm sorry," I grin.

"I don't think you are, judging by that cheeky, gorgeous smile on your face," she replies.

The sexy and sultry look she gives me causes immediate chaos, deep down below, yet again. Quickly jumping up, I take hold of her right hand and pull her to her feet.

"I think we both need to cool down, don't you?"

Chapter 39

"I'm not going any further, it's too bloody cold," I tell her, the cold sea water flowing freely around my knees.

"Come on, Jazz. Just two more steps," she pleads. The deep wet sand sucks at my feet, as the waves continue to splash droplets of freezing salty water all over me.

"I'll watch you from here, Mia. I for one, certainly don't want to catch a chill before tomorrow evening," I reply with a grin.

"Spoilsport," she laughs back.

"You're crazy," I call out, watching her dunk her whole body under the chilling sea water.

"You should try it, Jazz. It's exhilarating," she calls back.

I shiver. The thought of my body being completely immersed in this cold murky water is enough to make me want to turn around and urgently head back towards the warm golden sand.

Mia appears to be jumping up and down having a whale of a time. Eventually, she makes her way across to me. Her dark dripping hair dangles around her shoulders. The closer she gets, the more she laughs at the look on my face. "Come here and let me give you a cuddle," she says, a naughty look glinting in her eyes.

Oh my God. Just look at her breasts. Mia resembles the vision of a Goddess. Honestly, Jazz, how bloody lucky are you to have caught a stunner like Mia? "No bloody chance," I reply, quickly turning to head back to the shore.

Her sexy voice seems to be getting closer. "Spoilsport," she calls out.

Lifting my knees as high as I can, I try hard to take bigger steps, but my feet seem to be sinking deeper into the bottomless sand beneath, making my escape plan more difficult than I imagined. *'Ten more steps, Jazz,'* I say to myself, looking around to see where Mia is.

A mischievous grin covers her face, as she closes the gap and at that precise moment, I lose my footing, falling face first into the icy cold water, the whole of my body completely immersed within a split second. Spluttering and gasping to catch my breath, the shock of this sudden mishap sends shivers of coldness from my head down to my toes, as I struggle to scramble to my feet. I can vaguely hear Mia laughing hysterically, my ear drums completely blocked with gurgling water. The taste of salt is prominent in my mouth, slowly dripping down from my soddened hair.

"Are you ok?" Mia asks, appearing at my side, still laughing.

"What do you think? I'm freezing and feel like a bloody drowned rat," I reply, in between coughing and spluttering.

"You look like one."

Turning to look at the wide grin across her face, she slowly looks me up and down, trying not to laugh anymore. "Apart from your nipples, of course. It's amazing what kind of reaction the cold sea water can have on some of your body parts," she laughs.

Glancing down at my breasts, I can immediately see what she means. I have never seen my nipples look so hard and erect. Mia laughs again and I suddenly see the funny side. My cold wet feet finally touch the toasty grains of sand, the heat from the sun bearing down on me, and this feeling of warmth is priceless.

"Here," says Mia softly, wrapping a huge beach towel around me.

"Thank you," I tell her gratefully.

"I'm sorry, but that was really funny. The way you fell forward with a splash, was so unexpected," she teases, her towel massaging her beautiful dark hair.

"Tell me about it," I reply, turning to grin at her.

"Why don't you lie back on the blanket and let the heat of the sun warm and heal your beautiful, sexy body?"

I do as she suggests, unwrapping the damp towel from around me. Hopefully, the warmth from the rays of the sun will soon dry my damp clothes. I let out a sigh of relief, as I begin to feel half human once again, lying flat out on my back. "See, I told you, Mia. Me and cold water, do not get on." Closing my eyes, I allow the rays from the sun to do their job.

"Did you know that cold sea water increases the level of oxygen in your blood and it's rich in vital elements including vitamins and mineral salts? There are so many benefits to having a dip in the sea," she informs me.

"I would rather take the vitamins and minerals in tablet form," I reply, with a grin, keeping my eyes still firmly closed.

"You do make me laugh," she replies. Her salty lips brush lightly across mine, instantly blocking out the sun.

"Are you feeling nervous about tomorrow evening, Mia?" I suddenly blurt out, slowly opening my eyes.

She's lying next to me, her right hand firmly propping up her chin, looking lovingly down at me.

"In what way?" she queries softly. "You know, with it being my first time. I don't want to let you down by not knowing what I'm supposed to do."

"Jazz, remember, it'll be my first time, too. We can just take things slowly and see where it leads. There is no pressure on either side. Honestly, I would wait a lifetime to make love to you if I had to. That is how much I love you," she replies earnestly, her sexy green eyes piercing deep into mine.

I smile warmly back at her, the sexual urgings immediately returning with enthusiasm, deep down below.

"Oh, Jazz. You need to stop all this worrying. I reckon you're going to behave like a caged tiger who has just been released to freedom for the very first time.'

"You're right, Mia. I just don't want to disappoint you."

"That can never happen, I promise," she replies, her left fingers gently caressing my cheek.

"What have I done to deserve you?"

"I honestly don't know," she grins back.

"If you carry on with your cheeky comments, you know you will end up being back on my naughty list, don't you?"

"Bring it on," she replies, her fingers gliding downwards to the inside of my thigh.

"Bloody hell," I reply, her touch taking my breath away.

"How naughty would you like me to be?"

I know exactly where this could lead to. "Very, very naughty."

Her voice low and sexy, "Let's see how much willpower you really have."

Her hungry lips ravish the side of my neck, her tongue teasingly flicking against my skin. I take in a sharp breath, as her teeth gently pinch at my skin. Very slowly, I feel her fingers lightly move under my T-shirt. Tingling sensations flash intensely throughout my body. I moan, the heat of the sun warming my stomach, as she gently raises my T-shirt up and over my bra.

"Jazz, you are so beautiful," she whispers, before her lips move down to my bra, her hands playfully sliding up and down my stomach, hovering close to the top of my shorts.

My pelvis automatically pushes towards her and she moans with glee. An electrifying surge flows deep down below. Closing my eyes, I cherish and enjoy every single second of this mind-blowing moment.

"Honey. Come," I hear a voice calling out in the distance.

For a moment, I think, *'What an appropriate comment,'* just as Mia pulls away from me. Quickly sitting up to straighten my T-shirt, I'm surprised to see a small white fluffy dog heading straight towards us at great speed. I hear a high-pitched whistle, but the dog is not responding at all. Suddenly, this little ball of fluff lands firmly in my lap, her little tongue continuously licking my face.

"Hey little one, have you escaped?" Mia asks her, leaning forward to greet her. The dog turns to lick her face, too, as I try hard to hang onto her wriggling furry body.

"I'm so sorry," an out of breath female voice says, slowly coming to a halt directly in front of us.

"She's very cute," I reply.

"She may be cute, but she can be a right little monkey. I apologise for interrupting your relaxation. Come here to Mummy, Honey," she tells the dog, who is taking no notice at all, as she continues to lick my face. "Look what you have done. Naughty girl, you have covered these two ladies in sand," she gasps in horror.

"Honestly, it's not a problem. We were just about to leave anyway," Mia informs the anxious lady.

"Pass me her lead and I'll clip it on for you," I tell her calmly.

"There we go, Honey. Good girl," I say, giving her one last hug before handing the end of the lead to her Mum.

"Thank you and once again, I'm so sorry," she continues to say.

Honey reluctantly follows her Mum, occasionally stopping to glance back at the two of us.

"Now, that is what I call cute," I say, turning to grin at her.

"I totally agree, Jazz. Maybe one day, we could rescue a dog just like Honey?"

"I love that idea," I reply, a warm loving smile across my face.

"I suppose we ought to head back home. It's almost five o'clock," she says, placing her watch back onto her right wrist.

"I don't want to go yet. We still have some unfinished business to attend to," my lips tenderly brushing hers.

"Well then, I'm curious. How was your willpower holding out, before we were rudely interrupted?"

"Well, to be honest, not very well. I think the arrival of Honey was a Godsend. You were turning me on, driving me into a wild frenzied state and I doubt I could have held out for much longer," I tell her, with a naughty smile.

"That's what I like to hear. I aim to please," she replies, her tongue circling around her lips.

"Mia, you can't do this to me," I say, imagining her tongue circling, deep down below.

Standing up quickly, I turn my back to her, bending over trying hard to wipe the dried sand from my arms and legs.

Mia's pelvis pushes sexily against my backside; her hands taking hold of my breasts and my legs turn to jelly.

"You really want to end up on my naughty list, don't you?" I tell her.

"Yes, I do. What punishment do you have in mind, sexy girlfriend?"

"Be patient, Mia, and I promise you'll soon find out." I let out a deep disappointing sigh, as Mia removes her hands from my breasts and her hot body away from my buttocks.

Shaking the grainy sand from our towels and blanket, we reluctantly pack everything back into our rucksacks. We walk slowly across the golden carpet of sand. No words are needed. The loving glances we occasionally give each other, speak volumes.

"Are you looking forward to the show tomorrow?" she asks me, as we drive back through the glorious countryside.

"I guess, but tomorrow evening can't come soon enough for me," I reply, turning to look at her reaction.

The naughty, yet sexy grin on her face says, that she feels the same. "I'll message you later then, my horny little minx," she says, as the car comes to a standstill just in front of the yard.

I quickly glance around. Not a soul in sight. Releasing my seat belt, I lean towards her for one last kiss. Our lips linger gently for what seems a lifetime, before reluctantly parting.

"I love you," I declare, searching for the door handle. Taking hold of my rucksack, I open the door and climb out.

"I love you more than you could ever know and tomorrow evening I'm going to prove to you, just how much," she replies.

I sigh, as her car fades away into the distance.

Chapter 40

'Don't forget the clippers,' I suddenly remind myself. Diverting from the path towards the house, I quickly make my way across to the tack room. Thankfully, I cannot see anyone around. Feeling a bit like a burglar, I quickly rummage through the cabinet in search of the clippers. *Bingo.* Looking around to check the coast is still clear, I hurriedly open my rucksack and sneak the box inside. Zipping it up securely, I head back to the house with a smile. I need to get this job done, as quickly as I can, so I can return the clippers back to the tack room before anyone notices they are missing.

I sigh with relief to find the house completely empty. Glancing down on the table, I see a scribbled note from Aunty. *See you at seven for drinks. I hope you had a great time at the beach x.*

Move your ass, Jazz. You only have an hour and a half to complete your task. Racing back to the bedroom, I quickly lock the door behind me, before ripping my clothes off in a frenzy. *Oh shit. Where are the other blades?*

I feel panicky, as I rummage frantically through the clipper box.

There are no spare blades to be seen. The tiny metal teeth on the end of the clippers stare back at me. *Bloody hell. If I go ahead and use this blade, I'll have no bloody hair left. What the heck, do it, Jazz.* Plugging them in, I walk cautiously towards the bathroom, feeling grateful that the lead is long enough to reach. Carefully rinsing the blade with scolding hot water from the tap, I'm finally ready. Looking at myself in the mirror, I take a deep breath and say out loudly, "You can do this, Jazz."

Bending over, I'm shocked to see the amount of hair staring back at me from, deep down below. Feeling reasonably confident, I turn on the clippers and get down to work. The vibration from the clippers between my legs is a very pleasurable one, to say the least. I need to concentrate to avoid any serious injury with this sharp gleaming blade. I am amazed to see the huge volume of light curly hair dropping slowly down onto the bathroom floor. *Imagine Mia's face if I cut myself badly down here and needed to call her to ask for assistance!*

Turning off the clippers, I look down to check my handy work. I'm totally shocked to see the area all around my private parts, is now completely bare. *'Oh, dear Lord,'* I sigh. There is not a single thing I can do about it now, apart from pack the clippers away, get showered and quickly return them to their rightful place, back in the tack room.

The sponge glides softly between my legs. Moving my right hand downwards, I allow my fingers to explore my recent trim. I am happily surprised at the outcome. My skin feels smooth and clean to the touch. In fact, it feels so good, I'm beginning to turn myself on. I quickly pull my hand away, as the aching and throbbing starts. A hot, sensual flush instantly soars throughout my body. *Bloody hell.* I tut, looking down at the grains of sand sitting at the bottom of the shower tray, before blasting them down the plug hole with the powerful jet head. After thoroughly drying myself, I decide to rub a generous amount of coconut butter cream all over my naked body. My hand slides carefully down in between my legs, and the feeling of my soft and naked skin causes a tremor of delight. *I think Mia might be delighted with this result, too.*

Trying to ignore my naughty and erotic thoughts, I hurriedly get dressed. Packing the clippers safely away in my rucksack, I make my way slowly back to the tack room. I feel like a criminal, constantly looking around to check no one is in sight. A wave of relief flows through every single part of me, as I place the clippers back to their rightful place, before heading back to the house to put the damp, sandy towels into the washing machine.

***

"What a fabulous and rewarding day I've had," grins Aunty, before sitting back in her armchair, armed with a glass of what I assume, must be vodka and coke.

"I see you are on the hard stuff, once again," I grin. "How was lunch?"

"Lunch was absolutely awesome, thank you. We have so much to catch up on. Lucia told me about her future plans for the new stud and I must say, they sound, not only ambitious, but very exciting, too. How was your little trip to the beach? I hope you managed to relax?"

"We had a lovely time," I reply, before telling her all about my embarrassing moment, falling head-first into the freezing cold water.

"Jasmine, that's so funny. I bet your face was a real picture," she laughs.

"I can see the funny side of it now. Have you heard anything from Uncle?"

"No, but I have spoken with my solicitor and asked him to draw up the divorce papers. I plan to tell your Uncle tomorrow evening.

This is my final decision. We can then both move on with our lives. It shouldn't be too complicated, as the house and yard belong to me. We only have a joint account, which can be split equally between the two of us," she replies, matter of fact.

"Sounds like you've definitely made your mind up, Aunty. Good on you."

"I have and nothing will change my mind. Anyway, let's change the subject. Are you looking forward to the show tomorrow? And have you and Mia decided, how you will spend your evening?"

"Oh, yes, I'm looking forward to tomorrow. I do love local shows; they always seem to be relaxed and such good fun. It should just feel like a warm-up for, Breeze, compared to some of the bigger competitions we've recently competed in. Mia and I thought we would find a good old horsey film on *Netflix* and just chill out for the evening," I tell her, looking down at my glass, trying my best to avoid any eye-contact.

"A cosy night in sounds like a good plan to me, and totally the opposite to the one I'll be having", she laughs.

"You'll feel a lot better once you've got it all off your chest and told Uncle about the divorce. Do you think he'll still be expecting to come back here to stay, even after you've told him?"

"If he does, he's going to be in for a very big shock. There are plenty of hotels dotted around. I can tell you now, your Uncle will never, ever, be setting foot back inside here. Early next week, when I can manage to find a spare couple of hours, I plan to pack all his clothes and belongings into boxes. I'll give him seven days to arrange collection, and if he doesn't, tough shit! I'll just drop the boxes off at the nearest charity shop."

"Go, Aunty."

"I feel like a heavy load has been finally lifted off my shoulders. Once I have sorted your uncle out, I'm determined to look forward to the future and to making a fresh start."

"I love your determination and focus."

"Girl power," Aunty laughs, holding up her glass.

"Cheers. Here's to a brighter future ahead," I grin. "I think it's time for you to continue with your saucy story and before you ask me where we'd got up to, you'd just woken up to find Lucia fast asleep, lying lovingly in your arms."

"Oh, yes, I remember every second," she grins, her eyes instantly lighting up.

Glancing across at my watch, I was relieved to see it was only seven am. I can't even remember falling asleep, the whole evening felt like it had been just a wonderful dream. Looking down at Lucia's beautiful face, a peaceful smile across her perfectly shaped lips, I knew this was real. I still needed to pinch myself just to be sure. Lucia's eyes eventually opened, her striking green eyes hurriedly searching for mine. The heart-warming grin across her face when she first saw me, was priceless and it wasn't long before her lips hungrily found mine. The next hour flew by. We continued to make love in the most passionate way imaginable.

"Coffee?" I asked her when she eventually allowed me a take a five-minute break.

"I would love one, but only if you come back to bed," she replied with a sexy grin.

"It's a deal, but don't forget, we only have an hour before we're due back at the house to get ready to do some work," I told her.

"Oh, yes! I think we should have a practice run, don't you, officer Trudy?" she'd teased.

I glanced across at her sexy, naked body, looking irresistible against the satin sheets, immediately nodding in agreement, with a naughty look across my face. Climbing on top of her, holding her hands firmly above her head, I told her she was under arrest. How I kept a straight face, I don't know. She struggled and squirmed, as she tried to release her hands from my firm grasp.

"Are you trying to resist arrest?" I asked not daring to take my eyes off hers.

She provocatively pushed her naked pelvis up towards mine, and for a split second, I lost all concentration. Lucia quickly took advantage of my moment of weakness and before I knew it, her body wriggled around sexily on top of mine.

"I don't think I need to explain what immediately followed," she says, with that faraway look in her eyes, a happy grin across her face.

"Wow. You and Lucia certainly got to know a lot about each other in such a very short time," I giggle.

"Oh, believe me, there's still a lot more to follow," she laughs. "Anyway, somehow the two of us ended up on the floor with a thump, after managing to roll off the bed. We lay helplessly laughing."

"It's a good job, Nurse Lucia is on duty this morning, officer Trudy," she said, trying hard to stop her laughter.

I played along, trying to look pathetic.

"Oh, Nurse Lucia, thank goodness for that. Would you be kind enough to check me all over? I think I may have damaged part of my pelvis in a recent fall."

"Well officer Trudy, luckily for you, gynaecology happens to be one of my favourite subjects. I would be more than happy to give you a thorough examination," she replied.

"Honestly, Jasmine, the tears were streaming down my face with laughter."

"That is absolutely hilarious. I can just picture this scene in my head," I reply, trying hard to stop the tears running down my cheeks.

"To cut a long story short, it wasn't long before we ended up in the shower together. I have never known anyone, until I met, Lucia, who was not only loving, but also considerate and passionate in their love making, too. She was in a league of her own. We didn't have time for coffee in the end and it was just before nine, when we eventually arrived inside Ruby's kitchen," she says, taking a large gulp of her drink.

"Oh, so now we get to the dressing up part then?" I grin.

"Oh, yes, lot's more still to come."

"Good morning, you two love birds. Did you manage to get any sleep at all?" Ruby asked, with a huge smile, as we stood grinning in our beautiful, white, bath robes.

"We had some, enough to ensure that we're now fully recharged, isn't that right, officer Trudy?" Lucia, grinned back, turning to look at me with a wink, my mind drifting back to our recent sexual encounters.

"Coffee?" smiled Nicole, suddenly appearing in the kitchen looking as ravishing as ever.

"Yes please. We did intend making one, but somehow managed to get waylaid, didn't we, nurse Lucia?"

"I see the pair of you are taking your role play seriously, by the sounds of it?" Ruby laughed.

"Tell us more," Nicole pleaded, as the four of us sat around the kitchen table.

"Well, I tried to arrest, nurse Lucia, but she resisted and we both ended up on the floor with a big bang. I needed checking over. I was slightly concerned, I may have damaged part of my pelvis, so I called on nurse Lucia, for assistance," I told them.

The laughter became contagious, stopping only when Ruby spoke in a serious tone.

"I reckon, we can make some good money this morning,

ladies," she announced.

"What will we need to do?" Lucia asked, looking deeply into Ruby's sexy green eyes.

"Don't worry too much, Lucia. We tend to make it up as we go along. You just need to follow our lead," she grinned back.

"What I think would be a great teaser to start with, is for us all to get dressed up in our outfits. I can then take a selfie of the four of us posing, post it straight onto our site and wait for the requests to come flooding in. What do you think?" asked Nicole.

We turned and looked at each other with eagerness and excitement all over our faces.

"Drink up, and then follow me upstairs. Your outfits await," Ruby said seductively, before standing up, her slender hands running invitingly all around her gorgeous breasts.

"Let me put your empty cups into the dishwasher for you," Nicole said.

"We patiently waited for her to join us before racing up the stairs at great speed, like three naughty teenagers," Aunty says, a dreamy look across her face.

"You need to turn this into a book Aunty. Seriously, the adventures you managed to fit in, in only fifty hours is unbelievable and there is still more to come," I say eagerly, thoroughly engrossed in her story.

"I suppose, I should, but I don't like the idea of washing my dirty linen in public," she chuckles.

"This's why you use a pen name, Aunty, so no one knows who you are."

"Maybe an idea I'll consider when I retire then, eh?"

"I'd be the first one to demand a signed copy," I tell her seriously.

"Let me get a top up and I'll tell you the rest of the saga."

"No, stay there. I'll grab you one," I reply, walking over to pick up her empty glass, before rushing to the kitchen.

"Thank you. Are you ready?"

"Bring it on," I reply.

Lucia's face was a real treat when she walked into Ruby's bedroom. She reacted the same as I had, slowly looking around, completely spellbound. Her striking eyes stared at the magnificent waterbed sitting proudly in the centre, the tranquil candles flickering all around, soft music playing in the background. Our outfits were hanging ready in Ruby's dressing room. This was real and happening soon. To be honest, I didn't even feel nervous this time, probably because Lucia was with me. We looked at our clothes and grinned.

"Are you ladies ready to rumble? Get your clothes off and let's get naked. No rush, we have plenty of time. I've put the time back to ten-fifteen to keep our customers in suspense," Ruby said, with a naughty look across her face. Lucia and I looked at each other lovingly, as our robes slowly slid down to the floor. The sexual chemistry between us was obviously visible to both, Ruby and Nicole.

"You'll have plenty of time to have red hot sex afterwards, you pair of horny beauties," Ruby told us, gently slapping my backside, as I bent over to put on a pair of blue crotchless briefs.

For a split second, I thought Lucia looked slightly jealous, but I ignored her and carried on getting dressed. I could see Nicole bending over, with her head between her legs, her gorgeous backside pointing invitingly, her long silky hair touching the carpet. She winked at me sending me into a fit of giggles. Lucia and Ruby joined in too. It didn't take us long to add a splash of make-up and tie up our hair. The four of us were ready. We looked at each other in wonder, before pouting our vibrant, hot lips, as Nicole took a selfie of the four of us.

"Shall we do this then, ladies?" asked Ruby, with a huge sexy grin."

Chapter 41

"It sounds like a lot of fun and antics are yet to come."

"You're spot on. Here's what happened next," she grins, taking a sip of her vodka. "We raced downstairs, and Nicole popped open another bottle of bubbly."

"Only a small one for me, remember I'm driving later," Lucia

said.

For a second my heart sank at the thought of her leaving. I quickly put the thought to the back of my head, deciding to make the most of the time we had left together. Honestly, Lucia looked incredible, and my body ached for her. She wore a figure-hugging white dress, only just covering her crotch. Her mouth-watering breasts heaved outwards through the material. A single red belt with a gold buckle enhanced her sexy slender waist and the red fishnet stockings showed her beautiful legs off to perfection. A small white nurse's hat sat perfectly on top of her head, and her long curly auburn hair flowed beautifully down towards her breasts. Seriously, she looked like a film star. My heart rate went completely off the scale, causing me to feel sweaty and warm, especially down below, and talk about being turned on, well, that's an understatement. Ruby walked towards her, placing a stethoscope around her slender neck. She went to kiss Lucia on the lips, and I was surprised, but glad in a funny sort of way, when Lucia turned her head away and looked lovingly towards me. The kiss eventually landed on her right cheek."

"Blimey, go Lucia. Did you manage to get a copy of the photo with all four of you? What was your outfit like?"

"Do you know what? I didn't even give that a thought. What a fabulous keepsake that would have been," she sighs.

"My outfit was absolutely brilliant. Seriously, it was so sexy. A tight-fitting black mini dress, with a zip down the front allowing my breasts to bulge out and a police badge sat proudly on the upper right side. I wore a black peaked police cap and long black boots with four-inch-high heels which ran just above my knees. My finishing touches were a thick black belt, supporting two silver metal rings, one holding two pairs of plastic handcuffs and the other a long black truncheon. Lucia couldn't take her eyes off me. It was hard to control our sexual feelings and the intensity between us began to escalate," she says.

"I'm not surprised! What were Nicole and Ruby wearing?" I ask. The temperature seems to be rapidly rising. The thought of Lucia in that nurse's outfit is beginning to create a few flutters here and there. *Bloody hell, Jazz. Just behave yourself. What about Mia?*

"Nicole wore the same maid's outfit as the previous day and Ruby, well she looked good enough to eat! I have never seen a plumber look so sexy. If they really existed, trust me, I would be calling one out every day! She wore a tight black leather mini skirt, a skimpy red blouse, the buttons left open for her big Mamma's to seductively hang out, and a black leather toolbelt with screwdrivers and other tools neatly slotted in. Black fishnet stockings, long leather boots and a builder's hat, completed her outfit."

"Wow," I blurt out.

"Our site is going crazy since I posted the photo of the four of us. We have seventeen people waiting patiently in the queue. This has never happened before," Ruby grinned, before taking a large sip of champagne.

"Trudy and Lucia, would you mind sitting on the sofa for now? Nicole and I need to get our regulars out of the way first. You two can take part in the last fifteen minutes of the show. Trust me, this is going to be an hour's work none of us will never, ever forget. Is that cool with you?" she continued.

Lucia and I nodded, before making our way across to the sofa to watch the upcoming entertainment.

"You mustn't laugh," I told her seriously.

"You had better keep my lips busy then, hadn't you?"

I moaned, as her lips hungrily found mine.

"Watch the lipstick ladies," Ruby had called out.

We quickly pulled apart.

"Three, two, one and we're live. Good morning, Samantha and

what can the gorgeous, Nicole and I do for you today?"

There was a pause.

"Ok, I'm sure that can be arranged. This performance will cost you fifty."

We watched Nicole, put her thumb up to Ruby, confirming the payment and then the action really started.

"So, you think we have a blockage in our sink? I would be more than happy to deal with this, although I will of course, require Nicole's assistance," Ruby told her.

"I'm happy to help in any way I can," Nicole replied, in a low sultry voice.

Lucia looked at me, her eyes wide open in complete surprise before turning back to watch the maid and the plumber in action.

Ruby used the plunger vigorously in the sink drain with both hands. She stood sideways at an angle, her heavy round breasts bouncing up and down with every movement, a perfect angle for the camera.

"Holy shit," Lucia gasped.

"I don't think it's working. Samantha, what do you suggest I should try next?"

Another pause.

"Ok, that sounds like a plan."

Ruby opened the cupboard directly under the sink, kneeling down with her magnificent backside pointing cheekily at the camera.

"Could you help me please, Nicole?" she said.

"Of course. What would you like me to do?" Nicole replied, her hands slowly massaging her own breasts.

"Could you just kneel down next to me and have a fiddle around in my toolbelt? I desperately need a flat headed screwdriver," she told her.

Nicole slowly and sexily knelt next to Ruby, her hands seductively searching all around the tool belt.

"Oh yes, that feels really good. Do you agree, Samantha?"

There was a five second pause, before Ruby replied, "Really? You think the screwdriver is hidden between my huge, firm breasts? Of course, I'll ask Nicole to double check."

The two of them still on their knees slowly turned to face each other. Nicole leant forward, both hands massaging Ruby's breasts which were firmly hanging out of her red skimpy blouse. Nicole's mouth moved slowly towards them.

"You want to watch the gorgeous, Nicole, suck both my nipples? That will cost you an extra thirty, Samantha."

I watched, holding my breath, as Nicole put her thumb up before teasingly undoing the rest of the buttons. Her eyes looked hungrily into Ruby's, as she slowly removed the blouse, her hands reaching around Ruby's back to unfasten her bra.

Ruby slowly turned her body, her protruding nipples pointing directly at the camera. Nicole cupped her right breast in her hand, before leaning forward, her tongue lightly flicking against Ruby's right nipple. Ruby threw her head back, moaning in ecstasy, as Nicole tenderly sucked her nipple before moving across to the left. It was such a turn on watching this happen right in front of our eyes. I know for sure Lucia was enjoying it too. Her left hand occasionally ran up the inside of my right thigh, causing mini earthquakes to surface.

"I am glad to hear you enjoyed your time with us, Samantha. Nicole and I hope to see you again, very soon," Ruby said, letting out a huge sigh, before she and Nicole quickly got up to straighten themselves ready for their next client.

"So that was eighty pounds in total and how long would you say the session lasted? I ask, feeling intrigued.

"Maximum five minutes," Aunty replies.

"Wow!"

"Some of the things that followed were hilarious," laughs Aunty.

"Please tell me," I beg.

I watch Aunty glance down at her watch.

"It's not even nine-thirty yet. Don't forget, I'm going home tomorrow, so I need to hear the rest of the story tonight," I plead.

"Ok, you win," she smirks.

"Ruby took a very unusual request, but it didn't bother her at all, she just got on with it. Lucia and I thoroughly enjoyed watching it, too. It involved whipped cream and strawberries," she smiles.

"Just like when, Maddison caught out, Lucia and her groom?" I ask.

"Very similar. Maybe that's where she got the idea from!"

"Good morning, Mr Johnson, and what can I and my lovely assistant do for you today?"

There was a slight pause.

"You want me to call you Dick? Then Dick it is!" she replied, grinning at the camera, her hand slowly moving down in between her legs.

"Nicole, my darling, would you be good enough to get me the whipped cream from the fridge. Oh, and a couple of strawberries. Don't worry, they are already washed and prepared. You do realise this could get a little messy, don't you, Dick? Something of this nature, will cost you ninety pounds for, five full minutes."

We watched, as Nicole put her thumb up confirming the payment.

"Nicole, please remove all your clothes, just leaving your sexy red knickers on and I'll do the same. Hold on, Nicole. Well, Dick. That would be possible, but that will cost you another twenty," Ruby said.

Nicole put her thumb up, once again to confirm, and Lucia and

I waited in anticipation to see what would happen next.

"Dick would like me to undress you, very, very slowly," she told Nicole, standing directly in front of the camera.

I held my breath, as Ruby slowly and seductively removed Nicole's clothes. She sexily peeled down her hold up stockings, finally leaving her standing in just her briefs. Nicole then flirtatiously undressed Ruby.

"Nicole, lie down on your back, now," Ruby commanded.

Lucia and I quickly stood up, so we could get a better view. Ruby glanced over and winked at us.

Holding the container of whipped cream, Ruby slowly unpeeled the lid, her tongue seductively licking the inside of the lid.

"Oh, yes, Dick. It does taste cold and creamy on my tongue," she grinned at the camera.

I seriously don't know how Nicole, managed to keep a straight face, as Ruby began to massage the whipped cream into, Nicole's so called, big Mamma's. Nicole squealed in joy, wriggling her body whilst moaning with ecstasy, and just like me and Lucia, apparently, Dick was finding this a huge turn on, too.

Very slowly, Ruby leant over Nicole, hungrily licking the cream from around her breasts. Ruby's gorgeous backside pointed high up towards the camera. She paused for a moment, whilst she reached out to grasp one of the strawberries, before placing it gently into Nicole's awaiting mouth. She sexily moved around to sit at Nicole's head with her body, now facing the camera. She then leant over Nicole once more. Her breasts rubbed firmly against Nicole's face, before gently sucking the strawberry out of her mouth with her beautiful red lips.

"Oh, yes, Dick. It tasted sweet and wet. I'm pleased to hear you are having a wonderful time," Ruby told him in a sultry voice.

There was another slight pause.

"You need another five minutes, Dick? I'm sure Nicole would

be delighted to rub whipped cream into my warm and wet vagina, before gently licking it off, but I'm afraid, due to our tight schedule, that would cost you another hundred," she told him firmly.

We couldn't believe it, when Nicole put her thumb up to confirm.

Lucia and I quickly sat back down onto the sofa. It was such a huge turn on, and we had to look away, or we knew we would be in big trouble.

I vaguely heard Ruby calling out, "Yes, that feels so good, please don't stop," but the rest was a blur.

Lucia's lips hungrily landed on mine, her hand slowly teasing the inside of my inner thigh. I thought I was about to explode.

"Trudy, could you quickly grab the packet of baby wipes from the table please? We have a quick five-minute break," I heard Ruby call out, in a hurried voice.

I sighed, as Lucia's lips left mine, quickly jumping up before rushing across to the table.

Nicole laughed, as she struggled to remove the whipped cream and Ruby took a large gulp of champagne before cleaning herself up too.

"What did you think of that?" Ruby asked, grinning.

"That was pretty hot stuff. Honestly, we couldn't bear to watch the last five-minutes; it was making us both feel too horny," I said.

"There's still more to come, Trudy. Sit back down and enjoy yourselves, ladies. It might be worth you both applying a little more lipstick, as it won't be too long now, before we'll be needing you," she smiled, before taking the next call.

"With my reckoning, those two sessions earnt them two hundred and ninety pounds," I gasp, not quite believing the amount of money they both made in just fifteen minutes.

"I know. A bit bizarre, isn't it? By the time, Lucia and I joined in, they already had six hundred and fifty pounds in the kitty, after forty-five minutes work. Can you believe that?" Aunty says.

"Just think if the two of them had carried on doing this for even five days a week, over the last fifteen years, they could both be happily sitting somewhere in the Bahamas, sipping champagne aboard a luxury yacht", I reply.

"Maybe they are. Who knows? Time for me to get a top up, would you like one?" she asks.

I nod slowly. My head spinning at the thought of the unbelievable amount of money they had earned.

Chapter 42

"That's better," I hear Aunty say, as she plops herself back down into her comfy chair.

"Thanks for the top up," I say, raising my glass.

"I bet you need it, after listening to my mischievous antics. I'd forgotten how much fun we had during those fifty hours," she replies with a sigh.

"Come on, Aunty. Please don't keep me in suspense. I want to know what happened next."

"Well, our session ended up lasting twenty-five minutes in the end. Mr Shackle and his friend who was with him, Roberto, kept upping the ante and we couldn't refuse. Honestly, it was crazy money," she laughs.

"How much did you earn?"

"I'll tell you at the end of the story," she grins.

"Mr Shackle, how lovely to hear from you, once again. That's two days running, so business must be good. Of course, it's ok to have a friend with you. What is his name?"

There was a slight pause.

"Hi Roberto. How lovely of you to join us. Yes, Mr Shackle, we do have a maid, nurse, plumber, and police officer to attend to your every need, but the price I am afraid, is not negotiable. We need a starting bid of at least five-hundred," Ruby told him.

I held my breath, not quite believing what I was hearing. Ruby kept her cool. What a fabulous business lady she was. Nicole soon put her thumb up and we were off.

"So, let me get this right, Mr Shackle and Roberto. You would like me to place a chair in the centre of the kitchen, then politely ask, officer Trudy to arrest and handcuff, nurse Lucia and maid Nicole to the chair? Ok, I'm sure this can be arranged," she told them, with a beautiful smile.

We watched, as Ruby centred the chair before calling me, Lucia and Nicole, forward.

She signalled for Nicole and Lucia to stand either side of the chair.

Pulling her heavy metal wrench from her tool belt, she stood in front of the two of them.

"I'm disappointed in the pair of you for deceiving me. You deserve to be punished," she told them, in a very firm voice.

"Officer Trudy, please could you arrest these two guilty sluts and handcuff them to the chair?"

I was shocked with the sharpness of her voice, not only was she a shrewd business lady, but a brilliant actress, too.

Walking sexily across to Nicole and Lucia, I slowly showed them my handcuffs. Both played along, letting out a gasp, pretending be shocked, before placing one hand firmly over their mouths. It's a good job I had my back to the camera, as I wanted to giggle, but I quickly got my concentration back.

"You do not have to say anything. But it may harm your defence, if you do not mention when questioned something which

you later rely on in court. Anything you do say, may be given in evidence. Do you both understand?" I told them in a stern manner.

Lucia and Nicole nodded.

I walked across to Nicole, in an authoritative way.

"I'm sorry, I didn't mean to do it," she pleaded.

"Silence," Ruby told her, winking at me.

Making sure I stood behind her, so I was facing the camera, I took hold of Nicole's left hand. Holding it out, I placed the first bow of the cuff firmly around her wrist, and the other end around the metal arm of the chair. I then handcuffed Lucia's right hand to the other arm, unable to resist running my hand lightly up the outside of her leg.

"That would cost you another fifty," Ruby said.

I watched Nicole's right hand, slide down to her phone before raising her thumb.

"Officer Trudy. Please could you hand me your truncheon?" Ruby told me.

I retrieved the plastic truncheon from my belt and handed it over to Ruby.

"Oh my God Aunty, this is just unbelievable. How on earth did you manage not to laugh?" I ask, tears streaming down my face.

"Trust me, it was hard," she laughs.

"I need your assistance with this, officer Trudy. The maid and the nurse will receive ten lashes each. Please could you make them lean over, so I can see their sexy, and naughty backsides," she asked.

Gently taking hold of Nicole, I slowly turned her body at an angle where the camera could see her beautifully shaped backside.

"Bend over," I told her.

She immediately obliged. I couldn't even look at Lucia, in case I had a fit of giggles.

"Mr Shackle has informed me, that this is the punishment you deserve," Ruby told Nicole, seductively rubbing the plastic truncheon all around her bum cheeks.

Ruby gently tapped the truncheon against Nicole's beautiful flesh, ten times.

"I'm glad you're happy, Mr Shackle, and of course, I'll tell her you have decided to drop the charges. I'm sure she will be very grateful. Officer Trudy, please release the maid. She is now, free to go."

I did as she asked, although it felt a bit bizarre finding myself unclipping a set of plastic handcuffs.

"Off you go, Miss," I told Nicole before placing the handcuffs safely back onto my belt.

I watched the gorgeous Nicole, walk away with her head bowed low to the other side of the kitchen, completely out of view of the camera. She picked up a champagne glass, took a sip and held it up to me.

"Time now to dish out the punishment to our lovely nurse. Officer Trudy, could you ask her to bend over? Roberto has told me, how you rudely stuck your thermometer up, high inside his hairy anus. Is this correct?" Ruby demanded.

Lucia kept her head low, nodding guiltily.

My hands gently took hold of her waist. I could feel the excitement flowing between the two of us, as I whispered to her to bend over. I leant over her arched body, my hands firmly on her back, as Ruby rubbed my truncheon all around her beautiful bum cheeks. I heard Lucia gasp and I couldn't resist my hands moving upwards to her shoulders.

"If Roberto wants officer Trudy to pull the nurses hair whilst I dish out her punishment, then that will cost an extra twenty," Ruby said, her truncheon still busily caressing Lucia's backside.

Once again, Nicole put her thumb up.

I stood for a second, not quite sure, if I wanted to take part in this.

"Officer, please wrap your fingers around this naughty bitch's curly auburn hair and pull it hard, as I dish out ten lashes," Ruby told me.

"Bloody hell. Are you serious?" I gasp.

"It isn't as bad as it sounds," Aunty laughs.

I gently took hold of her soft red locks, as they draped beautifully, all around her.

"When you are ready," Ruby called.

I'm so glad Lucia had this all planned out in her head. With every tap of the truncheon, she lifted her head and moaned, as though she was in incredible pain. To the camera it must have looked very convincing.

"Roberto has also decided to drop the charges against you. You're free to go now, nurse" she told Lucia.

I unclipped the handcuffs and as Lucia turned to face me, I couldn't stop my lips from ravishing hers.

"Now, hold on a second, Mr Shackle, you need to think about this seriously. What you are asking for, would cost at least, five hundred on top. Our hourly slot is coming to an end, and we have never, ever, done any overtime for anyone," Ruby said.

There was another pause.

"Yes, Mr Shackle. No, there is no chance you would ever get another opportunity to see anything like what you have just asked for. Our gorgeous nurse and our luscious sexy, officer Trudy, will both be on other professional duties for the foreseeable future." Ruby told him.

I was shocked to see Nicole raise her thumb.

Lucia and I looked at each other questioningly. We hadn't a clue what lay ahead, but Ruby was grinning widely.

"Oh Aunty, this is such a fabulously entertaining story. What a fun and adventurous fifty hours! What on earth happened next?" I ask, still chuckling away.

"To be honest, I was feeling slightly concerned and hesitant, but I needn't have worried," she laughs. "Apparently, when I kissed Lucia, Mr Shackle and Roberto both demanded more and wanted to see all four of us in action."

"Mr Shackle and Roberto would like to see the four of us, slowly undress each other. Apparently, one of their biggest unfilled fantasies, is to see four beautiful sexy and naked women, touching each other. What do you think ladies?" Ruby asked.

"Bloody hell. Phew. I thought for a moment it might be something a little bit more sadistic," I sigh with relief.

"Jasmine, this was easy money. Trust me," she giggles.

The three of us nodded in agreement at Ruby, and then, that is where the fun started. I still cannot believe two men were willing to pay this amount of money, for something we would usually do and enjoy anyway.

Nicole removed the chair, and we all took our positions.

"Ok sexy, ladies. Let's give Mr Shackle and Roberto the performance of a lifetime," Ruby grinned.

Lucia made the first move, walking sexily across to me. Her soft and slender hands removed my police cap, before throwing it completely out of sight. My eyes dreamily stared into hers. I felt my black belt slowly unfasten. Nicole stood behind, Lucia, her arms reaching high to take off her nurse's hat. Lucia teased me, as she slowly unzipped the front of my dress allowing my breasts to come into full view of the camera.

"Yes, Mr Shackle. I'm glad to hear you and Roberto are enjoying yourselves," Ruby breathed heavily down the phone.

It wasn't long, before we were all left standing in only our briefs.

I bent down in front of Lucia, slowly peeling off her red silky briefs. I gasped at the beauty of her slender and sexy body.

We watched as Ruby stood behind Nicole, wrapping her arms tightly around her gorgeous waist. Lucia and I gasped. Ruby peeled her briefs all the way down using just her teeth, before flinging them through the air to join our other discarded items of clothing.

Next, Nicole walked across to me and soon I also, stood completely naked. Only Ruby was left.

"How would you like to see, all three of these sexy ladies remove my skimpy crotchless briefs? It would cost you another twenty though."

There was a slight pause, as Nicole looked for her phone.

Thumbs up.

Nicole, Lucia, and I knelt down at different angles, next to Ruby's long, slender legs.

"After three," Ruby whispered.

On the command of three, we took our time removing her flimsy briefs, before allowing our hands to seductively caress her naked body.

"I'm so glad that you and Roberto had the most mind-blowing orgasms. As you know, we aim to please. Goodbye for now, Mr Shackle," Ruby told him, before safely placing her phone down onto the breakfast table.

She turned to face us with a massive grin on her face.

"We did it, sexy ladies. We did it," she screamed out, as we all moved in for a group hug.

A group hug was the wrong move.

Having three sexy naked bodies pushing firmly against mine, was sending me to a place of no return.

We eventually and very reluctantly pulled apart.

Lucia's lips immediately pressed hungrily against mine.

"Go on you, two randy ladies. I can hear the bed calling out your names. Nicole and I will round off our unfinished business down here, after we've had a little tidy up. Have fun," Ruby told us, as she and Nicole grinned.

Lucia grabbed hold of my right hand and we scrambled up the stairs laughing like two naughty teenagers.

I threw the bedroom door wide open and ran towards the bed with Lucia in hot pursuit behind me.

"Do you know, you are the sexiest lady I've ever met?" she told me, looking lovingly into my eyes, before lifting me gently onto the bed.

Our love making that morning was passionate and sensual.

It was one o'clock, before we decided it was time to try and locate our original clothes. Reluctantly, we got dressed and made our way downstairs. Nicole and Ruby were curled up on the sofa with a cosy blanket wrapped tightly around them.

"Ruby, Nicole. Sorry to disturb you, but Trudy and I need to make a move soon. I'm due to be back at the yard by six at the latest," Lucia told them softly.

"Well ladies, I hope you have both had a wonderful time. We certainly have. Hand on heart, we're sad to see you leave," Ruby said, slowly standing up.

"Can you believe, wait for it, we made one thousand, seven hundred and forty pounds from our hourly session earlier? That means you have a quarter share, so four hundred and thirty-five pounds each, to take away with you," Nicole grinned, getting up to stand by Ruby's side, her hand tenderly wrapped around her still

naked waist.

"We can't possibly take any money. You two did most of the work on your own. Plus, we've had such a fun and awesome experience, haven't we, Lucia?" I replied turning to look into her green mesmerising eyes.

"It's not negotiable Trudy. Both of you earned every single penny. Your money is on the table, over there," she told us.

"B-but," I started to say.

"Shush, no buts. Come here and give me a goodbye hug and make sure you keep in touch, eh?" Ruby told me.

I slowly walked towards her, feeling sad our adventure was finally coming to an end. She gently cupped my chin in her right hand, looked deeply into my eyes and kissed me tenderly for what turned out to be the very last time. A tear welled up in my eyes, as I said my goodbyes to Nicole. Lucia gave them both a hug and thanked them for their hospitality, before gently taking my hand, to lead me towards the front door.

Just as Lucia went to open the door, Ruby appeared.

"Don't forget your money," she said, handing us each a white envelope.

"Her hand purposely lingered on mine. I could feel the chemistry between us, as she gave my hand one last squeeze," Aunty says sadly.

"Did you never see them again?" I ask, now feeling sad, too.

"Not Ruby and Nicole. I made a firm promise to Lucia, that I wouldn't visit their house, ever again. Lucia and I saw each other every single day, that is, until she got onto the plane to start her new life in Australia. I was gutted when she left," Aunty continues, with a tear forming.

"I'm sorry, Aunty," I reply.

"Don't be, those precious days we spent together before Lucia left, are special and precious memories. They can never be taken from me and I'll always treasure them. At the time, Lucia had a bedsit above one of the stables where she worked. After she left, one day I sat and counted, out of curiosity how many times we had made love during that very short time. Can you believe, the total was fifty? Most of our love making took place on stacked bales of hay in an old run-down barn. We always called that, our special place," she says.

"That is an even better title for your book, Aunty. Fifty bales of hay," I suddenly blurt out.

I watch a huge smile start to emerge on Aunty's face. "I like that. Fifty bales of hay. If I ever decide to write a book, I promise, that will be the title. Now off to bed you, it's gone eleven and we both have an early start, not to mention a long and interesting day ahead of us," she says.

Slowly getting up, I walk across to Aunty and place a kiss gently onto her right cheek. Taking hold of her hands in mine, I look deeply into her eyes. "Aunty. Promise me, from now on, you will follow your heart," I tell her.

She squeezes my hand, tears slowly welling up in her eyes. "I promise," she whispers.

Chapter 43

My body feels hot and sweaty. I move the duvet cover over to one side, whilst trying to work out where I am and what day of the week it is. The little hands on the ticking clock tell me it's only ten past five, yet the sunlight is already streaming through onto my bed. *Oh, Lordy, now I remember.* Today is the day of the show and possibly my first ever, sexual encounter. A nervous shiver runs through my body at the thought of Mia making love to me. Closing my eyes, my mind drifts back to the filthy dream I just had, and I immediately grimace with guilt. In my dream, Lucia turned out to be a very bad influence. She slowly seduced me, playing me along, before stealing my virginity. The shock on Aunty and Mia's face when they walked into my bedroom to discover me and Lucia lying naked in each other's arms, was truly heart-breaking. I shudder once again at the thought. *How terrible is this?*

I must have dozed off. It wasn't long after, the alarm screeched loudly in my ears, making me jump. Half past six and time for me to move. Dragging myself out of bed, I quickly shower the dried sweat from my body, grinning to myself when I suddenly remember yesterday's episode with the clippers. The area down below feels tender and soft. An instant flutter flickers between my legs at the thought of Mia's naked body, on mine. I try hard to remove any sexual thoughts from my head, but to be honest I'm finding it very difficult. Looking at myself in the bathroom mirror, a massive grin appears on my face, that is, until I see the colourful bruising marking my arm. Most definitely, a long, sleeved blouse will be required for the show today. The last thing I want, is complete strangers constantly staring at my arm.

I glance over at my phone. Who could be messaging me at this time of the morning? *Mia, of course!*

'Good morning, my sexy girlfriend. Where are you hiding? I am already here ready and waiting for you. The kettle has just boiled. Shall I come and get you? Lol xxx.'

Grinning, I quickly get dressed, grab my phone, and race towards the kitchen.

"There you are," Mia says, with a smile to die for.

My heart instantly aches with the love I feel for her. Heading towards my beautiful girlfriend, my legs suddenly feel weak, and as her soft tender lips immediately find mine, the passion burning inside, bubbles like a volcano about to erupt.

"Are you ok, my lover-to-be?" she asks me tenderly, her lips moving around to my right ear. Her tongue flickers teasingly around my earlobe and I gasp at the sensations she is causing.

"Mia, I want you now," I moan, not feeling in control of my sexual urgings.

"Your coffee is getting cold."

"I don't care," I murmur, lost in a world of ecstasy.

"Not long to wait now, my love," she says, pulling away, before looking lovingly into my eyes.

"Don't stop," I plead.

"Jazz, Lucia and Trudy will be back soon. They left about an hour ago to do some schooling with Autumn Wonder and don't forget, we have a show to get ready for," she grins.

"Good morning, ladies," Lucia says, as she strolls into the kitchen, with Aunty following closely behind.

A vision of Lucia wearing her sexy nurse's outfit, complete with black fishnet stockings, flashes through my head, followed by a massive rush of guilt.

"Good morning all. Oh, Jasmine, by the way an *Amazon* parcel has just arrived, with your name on it," Aunty says, placing the cardboard package on the table. "What have you been ordering?"

Blood instantly rushes up into my cheeks. "I can't remember," I mumble

"Aren't you going to open it?" Mia asks.

"Later," I reply, avoiding her eyes.

"Well, I must say, Autumn Wonder was an absolute star earlier," Aunty says, turning to grin at Lucia. Their eyes look longingly into each other's, before Lucia eventually turns away to reply to a message on her phone.

"Are you planning on plaiting your horses for the show?" Lucia asks, Mia and me. We look at each other before shaking our heads. "I'd be more than happy to plait their manes for you. In fact, to be honest, it's one of my favourite tasks," Lucia says.

"Cool. That would be wonderful if you are sure you don't mind. Ebony has never been plaited before, I bet she'll look gorgeous," coos Mia.

"What about your boy, Jazz?" Lucia smiles, her seductive green eyes piercing sexily into mine.

"Yes, please. Breeze loves to be plaited. I think he finds it therapeutic," I reply, trying hard to make my eyes leave hers.

"That's sorted then. It's only twenty-five past seven, so we have plenty of time on our hands," she replies.

"I have lessons booked in for eight and nine. Lorna is then covering until three which leaves me with just one lesson to teach, before I need to get myself ready, so I can be on my way, by six," Aunty says.

Lucia puts her hand tenderly over the top of Aunty's, squeezing it softly, before quickly moving it away.

Glancing across at Mia, I am relieved to see that her head is turned the other way. Surely, if I can see the sexual chemistry flowing freely between the two of them, then I'm confident, Mia would spot it too.

After placing my empty mug in the sink, I casually pick up my parcel. "I'll be back in two seconds," I call, quickly dashing out of the kitchen towards my bedroom.

Ripping open the cardboard in excitement, I smile down at the three separate items neatly packaged in polythene bags. The first bag I open, is the pair of red crotchless knickers. I hold them up to inspect them. *It hasn't taken much material to make these, that's for sure! They are not something you'd be wanting to wear on a windy day either.* Placing them safely to one side, I open the next item to reveal a pair of silky hold up stockings. I've never worn anything like this before in my life, but after hearing the effect they had on Aunty and her girlfriends, I'm willing to give them a go. I'm not quite sure what material they are made of, but they feel soft and sleek to my touch. I eagerly open the third package, and my eyes shine with glee. The red silky corset is just how I expected it to look. Two silk shoulder straps, leading down to a stunning figure-hugging bodice. Beautifully made, with warm red lace entwined underneath the supported breast area. *Perfect, let's just hope it fits!* Quickly, picking up my recent purchases, I hide them safely away underneath a pile of clothes inside the wardrobe. Grinning, I make my way back to the kitchen.

"There you are," Mia smiles.

"I was just applying some more arnica cream to my arm," I lie.

"I could have done that for you," she answers with a sexy grin.

"Shall we go and make a start on Ebony and Breeze?" I reply, seductively licking my lips, knowing we are completely out of Lucia and Aunty's view.

Mia stands staring directly at me, her gorgeous eyes fixated on my tongue. She moves her hands upwards to her luscious breasts, caressing them in a way that is really turning me on.

"Mia!" I exclaim.

"Are you two, ok?" Aunty calls out.

"We're fine, thank you. I'm just going to bring Breeze in from the field," I reply, trying to buy myself enough time to allow my sexual urgings to decrease.

Mia laughs, as she walks towards me, her hands still sexily caressing her breasts. "Shall we go?" she whispers, her right hand squeezing my buttock.

Taking a deep breath, I turn to walk back towards the table where Aunty and Lucia sit, looking deep in thought.

"I'll be over in around ten minutes," Lucia says, not lifting her head up from her phone.

Mia follows closely behind, as I hurriedly head towards the back door. Her hot breath blows softly against my neck, causing shivering sensations to run down my spine.

"Mia, what the bloody hell were you trying to do to me back there? Watching you touch your breasts in such a sexy way, was driving me bloody crazy." I turn her to face me, my lips eagerly reaching for hers.

"So, my horny girlfriend, you enjoyed watching me then? Just you wait until you see what I've got in mind for the two of us this evening," she whispers seductively.

"Please tell me, it doesn't entail nipple clamps or bondage," I reply seriously.

She immediately pulls away. The look on her face is priceless.

"Only joking," I tell her with a grin. "Bloody hell, Jazz, you really had me going for a moment then. You have such a dirty mind," she says sternly. The tone of her voice makes me burst out laughing.

"Ha, ha, bloody ha," she mocks, her face covered with a huge grin.

"I'll see you shortly," I tell her, before placing a tender kiss on those beautiful lips of hers, my right hand unable to resist a cheeky feel of her sexy buttocks.

"Behave yourself," she calls.

I make my way across to the field. "Oh, Breeze, I can't tell you how pleased I am to see you. Honestly, my head is all over the place this week," I confide to him, his soft muzzle gently resting in my hands, looking deeply into his stunning blue eyes. "Anyway, less of my problems. What about you, my boy? I hope you are looking forward to the two of us doing a spot of show jumping later. Shall we show the locals what we are capable of? Breeze snorts into my hands and I laugh. He understands everything I say and always responds to me in his own little way. "Have I told you lately, how much I love you?" He snorts once again, and I giggle. "Come on, let's go and get you all spruced up," I tell him, before placing his head collar on.

Blossom whinnies to him, as we walk through the gate.

"Don't worry, Blossom, Breeze will be back with you sometime this afternoon," I assure her.

The sun shines warmly high above, fluffy white clouds dance lightly around in the sky, occasionally blocking out the rays. There is a light breeze flowing all around, so perfect conditions for the show ahead. I felt relieved when I checked the weather channel earlier to see their prediction for today. The temperature shouldn't reach any higher than twenty degrees. I adore this time of the morning, birds singing sweetly, horses and ponies whinnying far away in the distance. The beautiful scent arising from the numerous colourful flowers planted all around, waft slowly up my nostrils. I ask Breeze to stand for a moment, appreciating our glorious surroundings and I sigh contently. Breeze stands close to me, looking totally relaxed with his handsome head resting low. Patting him softly on his stunning, silky neck, before kissing him gently on his velvety muzzle, we slowly make our way to the yard to find an empty stable.

Chapter 44

Mia glances across the yard to wave to me. My heart instantly skips a beat. We had already agreed to have our horses ready by nine-thirty, allowing us plenty of time to get changed. Smiling, I leave Breeze happily munching on his hay net, before heading across to the tack room to grab my grooming kit.

"I remember that so well. Your face was a picture of horror," I hear Aunty laughing.

"I can't believe, I fell for their story," laughs Lucia. Lucia looks up at me, as I enter the tack room, giving me one of her special smiles.

My legs instantly turn to jelly. *Why does she have this effect on me?* Avoiding any eye contact, already feeling hot and flushed, I bend over to pick up my grooming kit.

"Very nice," says Lucia.

For a slight second, I freeze. Surely, she cannot be talking about my bum in front of Aunty of all people. Little spasms run through my body, as I try hard to compose myself, before standing up.

"I agree, Trudy, navy blue will suit him. Shall we go with that colour then?" Lucia replies.

I turn around, feeling slightly relieved to see them both deeply engrossed with Aunty's phone.

"We were just ordering Autumn Wonder, his very first numnah," Aunty says, with a grin.

I feel so stupid. *Why do I seem to be obsessed with Lucia?* Another wave of guilt flows through me.

"I can't wait to meet, Breeze, Jazz. I'll make a start on Ebony first and will be over to you in around forty minutes, if that's ok?"

I nod gratefully, before hurrying back to Breeze. Shuffling back to the stable, feeling angry and disgusted with myself, I throw my arms around Breeze's neck and close my eyes, taking long, deep breaths. The therapeutic sound of him crunching on his sweet green hay, instantly has a calming effect on me. "Right, my handsome boy. Let's get this show on the road," I tell him, finally feeling positive and focused. My body brush glides over his golden frame, and down underneath his belly. I smile at the unusual white pattern that sits prominently from his chest running all the way around to his nearside, past his girth area. This has always fascinated me. The shape reminds me of a map, or maybe an artist who has just added the final touches to his latest masterpiece. His striking gleaming white socks rise proudly high above his knees, resembling a pair of hold up stockings. I laugh out loud, at the thought of me wearing precisely the same this evening, in my readiness to seduce, Mia.

A dreamy look covers my face, just as Lucia appears, making me jump. "That sounded like a naughty laugh, Jazz. Wow, so this must be Breeze?"

I watch in complete silence, as her enchanting eyes slowly

glance over the length of his gleaming body.

"I don't know what to say. He is absolutely stunning," she finally says.

I beam with pride at her recent comment. Her beautiful slender hands run seductively up and down his neck, before flowing gently down to caress both his striking, front legs. *Oh, Lordy.* Breeze momentarily stops crunching on his hay, slowly turning his head to investigate, Lucia's gorgeous backside. I giggle nervously, trying to control the naughty thoughts that have just arrived in my head. She eventually stands up straight, turning to look into Breeze's unusual and captivating blue eyes. I hold my breath, as the two of them hold each other's gaze, with a mutual understanding, before Breeze whinnies lightly, placing his head into her soft waiting hands. I have never seen him act with anyone in this way before. He must be able to sense what a great horsewoman she is, is all that I can conclude.

"Good boy," she tells him softly.

"He must like you, Lucia. He has never responded to anyone he doesn't know in such a warm and welcoming manner," I say.

"You've got a good one here," she says, still holding Breeze's contented head in her hands.

"I'm very lucky to have found him," I reply, feeling on top of the world.

"How about you tell me, how the two of you came together, whilst I get cracking on plaiting his mane?" she smiles.

Oh, that smile. I carry on grooming Breeze's near side, as Lucia carefully listens to my story, letting out the odd gasp here and there.

"Sometimes, I really do despise humans. Give me animals any day of the week. I believe in fate, Jazz. The two of you were meant to find each other that day at the sales," she says, after I finish my story.

"I agree. I have never felt such a strong connection with any horse like I do with Breeze. I would trust him with my life."

"Having the trust of a horse is one of the greatest gifts you can receive. Many are misunderstood, due to their owner's ignorance. A couple of years ago, one of my colleagues called me. She had rescued a thoroughbred mare from a sale who was doomed for slaughter. I had never seen an animal looking so distressed in the whole of my life. It isn't often that I cry, but that day, I did. She was only seven years old, with not a single ounce of flesh on her. All four hooves were completely overgrown, to the point where they were curling up. Her eyes looked empty and sad. There was no hint of life in them at all. This mare was shut down and had completely given up." Tears instantly fill my eyes. Lucia glanced across at me. "Oh, Jazz. I didn't mean to make you feel sad. I haven't finished the whole story yet. Wait until you hear the rest, and I'll guarantee, you'll be smiling," she says softly.

No wonder Aunty fell for Lucia, she has such a caring and loving side to her.

"We padded a stable out in deep golden straw, and slowly led her inside. She took no interest at all, just standing there looking empty. The best quality hay sat in the manger, but even that wasn't enough to tempt her. I knew we needed to get some nutritional food into her, to give her a fighting chance. Eventually, I came up with an idea. My friend had an elderly Shetland called, Boris, who had recently lost his lifetime friend and was grieving. That precious moment, when we led little Boris into her stable, and she slowly lifted her head up for the very first time, I knew there and then, she would make it. The two of them became inseparable, and over the next six months, the change in the mare, who we named Faith, was truly incredible. Watching her change from a lifeless empty soul into a confident gorgeous Goddess was priceless. We searched through her history and were shocked to find out, she had once been a top-class racehorse on the flat. During her three-year career, she had accumulated over forty-five thousand pounds in prize money, before retiring to stud at the age of five. From what we can gather, the breeders couldn't get her in foal, and she was given to a so-called friend of the stud's owner, for a riding horse. Her new owners obviously didn't care for her and that is how she ended up at the sales. To be honest, she shouldn't have been allowed through any sale ring in that condition. This is the reason why I admire and respect any human who is willing to give a rescue horse a second chance. Just like you have with Breeze, Jazz."

The colour quickly rises to my cheeks at her lovely words. "What happened with Faith in the end?" I ask, feeling curious.

"You won't believe this, but last year she won her first dressage competition and guess what? Boris was there to cheer her on. The two of them are still inseparable and continue to share the same stable. How wonderful is that?" she asks.

"I love to hear stories like this. So, heart-warming. It gives me back a little faith in the human race," I reply.

"Once I have my stud up and running, my end goal is to build an extra stable block, so I can offer rehabilitation and training for ex-racehorses. This is something I'm very passionate about."

I'm beginning to adore Lucia more and more. "Aunty has always wanted to take in rescue horses and ponies too. She has always said, when she gets old enough to retire, this is something she would love to do."

"Trudy is a very special lady. I know she has told you all about how we met and what we got up to all those years ago. I bet you were a little shocked, but to be honest, Jazz, I have kicked myself every single day since we said goodbye. One of my main regrets in life, was letting your Aunty go," she confesses.

"Have you told Aunty any of this?"

"No. She has enough on her plate at present. I just hope she keeps her cool this evening when she meets, William. What a complete arsehole he is, although I can't talk, as I was as bad as him cheating on my poor wife, Maddison. I would never, ever do anything so terrible again."

"Maybe, Maddison wasn't the right one for you. Sometimes, things happen for a reason and then suddenly you start to look at life in a different way," I reply.

"Your Aunty has always spoken very highly of you and you have made her very proud with everything you have achieved. Honestly, when you secure your place in the *Olympic Team*, treasure every single second. Trust me, opportunities like this don't come along that often. Just be yourself and show the world what you are capable of."

"What was it like when you were at the height of your career? I must confess, I even had a poster of you in my bedroom," I giggle nervously.

"Really? To be honest, I was young and stupid; letting fame and fortune go straight to my head. I had the press and groupies following me everywhere; absolutely no privacy at all. It was fun and exciting to start with, but after a few years, I began to detest it. Spending weeks on end travelling all over the world to different events, believe me, eventually takes its toll. Before my accident, I went through a stage, where I would have given anything, to have a nice house, somewhere I could sleep in my own bed every night and a quiet life to go with it. Reality was, staying in different hotels, constantly packing, and unpacking my suitcases, not having anywhere I could call home. Don't get me wrong, I made big money from my career, but trust me, as you get older, none of that seems important anymore. A quiet life, spending quality time with the people you love and doing a job that you enjoy, to me, is priceless and I wouldn't change it for the world."

"I hadn't thought fame and fortune could make anyone feel so isolated, Lucia. The pressures you must have been under daily, do not bear thinking about. When I read the articles in the equestrian magazines, they made your life sound like a fairy tale, everything just so lovely and rosy," I reply, suddenly feeling sorry for her.

"Never believe anything you read in the press," she replies.

"Not even the strawberries and whipped cream?" I ask without thinking.

Lucia's laughter fills the stable. I feel embarrassed at what I've just said. "I'm afraid that bit was true, and so was the chocolate spread," she replies in between her laughter.

"Sounds like the two of you are having fun," Mia suddenly announces in an offish tone, standing with her hands firmly on her hips.

I turn to smile at her, but she doesn't look overly happy with me.

"Hi, Mia. I just have the last plait to do and then this handsome boy is all finished. Are you nearly ready?" she asks.

"I just need to get changed and tack Ebony up," she replies, avoiding my gaze.

"Why don't the two of you nip off and get changed? I can stay here with Breeze," Lucia kindly offers.

"Thank you, Lucia, that would be a great help," I smile.

Mia just nods, before turning to walk back towards the house.

"See you shortly," I tell Lucia, quickly getting up to chase after Mia. "Hey, Mia stop," I call out, watching her sexy backside wiggle from side to side.

She completely ignores me and carries on walking.

Running as fast as I can to catch up with her, I take hold of her shoulders and turn her firmly towards me.

"Mia, what on earth is the matter?" I ask, feeling concerned.

"You and Lucia. That's what's wrong," she replies, avoiding my eyes.

"What about me and Lucia?" I say feeling confused.

"I heard the two of you laughing and flirting with each other. I know you used to lust after her, Jazz, and now you have your perfect dream woman making a play for you," she blurts out.

"Mia, you've got this all wrong. You trust me, don't you?" I say sincerely, gently taking her hands in mine. Her gorgeous sexy eyes finally look directly into mine.

"Of course, I do," she mumbles.

"Mia, I promise you, hand on heart, there is nothing going on between me and Lucia. You are the only woman I love and the only one I will love with the whole of my heart, for the rest of my life. You do believe me, don't you?"

"Yes. I'm sorry, Jazz. I suppose I just felt jealous seeing you enjoying yourself with another woman," she confesses.

"Oh, Mia, come here you silly little so and so," I tell her, wrapping my arms firmly around her, holding her as tightly as I can.

"I'm sorry," she mumbles once again.

"Look, we have a show to get to. Let's put all those silly thoughts about me and Lucia firmly out of your mind and just look forward to our day ahead," I tell her, before pressing my lips firmly against hers.

"You're right," she says, her beautiful heart stopping smile thankfully returning.

Checking no one is around, I take hold of her left hand, as we walk towards the house to get changed. *Not long to wait now, Jazz.*

Chapter 45

Mia grabs hold of her show clothes, before following me closely to the bedroom. She stares at the cardboard and the empty polythene bags scattered across my bed. "What was in your package?" she asks curiously.

"That's for me to know and you to find out," I grin, pointing to my nose. The smile she gives me, melts my heart. Walking towards her, I kiss her tenderly on her sweet, red lips.

"You do realise, we are all alone in your bedroom?" she whispers.

"This is the moment I've been dreaming about," I reply, before my tongue searches for hers.

"But, my sexy girlfriend, we do have a show to attend," she reminds me.

Reluctantly pulling myself away, I look into her eyes, and sigh.

"I think I'll get changed in the bathroom. If I see your gorgeous half naked body standing in front of me, there is no way on earth, I'll want to go to the show. Maybe, we can have our very own erotic little show in here, later," she says, pointing to my double bed.

"You cannot put thoughts like that into my head right now, my horny, lover to be," I grin, a craving and burning sensation already surfacing, deep down below. *You just need to hold out for a few more hours, Jazz.*

"Spoilsport," she says, before heading towards the bathroom with her clothes.

Letting out a frustrated sigh, as quickly as I can, I change into my clean white jodhpurs, perfectly pressed cream blouse and my favourite item, what I call my lucky tie. Slipping on my shiny tanned jodhpur boots, I look myself up and down in the mirror. *This time tomorrow, you may have lost your virginity.* As these words run through my mind, instant aching throbs pump strongly, deep down below. *Concentrate, Jazz.* My eyes turn to Mia, instantly lighting up, as she walks out from the bathroom. The beautiful vision of her standing sexily in her riding gear, posing with her riding whip, not only turns me on, but causes a new pleasurable feeling, deep down below, one I have never experienced before. "Bloody hell, Mia. What are you trying to do to me?" I ask, already feeling slightly moist down below.

"You look good enough to eat," she replies, her fascinating green eyes taking in every inch of my slender body, before fixating firmly on my breasts.

"You can eat me later," I reply sexily.

Mia giggles, her cheeks looking flushed and that smile, oh, that smile.

"Come on, we'd better make a move," I grin, heading towards the door.

Suddenly, I feel a slap on my buttock. "Ouch," I say turning towards her, to see her armed with her whip in her right hand.

"Did you like me spanking you, girlfriend?"

"Strangely enough, I did," I laugh.

***

"We'll see you shortly then," Aunty tells us, before waving us off.

I feel as proud as punch sitting on Breeze. Not only has Lucia done an amazing job on his mane, but somehow, she has managed to bring the oils, normally hidden beneath a horses' coat, out to the top, making it shine and glow with health. The finishing touches are the unique quarter marks on either side of his hind quarters. The prominent images of the shark's teeth shapes, glisten proudly in the early morning rays from the sun. Ebony too, looks truly stunning, her dark glossy coat radiant, and the diamond shaped markings on her hind quarters look superbly positioned. The neat perfect plaits line the full length of her crest, making her neck look stunningly elegant. What an amazing transformation, and all thanks to, Lucia.

As we ride through the glorious countryside towards the next village, I tell Mia all about the rescue story Lucia had recounted.

"What a wonderful ending to such a sad story," she replies, looking slightly emotional.

Maybe I shouldn't have told her. I change the subject and we are still laughing at one of my silly jokes, as we enter the already busy showground. It's heaving with activity. There are so many different sizes and colours of horses and ponies moving all around. What sounds like hundreds of different tones of whinnying fill the air. I'm sure I can smell the burning cinders of a burger van close by. I smile at a tiny Shetland, whose rider cannot be any older than two. Her riding outfit looks so cute, if slightly on the big side.

Breeze's solid frame strides out beautifully and proudly beneath me, with his head held high. His golden ears pricked forward and alert, whilst his stunning blue eyes eagerly take in the busy surroundings. "Shall we register?" I ask Mia. She smiles and nods.

We have already prepaid for our entry, so we only need to

collect our numbers. Jumping off at the secretary's tent, Mia hands Ebony's reins for me to hold, before patiently joining the queue. I glance around with a grin on my face. I love the atmosphere of horse shows, the buzz, and the excitement is like a drug, slowly getting you addicted.

"Here we are," smiles Mia, handing me over a square piece of paper with two bold blank numbers on the front, with tiny threads of red ribbon punched through either side.

I laugh as I look down at my number. *Very apt, sixty-nine.*

I'm just about to let my naughty thoughts run riot, when Mia notices my number. A big grin appears across her face. "Bring it on, girlfriend," she says with a wink, as she remounts Ebony.

It isn't too long, before we spot Aunty and Lucia standing close to the 'clear round' jumping ring. They seem to be surrounded by quite a few youngsters, along with their Mum's. Intrigued, we head towards them. Poor Lucia looks to be busy signing numerous sheets of show schedules, in between posing for selfies, mainly with the Mum's, I might add.

"That's all for now," Aunty kindly tells the groupies. "I'm afraid Lucia has work to do," she continues, before linking her arm in Lucia's and walking towards us.

"Thank you for rescuing me," grins Lucia to Aunty. "You four look like superstars," she says turning to me and Mia, with a look of approval.

"Thank you for your help earlier. I have never seen such perfect and beautiful quarter marks," smiles Mia.

"Great job," nods Aunty.

I still feel a strong sense, that numerous sets of eyes are staring at us.

"I want to see the both of you warming up your horses properly," Aunty announces, suddenly going into teacher mode.

"Yes, Mam," I reply cheekily, doffing my hat.

"What time are your classes?" asks Lucia.

"Mia's starts in forty minutes in ring two and mine in fifty minutes, in ring three," I reply.

"Do you know how many entries there are?" enquires Aunty.

"Not yet."

"Off you go then," instructs Aunty, as Mia and I enter the warming up area.

Thankfully, it isn't too overcrowded. Feeling determined, I focus on the task ahead.

Breeze feels in great form, responding effortlessly to my silent commands, as I take him through his paces. Finally, after cantering beautifully, three times around the outside of the ring, I gently ease him up.

"That was truly magical to watch, Jazz" beams Lucia, gently stroking Breeze's arched and proud neck. "You two certainly share a rare and wonderful connection, one, most riders are never lucky enough to experience in the whole of their lifetime. Watching you reminded me of myself and my old steed Flickering Light in the good old days, when I was around your age."

I beam at her compliment, just as Mia and Ebony arrive at my side.

"You have a wonderful soft seat, Mia, and lovely light hands. Ebony responds to your every move, and the pair of you were a delight to watch," Lucia compliments Mia.

The grin on Mia's face is wonderful to see. This comment coming from the one and only Lucia, will have boosted her confidence massively, doing her the world of good.

"Now you are nicely warmed up, you should head over to the 'clear round' ring. Mia, you go first, as your class is due to start in ten minutes," Aunty says, with a huge smile.

I feel proud watching my beautiful girlfriend and Ebony clear the eight jumps. Her face beams with pride, as she collects her first ever rosette.

"Well done," I congratulate her, before heading into the ring.

Switching my brain onto serious focus mode, Breeze and I clear the whole course effortlessly. Collecting my rosette, I notice poor Lucia is being hounded again.

"Sorry ladies," says Aunty, "I'm afraid Lucia is in the middle of training two of her students."

"Great round, Jazz," Lucia grins at me, before taking hold of Ebony's reins and leading her across to ring two. Aunty and I follow closely behind.

"Seventeen entries, Mia. You are the third to jump. Memorise the order of the jumps in your head. Remember, look ahead, breathe, take it slowly, and focus. Most importantly, enjoy yourself," Lucia says softly.

Mia turns to me, looking slightly anxious. "You've got this," I tell her warmly. I hold my breath, as Ebony and Mia finally enter the ring. The first two riders both have faults, so fingers crossed Mia can get a clear round.

Over the cross rail they go. Mia looks totally focused, as they head towards the vertical. Just a slight hesitation, but they are over safely. Cantering around to the left, the double lies ahead, one stride, two stride and they are clear and already halfway round the course, with only four left to jump. Ebony soars over the white oblong gate, Mia takes a gentle tug at the reins, as they head towards the false wall. Ebony's off hind, lightly clips one of the top blocks, it moves slightly, but thankfully stays safely intact. The last two jumps consist of two cross rails and I nearly jump out of my saddle with excitement, as they fly safely over the final jump with inches to spare.

"I cannot believe we did that," Mia exclaims, trying to get her breath back, and eventually coming to a halt by our side.

Leaning over, I wrap my right arm around her shoulders in

congratulations. Her face is one full of joy and happiness.

"Excellent, Mia. Well done, Ebony," Lucia and Aunty tell her, happy grins across their faces.

"Look, my hands are shaking. I cannot believe that we are through to the jump off. I never dreamt anything like this could happen," she replies dazed.

"That's just the adrenaline. Nothing to worry about. Why don't you jump off and loosen your girth?" reassures Lucia.

"My legs feel like jelly," Mia replies, after dismounting, standing with her body bent over.

"Right, Jazz. Why don't you and Lucia make your way to ring three to see what's happening? Mia and I will be along to join you shortly," Aunty says, placing her arm gently around Mia's shoulders, before taking hold of Ebony's reins. I'm relieved to see Aunty is looking after Mia.

"It's quite a big class for a local show. Twenty-six entries in total and you are the eighteenth to jump, so unfortunately, quite a while to wait," Lucia informs me. "How about I pop and get us all a hot cup of coffee?"

"Did I hear the word coffee?" Aunty grins, popping her head over Lucia's shoulder with a huge grin.

"Would you like me to give you a hand, Lucia? Maybe I could save you from being mobbed by your groupies A walk and a stretch would probably do me good," Mia laughs.

"Go on then," Lucia smiles, as Mia hands Ebony's reins over to Aunty.

I watch the rider ahead complete a clear round; his horse looked keen and fast. Maybe they could be the ones to beat.

"How are you, Aunty?"

"I'm fine, thanks. Being here is good for me. It's keeping my mind occupied," she smiles. "Are you looking forward to your evening with, Mia?" A naughty glint suddenly appears in her eyes.

I feel the blood rush immediately to my cheeks. Making out I'm concentrating on the horse and rider who are now in the ring, I reply, "Yes, I'm looking forward to chilling out and watching a movie."

"Here we go," says Mia, softly handing me a polystyrene cup of coffee.

Phew! That was great timing. I wonder if Aunty has sussed me and Mia out?

"Four more to jump and then it's time for you and Breeze to show us what you've got," says Lucia.

Handing my empty cup to Aunty, I leave to warm up Breeze. Clearing my head, I focus solely on the job in hand.

Chapter 46

Breeze and I enter the ring feeling confident. "Are you ready, my boy?" I ask him, as he prances excitedly around looking at the colourful jumps. Heading towards the first cross rail, Breeze clears it as though it isn't there. Round to the right a combination lies before us, he soars over the first part, one stride, two strides and clears the third with inches to spare. The jumps are higher than Mia's class, but Breeze has jumped a lot bigger fences at regional events. A green and white striped vertical is our next one to tackle. Huge green and red wings hold the jump together, as my boy lifts the whole of his body effortlessly into the air. We land smoothly, and I gently pat his neck. Only three remaining. Looking ahead at the incoming false wall, our stride is perfectly timed. Breeze thrusts his powerful body over, clearing it easily. Just two to go, a double consisting of two parallel rails with a white oblong board firmly beneath it. We successfully clear both flawlessly. Easing him down to a walk, with a huge grin across my face, we proudly leave the ring to a round of applause.

"Wow, that was one exceptional performance," Lucia says,

firmly squeezing my thigh. *Oh Lordy!*

I grin across at Mia who is now back on board, Ebony. She leans towards me, with a huge smile, gently squeezing my hand. "Jazz, well done."

Aunty's face beams with pride as she throws her arms around Breeze's neck to congratulate him, too. "We'd better head back over to ring two and find out what time the jump off commences," Aunty says.

"Only five in the jump off, Mia. You and Ebony are second to go," Lucia announces. "It's due to start in ten minutes, so if I were you, I would start to warm Ebony up now."

"I'll watch Mia's jump off, before popping back to ring three, to see what's happening there. How exciting is this? My two special girls, both in a jump off," beams Aunty. Seeing Aunty so happy and relaxed is awesome.

"Remember, Mia, just focus and enjoy," Lucia says, as Mia nervously enters the ring.

"You've got this," I call out encouragingly. She turns to look at me with a loving grin before focusing on the job ahead. I stand with my arm around Breeze's warm neck, feeling slightly nervous. Holding my breath, I watch the two of them clear all eight jumps with ease. The time announced is forty-two seconds, which means she is now two seconds ahead, in first place. "Mia, you and Ebony were awesome. Well done," I say, as the two of them head back towards me.

She smiles, still not quite believing what her and Ebony have just achieved. After congratulating Mia, Aunty and Lucia head back across to ring three for an update. Unfortunately for Mia, the next rider is four seconds faster and the following one, two seconds quicker than her time. Mia is sitting in third place with only two left to jump. Poor Mia's face looks white. Rider number four has one refusal and, fortunately for Mia, rider five knocks two poles down, which means Mia and Ebony have finished in third place.

"I can't believe it," she says, looking emotional, her slender hands across her face.

"Go on, get back in the ring and collect your well-deserved rosette," Aunty says grinning.

I watch with pride, as Ebony and Mia are presented with a four-tier yellow rosette. Her face glows with happiness and joy.

"Jazz, I still can't believe we did it," she exclaims.

"We're both so proud of you, aren't we, Breeze?" I reply. "I would love to kiss your beautiful lips to congratulate you properly."

"Well, sexy girlfriend, I shall look forward to my reward later," she naughtily grins.

"Just look at your fabulous rosette," Aunty beams, patting Ebony's warm and slender neck.

"Could you pin both of our rosettes onto Ebony's bridle please? We have never won anything like this before."

"With pleasure," Aunty replies, placing the clear round rosette and her most recent one onto Ebony's bridle.

"Stand still and pose, Mia. I want to capture this very special moment on my iPhone," I say, asking Breeze to move forward to stand in front of the two of them. Glancing down, I smile at the most recent one I've just taken. Mia is going to be thrilled with these photos. Her gorgeous smile looking back at me, fills my heart with longing.

"Only fifteen minutes until your jump off, Jazz. Eight have got through, and you are seventh on the list to jump," Lucia informs me.

"We had better get you warmed up, hadn't we, my boy?" I tell Breeze, before heading off in the opposite direction towards the warming up ring. Clearing my head of any other thoughts, Breeze and I sail through our exercises, as though we are one. I find it fascinating how I have always been able to completely shut out everything going on around us, whilst in full concentration mode, including noise. As the two of us walk across towards ring three, I visualise the eight jumps ahead, knowing precisely where I can save some precious seconds off our time.

"Two more left to jump before your turn, Jazz. The fastest time to date, is thirty-nine-point nought three seconds, and they are well ahead of the second clear round of forty-two point five seconds," Lucia says.

I watch, the following finalists with great interest, planning my tactics in advance. We have one to beat and only one more to go after us.

"You've got this," Aunty calls out, before Breeze and I make our way into the ring.

Taking a deep breath, patting Breeze softly down his stunning golden neck, I whisper to him, "This is ours to win, let's go." Breeze thrusts powerfully forward clearing the cross rail like an ignited rocket. Quickly asking him to turn towards the combination, trying to save a couple of yards, he now knows we are in a jump off. Accelerating a gear, he times his take off to perfection, I count one huge stride and over the second part we fly like a bird sprouting wings. Taking another risk, I allow him only two strides instead of the usual four, as we head towards the vertical. He knows me well, and immediately adapts his body to accommodate my request. We clear it safely. I don't take any risks on the next vertical due to the awkward angle it stands at. I needn't have worried, as once again, I allow Breeze to find his own stride before gliding over effortlessly.

Only three to jump. Cantering at great speed towards the false wall, the strength from Breeze's powerful hind quarters, lift us up high up and over. Only two left to jump. Turning on a sixpence, I urge him towards the oncoming double. Clearing the final jump, I thrust my right arm up powerfully into the air, cantering around the ring feeling confident that our time has been exceptionally quick.

Elated, Breeze and I head out of the ring to a huge round of applause. I don't hear the time being announced due to the cheers all around.

"Bloody hell, Jazz. That was one of the most breath-taking jump offs, I have ever seen," Mia says, her eyes wide open in amazement.

The adrenaline is rushing around my body and all I can do is grin back.

"You knocked a whole five seconds off the leader's time. Way to go, Jazz," Lucia says, rushing over to congratulate us. Poor Aunty looks in shock.

"Jazz, you nearly gave me a heart attack, cutting those corners like you did. You have some guts and determination, that's for sure," gasps Aunty.

I grin at the three happy faces around me. A groan from the crowd brings me back to the present moment, a refusal by the final rider.

"You did it, Jazz. You won," screams Mia, looking as though she has just won the lottery.

A photographer suddenly appears from out of nowhere, a lady in her mid-forties standing closely by his side.

"Lucia Charlton?" the lady asks, turning to look directly at her.

"Yes, that's me. Who is asking?" she replies, still stroking Breeze's soft lathered neck.

"My name is, Emma McCall from *Local Rider Magazine*. I wondered if we could take up two minutes of your time. Is it true, you are moving to our part of the world? If so, could you tell us when? Is this one of your students, who has just won the jump off in a record-breaking time?" the lady questions, as the photographer continues to click his camera.

"Jazz, they are calling for you in ring three," Aunty says, firmly taking hold of Breeze's reins, to lead us safely away from the press.

"Thanks, Aunty. Poor Lucia, she must get fed up constantly

answering their questions."

"Off you go, Jazz. What a brave and tremendous performance the two of you put up. You have made me the proudest Aunty in the world today, do you know that?" she says tearfully.

Breeze and I make our way proudly into the ring to collect our prize. The lady sponsor places a stunning red sash around Breeze's chest with the words *Intermediate show jumping winner* standing out in thick bold white lettering, leaning forward to firmly shake my hand. I accept the beautiful red rosette and a shiny silver cup gratefully. Leading the lap of honour, Breeze canters spectacularly around the outside of the ring, as I proudly hold out our trophy towards the spectators, who continue to applaud us. Some are even standing. These are the moments that I will always treasure, as the atmosphere is second to none. Finally, making our way out of the ring, I'm thankful to see that the press, have finally left.

"Let's get a photo of us all," grins Mia, asking a random lady who is walking by, if she wouldn't mind doing the honours. The six of us stand closely together, grinning widely. Lucia and Aunty's arms are proudly wrapped around each other's waists, in prime position between Breeze and Ebony. Thanking the kind lady, Mia turns to give me one of her special smiles and I suddenly remember what could lie ahead in the next few hours for Mia and I. Shuffling uncomfortably around in my saddle, the strong pulsating feelings return, deep down below with a vengeance.

"Are you ok, Jazz?" Aunty asks, noticing my uncomfortable movement.

I grin at Mia. "Yes, fine thank you, just a little bit of cramp."

"Well, if we're all finished here, maybe we could lead Ebony and Breeze and have a leisurely walk home. Might be good for you to stretch your legs, Jazz," says Mia.

"Great idea, Mia. Aunty, would you mind taking my trophy home in the car with you, to save me carrying it, please?"

"Of course. Right, let's get you dismounted before we head off back to the yard. We might as well take your saddles and body protectors back too. It'll give Breeze and Ebony a chance to chill out after their hard work."

"Great idea, thank you." Dismounting, it feels good to have my feet firmly back on the ground. I hold my arms up high into the air to take a well needed stretch. I look towards, Mia, her gorgeous emerald eyes fixated firmly on my breasts, with a naughty grin on her face.

"Right then, we'll see you both later on and congratulations to you both, once again," Lucia says, taking my saddle from me, before lightly planting a kiss on my cheek. I watch for Mia's reaction, but thankfully she just smiles, as Lucia walks across to give her a kiss, too. After a kiss each from Aunty, Mia and I lead our horses through the exit of the showground.

Walking side by side across the long winding bridlepath towards home, Mia's hand gently takes hold of mine, and my life feels just perfect.

"Looks like we have a lot to celebrate later," Mia says, her eyes looking deeply into mine.

"Bring it on. What time are you coming out to play this play this evening?"

"What time, would you like me to come?"

"How about now?" I reply seductively, in a low sexy voice.

"You're so rude, Jazz, and a naughty little minx with sex constantly on your mind. Although, I'm not complaining."

"I can't help it. Anyway, it is completely your fault for having this uncontrollable, sexual effect on me."

We suddenly stop and turn to face each other, and our lips finally connect with hunger and passion. My left hand slowly moves up the back of her white nylon blouse, and her beautiful skin flutters under my touch. "I love you so much, Jazz," she groans, as my hand slowly caresses the back of her neck. Her tongue searches eagerly for mine, and momentarily, we are lost in a world of our own.

Breeze gently nudges my back, suddenly sending my tongue down the back of Mia's throat. Probably, his way of hinting, it's time to get home. Laughing, I turn to give Breeze a hug, apologising for ignoring him.

"Blimey, Mia, I didn't realise Breeze had pushed you. For a second, I thought your tongue had lost the plot when I nearly choked," she says giggling.

"I can't believe, I've got to start packing my suitcase later," I unexpectedly blurt out, feeling sad.

"Don't start worrying about that yet, Jazz. We have the rest of the day and evening together and tomorrow morning. I can't wait to see what if feels like to wake up with you lying next to me," she replies.

"Me neither," I say, a grin returning to my face.

"Remember, Jazz, we only live thirty miles from each other and we both drive so there is no reason why we can't see each other at least once a week and maybe the odd stay over, here and there," she continues.

"I hadn't thought about that, plus I'm only at college three days a week, and I'm sure when I tell my parents about us, they'd probably be ok with you staying over," I reply, suddenly feeling positive about our future.

"There you go then, stop worrying," she smiles, gently squeezing my hand.

Leading Breeze into the yard, I feel on cloud nine. I sing softly to myself, whilst grooming his beautiful coat before checking his feet. "Right, my boy, that's you all done for today. Now you can go and relax with Blossom and tell her all about your show stopping performance earlier," I tell him, as he chomps on his second well done carrot. Slowly leading him to the field, my stomach flutters crazily around at the thought of Mia, and our very first evening together.

Chapter 47

I lay my head on the post and rail fencing, my chin leaning in my hands, merrily daydreaming away, whilst watching Breeze and Blossom grazing. "There you are, sexy girlfriend," I hear Mia's voice whisper.

"Well, hello," I reply seductively, looking around to check that the coast is clear before tenderly kissing her waiting lips. "You taste so good, Mia," I whisper, my lips gently nibbling her neck.

"That's because I have an important date later," she whispers.

"Who with?"

"Well, if I tell you, you must keep it a secret. Her name is Jazz. I have been crazy about her for a very long time but didn't have the courage to tell her, that is, until recently. She is the sexiest lady I have ever met. Every time I look at her, my heart skips a beat. Her gorgeous eyes mesmerise me, her long blonde hair always smells beautiful and her lips, well, each time they touch mine, I feel like I'm in heaven."

"What else do you love her about her?" I mutter, my hands slowly disappearing underneath her blouse.

"I love her slender body, and those breasts, I long and yearn for them to be naked against mine, to feel our erect nipples pleasurably touching. My tongue longs to explore every single part of her perfect body, and my hands, well, they want to caress and drive her to a pleasurable place she has never been before," she continues, in a sexy whisper.

"Wow," I tell her, trying my hardest to take control of the sexual urges that begin to surge throughout the entirety of my body.

"My fingers long to touch and explore places where they have never been before," she continues softly.

"Mia, stop. My body is on fire, and close to exploding," I tell her, hurriedly removing my hands from underneath her blouse. I feel hot and flushed.

Mia looks at my face and giggles.

"You are such a tease," I tell her, waiting for my shallow breathing to return to normal.

"I just wanted to check that you're preparing yourself for the exciting events this evening," she smiles, her tongue slowly circling the outside of her gorgeous red lips.

"Mi, I can't look at you. What are you trying to do to me?"

"This is nothing compared to what I have in store for you later," she replies. We sit down on the warm green grass, lovingly staring into each other's eyes.

"There you two are," calls Lucia, heading towards us.

"Hi," we both say in unison, as Lucia sits her gorgeous sexy body down next to us. *This is all I need.* Her green eyes sparkle in the sun's rays and my heart skips a beat. A beautiful flicker burns, deep down below, her sheer beauty completely taking my breath away. *Bloody hell, Jazz, behave yourself.*

"I must tell you again, how awesome the pair of you performed today. Breeze and Ebony are a credit to you both. Trudy is just finishing off her last lesson before she gets ready for her evening out." she tells us.

Glancing at my watch, I can't believe it's nearly three forty-five. *Where has the time disappeared to? I still have so much to do, in readiness for my dreamy date with Mia.*

"How is she feeling about this evening?" I ask, purposely avoiding her eyes.

"She seems to be full of herself. To be honest, she's in great form and hasn't mentioned William at all today. Watching how you two excelled in your classes was just what she needed. I was popping over to say goodbye, before I head back to the lorry," she tells us.

"Where are you staying at the moment?" Mia asks.

"In my lorry. It has everything I need and its only for a couple of weeks. I have lived in it many times when I was out on the road. So much better than random hotels. I hear you two are having a movie night this evening. You can't beat a night curled up on the sofa in front of the television."

"Your lorry is pretty awesome, Lucia. What are your plans for this evening then?" Mia enquires.

'*Oh, Mia. Please do not ask Lucia to join us,*' I pray, holding my breath.

"I'm catching up with an old friend of mine. We plan on getting slightly tipsy and having a wonderful time reminiscing about the good old days," she replies, with a huge grin and a faraway look in her eyes.

I wonder if Aunty knows.

"Well, I'd better get back, too," Mia replies, slowly standing up.

"I'll walk to the car park with you," Lucia says, standing by her side.

"Have a great evening, Lucia, and I hope to see you before I leave tomorrow afternoon," I say.

"Don't worry, I'm sure you will," she grins back.

"See you at six thirty then," Mia smiles at me, as I say my goodbyes.

I watch the two of them disappear into the distance, before racing back to the house to get myself prepared. *Yikes, you have only two and a half hours to get ready, Jazz.*

First things first. Quickly changing the bedding in anticipation for what may lie ahead later, I smile down at the beautiful Egyptian bed linen, causing a flutter, deep down below. Clearing my head, I hoover thoroughly before running a hot bubble bath, ready for my next task. *One and a half hours to go, Jazz.*

I take great care whilst shaving my legs, the last thing I need, is to cut myself, today of all days. Slowly cleansing every single area of my body, I ignore the urge to touch myself down below, quickly jumping out of the bath. I cover my body in coconut cream, the silkiness of my skin making me long for Mia's touch. Throwing on my bathrobe, I wash my hair under the shower head, trying hard to keep my thoughts free from Mia. It doesn't take long to dry my hair, and I sit looking at myself in the mirror, patiently waiting for the straighteners to heat up.

I glance down at my phone to see Mum is trying to call me.

"Hi Mum, it's great to hear your voice too. I'm glad you and Dad liked the photo of our trophy. Yes, Breeze was an absolute star.

Of course, we are missing you all. Well, you just tell Buster, Starlight, and Buttons we miss them too and we will see them tomorrow afternoon. Oh, just chilling tonight, nothing special" I tell her, before saying our goodbyes. *If only Mum knew what I could be getting up to later!*

I quickly straighten my hair, panicking slightly, as I glance down at my watch to see it's already twenty past five. My stomach starts to do somersaults. I place a small amount of serum throughout my hair to define the layers, before deciding not to apply any makeup until after Aunty has left, as this would seem a little suspicious. Rummaging in my wardrobe, I find my three new items of clothing, that is if you can call them that. Allowing my bath robe to slide down to the floor, and looking at myself in the long mirror, I pull on the red silk crotchless briefs. They fit perfectly, although it feels slightly weird having an opening all along the bottom. I chuckle at the thought of Mia's reaction. Following the instructions on the packaging of the holdup stockings, I place my left foot onto the bed, roll it up and starting at my toes, I carefully roll the silky material all the way up to my thigh. Running my hand up and down my left leg, I am pleased with the result. My right stocking is safely on and now I have a matching pair! It's a strange feeling, with the silicone at the top holding these beautiful stockings in place. Now for the finishing touch, the corset. I stare down at the instructions, feeling relieved to see, it just slides over my head. Gently pulling the silken material over my breasts, I continue to ease the beautiful material all the way down until it sits perfectly just above the top line of my sexy crotchless briefs. Walking back across to the mirror, I stare at myself in disbelief. I never dreamt three new items could make me look so sexy.

My revealing breasts sit perfectly in the laced part of the corset, discreetly hiding my nipples. The stockings look fabulous, and I cannot believe that this is really me. Turning at different angles, I'm absolutely thrilled with the final outcome. Strong, sexual cravings slowly begin to emerge, as I run my hands up and down my sides. This reminds me of some of Aunty's stories and I can now see what a turn on this dressing up lark could be. *I wonder what Aunty and Lucia would say, if they walked in right at this moment.* I suddenly feel relieved, that I remembered to lock my bedroom door earlier.

A tap on the door, brings me instantly out of my daydream. "Jazz, the taxi will be here in around fifteen minutes. I wanted to see what you think to my new dress before I leave," calls Aunty.

"Just coming," I call back, panicking for a slight second. Racing across to the wardrobe, I quickly pull my long sleeve denim blouse off the hanger before grabbing a pair of dark blue jeans. My blouse is on in seconds, but I struggle somewhat with my jeans. The thick seam on the jeans rubs harshly in between my legs, and to be honest, it feels rather uncomfortable.

Another lesson learned, Jazz. Don't wear crotchless briefs with jeans. Tearing off my jeans and feeling relieved the discomfort has finally disappeared, I hurriedly grab hold of a pair of tracksuit bottoms and quickly slip into my trainers before heading off in search of Aunty.

Eventually, I locate her in the lounge, standing casually holding a glass of red wine. I do a double take, as my eyes take in the vision of beauty standing before me. Her sparkly black and silver evening dress is not only figure hugging, but completely takes my breath away. Thin silk straps lie sexily just off her shoulders. My eyes wander slowly down to her accentuated breasts, bulging in a teasing way. The beautiful, shimmering material flows magnificently all the way up to her knees. Black fishnet stockings lead all the way down to a pair of three-inch black stilettos with silver straps. A matching evening bag hangs loosely off her right arm and the smile across her face totally warms my heart. The way she has applied her makeup, has taken years off her, too.

"Bloody hell. I honestly don't know what to say. You look breath-taking and truly stunning. I have never seen you dressed up like this. You belong on the front cover of *Vogue*. Can I quickly take a quick photo to send across to Mum? Blimey, honestly you look ravishing," I gasp.

"Why, thank you," grins Aunty, as I quickly head back to the bedroom to grab my phone.

Aunty happily poses. I cannot believe how happy she looks, considering she is off to meet Uncle to demand a divorce.

I suppose people handle sensitive situations in different ways. What an utter and complete knob uncle is, letting a beauty like Aunty slip away. I would love to see his face when he sets his eyes on her this evening. *Serves him bloody right.*

"I've left you and Mia a vegetarian pizza in the fridge for later, that is, if you fancy it. Feel free to help yourselves to anything you want and, most importantly, have fun," she says, before glancing down at her phone.

"Thank you."

"My taxi's here. Have a great night and I'll see you in the morning. If I'm not up early, don't worry it will just mean I've got a hangover," she says, before finishing the rest of her wine.

Walking across to me, she firmly wraps her arms around me, hugging me tightly.

"Have fun, you, sexy little minx," I cheekily tell her, as she heads off towards the front door.

She stops momentarily, turns with a wink and replies, "You, too."

As soon as I hear the door slam shut, I race back towards the bedroom to add my finishing touches. My heart is beating ten to the dozen. Applying a small amount of mascara and ensuring I put on my favourite lipstick, I then use the red lip liner to define my full lips. After a few sprays of my favourite *Armani* perfume and a quick glance in the mirror, I sigh at the sight of my tracksuit bottoms. They will have to do. I can't bear the thought of that seam rubbing against my, you know what. *Jazz, don't worry. Hopefully, they won't be staying on for too long anyway!*

I giggle to myself, before a massive rush of nerves begins to flow all the way through my body. Taking deep breaths, I try hard to calm myself down. *What if I mess up? What if I make a complete idiot of myself? What if I let Mia down?* Thousands of thoughts rush through my head, leaving me feeling confused and unsure. Sudden heart palpations take me by surprise, a warning to calm myself down immediately. Closing my eyes, I concentrate only on my breathing, clearing any negative thoughts from my head. I picture myself riding Breeze across the beautiful, scenic countryside. The rays from the golden sun beat down on us, as a soft breeze flows against my cheeks and through the long strands of Breeze's white silken mane. I smile and instantly feel lighter. Slowly opening my eyes, I'm relieved to feel my breathing has at last, gone back to normal. Letting out a relaxing sigh, I slowly stand up. A feeling of calmness and wellbeing surrounds me. That is until the doorbell rings.

Oh Lordy!

Chapter 48

A smile sits beautifully across her face, as I open the front door. "Hey, sexy girlfriend."

Suddenly, all the worries and nerves I'd felt earlier, seem silly and irrelevant. My gorgeous, Mia, standing right in front of me, instantly makes me feel comfortable and safe, as her lips brush softly against mine.

"You smell gorgeous, Jazz. I love the scent of your perfume. Are you wearing this for any special occasion?" she asks.

"I hope so. Come on through," I invite her, holding my left arm out to usher her and her overnight bag in. The thought of her staying the night, turns my legs into wobbling jelly.

"And where would you like me to put my overnight bag?" she asks seductively.

"How about my bedroom?"

"I think I'd better drop it there on my own, Jazz. I don't trust you. I bet you're planning to throw me onto the bed, rip off all my clothes, and make passionate love to me," she laughs.

"Now, that sounds like a marvellous idea," I say, taking hold of her slender waist, pulling her towards me.

Our lips meet passionately. The urgency I feel, to have her naked body next to mine, is overpowering. My hands pull her even closer towards me.

Mia gently pulls away. "Now steady on you, horny, little tease. Remember, we have the whole night ahead of us."

"But?" I say, sorrowfully.

"No buts. Good things come to those that wait. Now, let me get rid of my bag and you can pour me a very large drink."

I laugh, as she hurriedly heads towards my bedroom, her cute, tight backside swinging from side to side. I patiently wait for her to return.

Gently taking hold of my left hand, she leads me towards the kitchen. "Wow," Mia says, as I turn to look to where she is staring.

"Where did they come from?" I ask, feeling confused.

We make our way over to the twelve red roses sitting beautifully wrapped in red and white heart-shaped paper on the table. A large box of milk chocolates is perched on the left, with beautiful red ribbon wrapped all around, forming the shape of a bow, and a single white envelope sits in the centre of the sweet-smelling roses.

"Who on earth are these for?" asks Mia, looking closely at the envelope.

"I've no idea."

Picking up the envelope, I read the writing on the front. "To Jasmine and Mia." I turn to look questioningly at her.

"Open it up," she urges.

Pulling out a handwritten note, my eyes quickly glance over the words, not quite taking them all in, and my mouth falls wide open.

"Read it to me, Jazz," Mia says impatiently.

"Jasmine and Mia, these little gifts are for the two of you to enjoy together this evening. I have watched the sexual chemistry flow between you this week. It is hard to miss. I know you have tried hard to keep the love you share for each other a secret, but as you both know, I never miss a thing and you never have to hide it from me. Have a truly wonderful evening and enjoy making some beautiful memories that, I promise, you will treasure forever. I am thrilled for the two of you and I want you to know, I love you both. You are both welcome to stay here anytime when you want to spend some quiet time together. All my love xxx. P.S. You'd better lock your bedroom door just in case I come home drunk in the early hours and cannot find my bearings! P.P.S. There is a cold bottle of champagne waiting for you in the fridge. Enjoy!" My voice croaks slightly at her kind-hearted words and a huge wave of relief runs all the way through me, knowing that Aunty is happy for the two of us.

"Bless her heart," mutters Mia, with tears in her eyes.

I place the note back on top of the roses with a huge smile. "I'll find a vase for our flowers whilst you crack open the champagne," I tell Mia, with a grin.

I rummage through the cupboards until I find a beautiful crystal vase. I walk over to the sink to half fill the vase with cold water, before taking my time arranging the twelve sweet scented red roses carefully into the sparkling glass vase. Placing them proudly on the centre of the kitchen table, I stand back with a smile, to admire them.

"They are truly stunning," Mia says, walking towards me, holding two champagne glasses, before handing one to me.

"Here's to us," I toast, raising my glass.

The adorable smile on Mia's face, instantly sets my pulse racing and a naughty grin immediately covers my face. "Let's take our drinks and chill out in the lounge," Mia says.

I walk across to switch on the electric fire, making sure I turn the heat button down to zero. I watch entranced, as the wonderful glow from the roaring flames turns the lounge into a magical and romantic setting. I walk over towards Mia and sit down next to her on the sofa.

"I love to watch the flames dancing around in joy. They totally fascinate me. I can't take my eyes off them," says Mia.

I look into her striking green eyes. "I know how they feel, because that's precisely the way I feel about you."

Mia's angelic face slowly leans in towards mine. Cupping my chin in her slender left palm, our lips touch softly to begin with, before intensity takes over and our kissing turns to one of hunger and need.

My tongue searches for hers. They dance and tease each other erotically. I gently push Mia backwards, looking at the beautiful smile across her face, as her head lands softly on a cushion. Leaning over, my fingers trace the outline of her perfect lips, my eyes staring deeply into hers. They drift downwards towards her neck, gently running through her long silky hair. Her eyes look full of passion and longing. I smile, before lowering myself forward to place my wet lips firmly on hers. Placing both hands around her succulent breasts, I caress and squeeze them, as Mia's light groan vibrates against my lips. Reluctantly withdrawing my lips, I whisper, "Let's go and lie by the fire."

Mia nods in agreement. Picking up our champagne glasses, she follows me towards the fire. The deep pile rug in front of the fire looks the perfect place for us to relax.

Our eyes burn deeply, searching into each other's souls. "Cheers," Mia says, our glasses clinking once again. Placing her glass carefully to one side, Mia's lips take me by surprise. "Lie down, Jazz." I do as she asks. The sexual urgings flurry hungrily deep within, as her body presses firmly against mine. Moving my long blonde hair to one side, her lips teasingly caress the entirety of my face, before roaming across to my left ear. Her tongue flickers close to my ear, and her hot breath causes goosebumps to appear across the whole of my body.

"Oh, Mia, that feels so good," I murmur.

"You haven't seen anything yet," she whispers.

I let out a gasp, as her teeth seductively nibble my neck. The throbbing deep down below commences. Her breasts push firmly against mine. Her teeth continue to drive me crazy, erotically pinching my skin, her mouth gently sucking before releasing. My hands run wildly up and down her back, stopping occasionally to allow my fingernails to press deeply into her skin with every bite she takes. She groans in delight at the forcefulness of my touch. My body wriggles around in ecstasy, as I try hard to control the crazy and wonderous sensations that seem to have taken possession of my body.

"Does this feel good?" she whispers in my ear, before coming to a sudden halt.

For a second, it feels like a rollercoaster ride, one that has got stuck mid-way. I look up at Mia, to see she is hot and flushed, too.

"We've plenty of time," she says softly with a cheeky wink.

"Spoilsport," I grin.

"Here. Take a sip of this and cool down for a while," she says, handing me my champagne glass. I drink it straight down like a glass of water. Mia laughs, before she downs hers, too. "Would you like a top up, my love?" she asks, in a low sexy voice.

"Oh yes, please. I'm dying for a top up," I reply, with a hint of naughtiness on my face.

"Good things come to those who wait," she reminds me once again, before allowing her tongue to slowly roll around the edge of her lips. I can't cope, and have no choice, but to look away, taking in a long, deep breath. I hear Mia laughing, as she heads towards the kitchen.

"Are you ready for round two?" she asks, upon her return.

"How many rounds are there in total?" I ask.

She looks at me in a mischievous way. "Only three." I feel

Mia's piercing eyes watching me, as I sip on the cold champagne. "Round two?" she asks seductively.

"I'm ready, if you are," I reply, before taking another deep breath.

She slowly walks across to me, her eyes completely transfixed on mine. I feel the heat radiating from her body, as she suggestively lies down next to me. Moving her hair from around her face, she announces, "The rule for round two is you are not allowed to remove any of my clothes. Your one and only job is to concentrate on seducing me. Do you hear?" she grins sexily.

I look lovingly at the suggestive way Mia's body lies, with her legs slightly apart, and her hands high above her head. *Where do I start?*

Kneeling down, my fingers lightly trace the length of her slender legs which are hidden away beneath her tight, fitting jeans. Moving upwards, my hands glide freely up and down the inside of her thighs, stopping inches away from her sacred area. Watching for the reaction on her beautiful face, my right hand pushes upwards in between her legs, slowly caressing to the left, then the right. She moans with pleasure.

"That feels good, Jazz."

Sneaking my fingers underneath the waistline of her jeans, I feel her body pulsate against my touch. Moving my hands upwards, I allow my fingers to lightly run up the outside of her sides. Her body trembles, as she moans in ecstasy. Concentrating on her beautiful face, my hands eagerly wander, before gently squeezing her breasts. Her hard nipples show through her bra and blouse. Watching the pleasurable emotions rush across her face, turns me on big time. The area between my crotchless briefs feels warm and moist, as delightful rhythmic throbs continue to pulsate deep down below, rising upward into my stomach. Leaning forward, my lips caress the nape of her neck, before lying my body lightly on top of hers, and slowly pushing my pelvis against hers. "Does this feel good, Mia?" I whisper, in between my teeth pinching her soft, delicate skin. Her hands firmly grip my bum cheeks, pushing me harder against her.

No words are needed. The intensity and passion triggers electrifying sparks to fly constantly between us. My hands caress her porcelain cheeks, before my lips search impatiently for hers. Small beads of sweat form across my face. The burning heat from Mia's sexy body the reason.

"Ok, ok, Jazz, you need to stop. Round two is over," she mutters breathlessly.

"Are you saying you are ready for round three?" I whisper.

"I'm more than ready," she manages to say.

Reluctantly pulling myself away, I quickly sit up, trying to calm myself down. Looking down at Mia's hot glowing face, a bolt of sexual excitement races through my body, the moist feeling, deep down below, escalating to wet and juicy.

Holding my right hand out, Mia gently takes hold of it, her eyes not leaving mine.

"Here," I tell her, my trembling hand passing her the champagne glass. "How was round two for you?" I grin.

"Pretty awesome, Jazz. You definitely scored ten out of ten for your incredible seduction techniques," she replies, slowly sipping her drink.

Finishing her drink, she takes a deep breath before scrambling to her feet.

"Follow me," she says, her left-hand taking hold of mine, leading me in the direction of the bedroom.

This is it, Jazz. The moment you have been longing for is finally here.

Chapter 49

"Jazz, please give me five minutes to quickly freshen up," she says softly, before releasing my hand to close the bedroom door behind us.

"Would you like some water?" I ask, unable to take my eyes off her.

"Yes please. Some randy little minx I know has managed to get me into a right old, flustered frenzy. Maybe bring the rest of the champagne bottle, too?" she grins.

The loving smile she gives me immediately reboots the sexual cravings, I hungrily desire.

Hurrying towards the main bathroom, I decide a quick freshen up for me too is most definitely required. Finding a spare toothbrush, I vigorously clean my teeth, before taking a handful of baby wipes to clean the area, deep down below. I am surprised at the amount of wetness I encounter. I have never experienced anything like this before. *That is pure love, Jazz.* With a grin on my face, I head towards the kitchen. Grabbing two glasses and a large bottle of cold water, I head back to the bedroom and place them on the floor, just outside the door. Racing back, I pick up the half bottle of champagne from the fridge, before tracking down our two empty glasses in the lounge. Quietly opening the bedroom door, I'm surprised to see that Mia still seems to be occupied in the en-suite bathroom. Pouring us a glass of champagne and a cold glass of water, I turn off the main light before switching on one of the bedside lamps. Quickly scrolling through the playlists stored in my iTunes library, I choose a relaxing album, press play and adjust the volume accordingly. Rushing across to the door to quickly lock it, I sit on the edge of the fresh clean bed, my heart throbbing loudly, as I wait with anticipation for Mia to appear.

"Are you ready?" I hear her voice call out.

Taking a long deep breath, I answer, "Bring it on, Mia." I cannot believe what I am seeing. Slowly, I start to take in the beautiful, sexy lady standing before me. I gasp, transfixed. *Wow!* My eyes stare at the slinky black and red silk bra, revealing the top of her perfect round breasts, peeping through the cotton white blouse, left seductively open, before leisurely moving to her slender stomach, leading to a pair of sexy laced briefs, the stunning material identical to her bra. The black fishnet stockings run neatly down to her knees before disappearing inside a long black pair of riding boots. The sight of her dressed like this, holding her riding whip, causes the whole of my body to erupt with a throbbing sexual desire.

"Come here, Jazz," she commands, her whip slapping against

the side of her boots.

As if in a trance, I urge my legs to walk towards her.

"Take off my blouse. Make it nice and slow," she continues, in a low sultry voice.

Looking deep into her eyes and moving my hands up to the top of her shoulders, I seductively peel off her blouse, pulling it gently over the riding whip she is still grasping. The sheer beauty of Mia, her perfect body waiting for me to caress every single inch, is truly mind-blowing.

"Take off your blouse," she instructs, pointing her whip towards me.

My shaky hands fumble with the buttons, her eyes watching my every move. A naughty grin appears across her face, as I pull off my blouse to reveal the top half of my red silk corset.

"Bloody hell, Jazz. I wasn't expecting that," she gasps with excitement. "Take off your bottoms."

I do as she asks, seductively removing my tracksuit bottoms to reveal the sexy crotchless briefs and the silky hold up stockings.

Her whip instantly drops down onto the floor. With her sparkling eyes full of lust, her lips urgently find mine.

"Jazz, you look delicious," she moans, her hands busily running up and down my silk corset.

"So, do you, Mia. I love you," I moan, unable to stop the pleasurable sensations rocketing through my body; my hands caressing her silky golden skin.

"Come here, my love," she whispers, before gently taking hold of my right hand and leading me towards my bed.

I can't take my eyes off her. I never thought that I could feel this way about another human being.

"Lie down on the bed for me. I want to appreciate every single part of your sexy body," she whispers, her tongue teasing the outside of my lips.

I watch completely entranced. She bends over unzipping her long black boots, her beautiful backside only inches away from my face. My breathing quickens, as the pulsating, deep down below escalates in excited anticipation. I want her to make love to me now. Holding my breath, she turns around to look at me. I slowly shuffle my way to the top of the bed, not wanting to take my eyes off her. Lying flat on my back, I watch her crawl sexily across to me, her stunning green eyes scanning hungrily up and down my body.

Every single part of me is completely aroused, even the ends of my nipples now pulsate uncontrollably.

The moment her lips caress my neck, and her right-hand glides softly up and down my silky stockings, the volcano deep down below, slowly starts to erupt.

"Oh, Mia. I want you so badly," I groan.

"I want you, too," she moans, gently lifting my corset upwards, her tongue circling my stomach, before urgently moving to my breasts.

"Sit up, Jazz. Let me whisk this off," she says, her breathing sounding shallow.

Within seconds the corset is off, and my breasts wait impatiently for her lips.

"Undo my bra, lover," she gasps.

My hands slowly move across her tender satin skin, around to her back, readily unfastening her bra. Her skin trembles at my touch, making me moan softly. Tossing her bra to one side, Mia slowly leans forward. The moment our breasts finally touch, I am in paradise. She wraps her arms tightly around me, pulling our breasts closer together. Her nipples touch mine, and an electric bolt strikes fiercely, deep down below, taking me completely by surprise. Gently forcing me backwards onto the bed, I hold my breath. Her hot pelvis thrusts rhythmically against mine. Her fingers lightly tease the top of my briefs, before moving playfully downwards in between my legs.

The touch of her hand rubbing softly against my sacred area, makes me gasp for air. Her lips continue to kiss my neck, her tongue flickering against my quivering skin. All I can do is lie here and surrender. My aching clitoris longs for her fingers to caress and explore. "Oh, Mia, what are you doing to me?" I half cry out.

"Hey. This is nothing. We're only just warming up," she whispers, slowly lifting her body off mine.

I lie still, breathing heavily for a second, the sweat already forming across my body.

"Your turn to seduce me, my love," Mia whispers, whilst easing her gorgeous body down onto the bed.

I look at her in awe. Her beautiful body lies patiently, waiting in readiness for me to set it on fire. My body leans towards hers, both hands slowly sliding up and down the silky stockings, my fingers teasing in circular movements as they go. Soft pleasurable moans escape from her mouth. I lean my body upwards, my lips softly caressing the area just above her stockings. The tremors from her skin vibrate softly through my lips. Taking my time, I tauntingly roll down the right stocking, ensuring I kiss every single part of her soft tender skin, before moving across to remove the left one.

Dropping the second stocking onto the floor, Mia whispers, "Oh, Jazz, you really know how to turn me on."

My hands once again run up the inside of her legs, teasing the wondrous tender area around the line of her sexy briefs, before moving slowly upwards to caress her gorgeous, succulent breasts. Licking her right nipple with the tip of my tongue, the passion inside me is almost at bursting point. Slowly, easing my body gently down on top of hers, the sensation of feeling her warm silky skin firmly against mine, is heavenly. Our lips finally meet, full of passion and wanting, as her hands run urgently up and down my back, pulling me closer.

I gasp. We are locked in our own private world. Her warm body seductively pushes her pelvis softly against mine. Our breathing is rapid, the passion and our love for each other apparent with every memorable touch. Moving my body in sync, my right hand slowly wanders towards her sacred region. My fingers finally touch the precious moist area below.

"Oh, Jazz, I love you. Please stay where you are. Don't stop. I want you so badly," she moans, her tongue searching for mine. My tongue flickers playfully against hers, as I allow my fingers to do the same all around her hot and yearning sacred area. I have never felt anything so magical. The warmth and wetness beneath my fingers, as they teasingly caress below, is not only driving Mia to a place of no return, but me too. Gently pushing her pelvis against my caressing fingers, she moans and groans, "Jazz, don't stop." Erotic pulses flow freely down below. Mia is close to erupting. Moving my lips, slowly downwards, I gently suck at the soft tender flesh on her neck. "Oh, Jazz," she cries out. Suddenly, her sacred area seems to pulsate and flicker strongly beneath my fingers before her body eventually becomes limp. She lies hot and flushed, trying to get her breath back.

My lips slowly move up to her beautiful face, kissing every single inch of her tender flesh on the way.

"My sexy girlfriend, that was the most mind-blowing and earth-shattering experience of the whole of my life. How did you manage to do that to me?" she gasps, her mesmerising eyes looking lovingly into mine.

"You like?" I tease, before pressing my lips softly against her.

"Give me a few seconds to recover and then let me see what I can do for you," she whispers, before gently pushing me over, until I'm flat on my back. My body quivers with anticipation. My stomach flutters, and my breathing becomes more rapid, as her soft lips slowly caress the right side of my neck. With my eyes closed, I feel one hand gently squeezing my breasts, before erotically teasing the tips of my nipples. Tiny bolts of sexual pleasure race crazily up and down my body. Her fingers caress my stomach. I wriggle with delight, as I feel them slowly make their way, deep down below. That very first touch, causes me to gasp in wild pleasure.

Her soft fingers caress all around the smooth and sensitive area, deep down below. "Wow, Jazz, you feel so beautiful down here," she whispers.

The sexual intensity continues to increase at a rapid rate. I'm unable to control the flickering and throbbing sensations. Her fingers continue to caress deep down below; their movements becoming firmer and faster by the second. The entirety of my body is about to explode.

Suddenly, I experience the most incredible explosion, deep down below. "Oh my God," I cry out.

Parts of my body clench and pulsate uncontrollably. I'm taken completely by surprise, with the incredible display of fireworks dancing all around, as, deep down below explodes like a volcano. My body quivers with magical ecstasy, the strong pulsations pounding against Mia's gentle fingers. This must be what paradise feels like.

"Did that feel good, my lover?" Mia whispers, laying her head softly onto my pounding chest.

I'm finding it hard to speak. The gentle flutters, deep down below and the delightful pumping sensations have yet to subside, but I'm not complaining. Searching for Mia's right hand, I squeeze it gently. She lets out a contented sigh, as the two of us take in the precious, life changing moment, we've just experienced.

"Jazz, I still can't believe what just happened. The only way that I can describe it is, a wonderful feeling of fulfilment. I love you with every ounce of my heart. You know this, don't you?" she says softly.

"Mia, I have never felt anything so powerful in the whole of my life. It felt like the two of us completely merged into one. You drove me to a place of ecstasy, and I will promise you now, that my love for you will last an eternity. You and me, are meant to be together, forever," I manage to reply.

Slowly running my hands through Mia's long silky hair, I tell myself I must be the luckiest woman in the world to have found not only my true love, but my best friend and soulmate too.

Our hands lovingly squeeze each other's. No words need to be spoken. The love and unbreakable connection we share, says it all.

"I want to stay like this forever," Mia eventually whispers.

"Me, too."

"I may need a shower," she continues.

"Me, too."

"Come and join me, then," she says, her head slowly lifting, her stunning green eyes looking affectionately into mine.

"Now, that sounds like a fabulous idea, although I'm not sure my legs are ready to stand up just yet," I grin.

"Shall we have another glass of champagne then?" she naughtily asks.

I nod eagerly. Watching Mia crawl off the bed, her stunning backside pointing towards me, I start to feel the sexual urges return with a vengeance. *Pull yourself together, Jazz, you haven't even got your breath back yet.* Struggling slightly to sit upright, I keep my eyes firmly fixed on my beautiful girlfriend. Her body is perfect, like that of a Goddess. *How lucky am I?* Smiling to myself, I watch her walk sexily towards me carrying two full glasses. Handing one to me, she holds hers up in readiness for a toast.

"To us," she smiles, as we gently clink glasses.

I cannot take my eyes off her gorgeous body. Her breasts call to me, longing for my tender touch to please them, once again. My stomach jumps with excitement. "Mia, guess what? Can you believe that we're no longer virgins?" I suddenly blurt out, with a naughty laugh.

"I know, and what a way to do it!" she exclaims, her lips hungrily reaching for mine.

Chapter 50

Mia's left hand continuously glides up and down my naked back, whilst sipping away on her bubbly. "Shall we shower?" she asks me seductively, as flickers of excitement race swiftly beneath my skin.

"Oh, yes," I murmur, another sexual twinge arising from deep down below.

"Follow me, sexy girlfriend," she says. Gently taking my hands, she pulls me up from off the bed. Our champagne tasting lips collide, sending a sudden surge of urgency throughout my body.

Pushing my body as closely to hers as I possibly can, the flutters and pulsations slowly begin to recommence, deep down below.

"Wow, Jazz, you are a right horny little minx tonight, aren't you?" she whispers, her fingers teasingly wandering downwards. I groan at her touch, as she seductively guides me towards the bathroom.

Grabbing a couple of towels, I wait patiently whilst she tests the water temperature of the shower.

"Are you ready?" she asks, with a naughty look in her eyes. "Here, let me sponge you down," she whispers, taking hold of my right hand.

Standing in the shower, Mia's lips press firmly against mine. The warmth of the water trickles slowly down my body, whilst her hands caress me, immediately turning me on.

"Turn around, Jazz."

I do as she asks, allowing the front of my body to lean lightly against the black wall tiles. A soapy sponge slowly massages my neck, flowing softly around my back, before flirtatiously circling the cheeks on my backside. Holding my breath, the sponge makes its way down the back of my legs, before returning upwards, hovering momentarily in between my legs. "Mia," I gasp, the area deep down below feeling aroused and ready.

"Hey, steady on girlfriend," she laughs. "Now, turn around."

Immediately obliging, our lips meet once again, the water from the shower head flowing over us like a beautiful waterfall.

Reluctantly her lips leave mine. I watch in anticipation, as she squeezes more shower gel onto the sponge. The soapy sponge flows all the way around my tender breasts, my nipples feel hard and ready. I hold my breath once again. Mia guides the sponge downwards, before swapping it across to her other hand. Her fingers touch me deep down below, and the bubbling volcano feels ready to erupt, once again.

"Mia," I gasp.

"Does this feel good, my lover?" she whispers, her crisp emerald eyes looking longingly into mine.

"Oh, yes," I murmur.

"I aim to please," she replies, her tongue searching for mine, her fingers teasing gently, deep down below.

My pelvis pushes lightly against her beautiful fingers, making the throbbing grow even stronger. Closing my eyes, her teeth suck gently on my left nipple, causing a wave of vibrations to flurry uncontrollably throughout. Her fingers move up a gear, as does my thrusting. The build-up to the imminent explosion is taking my breath away. A gigantic pulsating wave rushes throughout my body. The pleasurable release takes me completely by surprise, as I continue to pulsate against Mia's gentle fingers.

"Wow, Jazz, that felt so good," she whispers, her fingers slowly moving away from my throbbing parts.

Keeping my eyes closed, I cherish the beautiful lingering sensations still flickering throughout my body. My legs feel like jelly, my breathing shallow, but my body feels fulfilled.

"Mia, that was incredible," I whisper.

"I'm glad to be of service," she replies, in a low sexy voice.

The trickling of the warm water has a reviving effect on my body and suddenly I feel recharged. Time for me to concentrate on, Mia.

My hungry lips take Mia by surprise, as I slowly turn her around with her back towards the tiles. Releasing my lips, I quickly bend over to retrieve the sponge, squirting shower gel onto the top, before turning back to concentrate on my beautiful woman standing before me.

"Where would you like me to start?" I ask her suggestively.

"I'll leave it completely up to you, but please don't take too long, Jazz. After feeling your beautiful love juice all over my fingers, the sexual build-up inside is not far from exploding," she grins.

"Let me see what I can do to help." My lips move down to her succulent breasts, my sponge roaming freely around her back. Her body shivers with pleasure at my every touch. Teasing her erect nipples with the tip of my tongue, I slowly redirect the sponge back around to her front. I look up at the angelic smile on her face. With her eyes closed tight, her lips moan softly with delight. Moving my lips downwards, her stomach quivers beneath them.

"Oh, Jazz," I hear her mutter.

Feeling fully turned on once again, my lips seductively move further downwards. My tongue teases gently all around. Mia gasps. The warmth and the wetness against my tongue is a wondrous feeling. Her body trembles and flickers, before a huge release surges all over her body.

"Bloody hell," she cries out, her hands firmly grasping the top of my head, warm water continuing to flow over us.

What a truly satisfying experience and, one I will never forget.

Moving upwards to look at Mia, she immediately cups my cheeks gently in her hands. Her eyes sparkle, as they gaze lovingly into mine. "Jazz, that was unbelievable. Wow, you certainly know how to turn me into a happy and contented woman," she says, before her lips tenderly kiss mine.

Pulling my lips away, I tell her meaningfully, "I love you, Mia."

"My legs won't work," she laughs, trying to move her body away from the shower spray.

"I'm not surprised. Here, let me give you a hand," I reply, in a sultry voice.

"You mean you want more?" she asks, looking suitably amused.

"I think that I may need a little more recovery time, and if we don't get out of this shower soon, we'll both end up being completely shrivelled," I reply laughing, before quickly turning the shower lever to the off position. Taking her hand, I slowly guide her out of the shower. Quickly grabbing hold of a clean towel, I lovingly wrap it all around her wet naked body.

"Why, thank you, my sexy lover."

We start to towel ourselves dry. Our eyes occasionally glance across at each other, as a strong sexual chemistry flows freely between us. "You dry your hair first, Mia, and I'll top up our glasses," I tell her, before gently kissing her soft red lips.

Sitting naked on the bed, I still cannot believe what has just happened between us. I never thought anything like this could be possible. The volcano inside, which had been lying dormant for months on end, and the intensity of it finally being allowed to erupt after all this time, was beyond my wildest dreams.

"All done," Mia says softly, momentarily interrupting my thoughts.

Turning to look at her, the love that rushes through me, almost hurts. Planting a tender kiss on her waiting lips, I look deep into her eyes. No words are needed. The connection we have is unbreakable.

Drying my hair, I feel on cloud nine. *This is how true love feels.*

"Hey, sexy girlfriend, are you ready for some more action?" Mia asks seductively.

A shocked look suddenly appears across my face.

"Only joking," she laughs, "The look on your face was hilarious, Jazz."

"I thought you meant it for a moment," I reply, joining in with her laughter.

"We ought to get some sleep; you've completely worn me out," she says, glancing across at her watch.

"What time is it?"

"Five to eleven."

"No way. It can't be," I reply, not quite believing her.

A sudden panic of guilt rushes throughout my body. I haven't even given poor Aunty a thought. I wonder how she is getting on with uncle.

"Are you ok?" Mia asks, looking concerned.

"I was just thinking about Aunty."

"I'm sure she'll be ok. Have you checked your phone?"

Hurriedly looking down at my phone, a huge wave of relief overcomes me, no messages or missed calls. *Relax, Jazz.*

"Shall we get some sleep and see what tomorrow brings?" Mia asks, with another naughty look across her face.

This feels so right. Mia wrapped tightly in my arms; her beautiful head resting against my chest, her sexy naked body lying next to mine. I sigh with contentment, as tiredness overwhelms me.

***

My eyes flicker, as sunlight sneaks into the bedroom. For a moment, my head feels fuzzy, and I can't remember what day of the week it is. Opening my eyes, seeing Mia fast asleep next to me, suddenly the mind-blowing events of last night come flooding back. A huge grin immediately spreads across my face. *How lucky am I?*

Taking my time, I allow my eyes to lovingly glance over every single part of Mia's perfect body. Her beautiful head lies peacefully on the pillow with her gorgeous long dark hair spreading all around her face. The smoothness of her skin, completely taking my breath away. My thoughts flash back to the erotic and sexual encounters we enjoyed last night. Twitches and flickers begin to emerge, from deep down below. Watching my naked, sexy, girlfriend is turning me on. My right hand reaches out to touch her soft silky skin. Her body trembles. My hand glides lightly up and down her back. Mia slowly turns her sleepy head around towards me. The loving smile she gives me, when she eventually opens her eyes, is one that I will never forget. The expression on her face is priceless.

"Good morning, sexy girlfriend," she grins, "What time is it?"

"Time for a kiss," I reply in a whisper, my lips gently brushing hers.

"Now, that's what I call a good morning welcome," she grins.

My body slowly moves on top of hers. The feel of her naked breasts firmly against mine, our lips hungrily kissing, in between our tongues naughtily teasing, is setting my body on fire.

"Oh, Jazz," she moans.

"Would you like me to send you to that magical place once again," I whisper seductively into her ear.

"Oh, yes please."

"Jazz, did you hear that?" Mia suddenly asks, trying to sit upright.

"No," I reply, my body urgently wanting hers.

A loud bang suddenly brings me to an immediate halt.

"I wonder what on earth that was?" I say, reluctantly pulling my body away from Mia's, the pulsations and flickers still racing through my body. "I'd better go and take a look."

"Shall I come with you?"

"No, Mia. You wait here. Why don't you make a list of everything you long for me to do to you, and when I get back, we can work our way through it?" I grin, with a wicked look in my eyes.

"You are on. It's only quarter past seven, so we have plenty of time. Maybe you could bring me a hot mug of coffee on your way back? I think I may need a caffeine boost before our next session," she replies, her tongue teasingly licking the edge of her lips.

Trying hard to fight my sexual urgings, I quickly nod before grabbing my dressing gown and unlocking the door.

"Don't be long," Mia winks.

"Don't you worry. Just get cracking on that list," I reply, with a naughty look.

Creeping quietly through the lounge, all seems to be in order, although I can hear a slight noise coming from the kitchen.

Cautiously walking forward, I am surprised to see Aunty busy making two mugs of coffee. *Now that is very interesting.*

"Good morning," I say, trying hard not to make her jump.

"Jasmine, a very good morning to you, too. Well, how was your evening?" she asks, with a huge grin across her face.

"I'll tell you, if you tell me," I reply cheekily.

"Is Mia still here?"

"Yes."

"Awesome news. Congratulations," she grins.

The blood rushes quickly up into my cheeks, and my heart is beating so loudly, that I am sure she can hear it. "Thank you, Aunty. Well, come on, out with it. How was your evening? What happened with Uncle?"

"I had the most awesome evening, thank you. We didn't get in until three am", she replies, avoiding my eyes.

"Well, I must say that's a surprise. Is Uncle here then?"

"No, he didn't come. I called him yesterday morning and told him I never wanted to see him again. I needed to tell him before he got on the plane."

"But why didn't you tell me?"

"I didn't want to ruin the evening you had planned with, Mia. I still went along to the restaurant, as the meal and drinks were already paid for," she says, with a huge grin.

Didn't she just say, WE didn't get in until three am? I'm confused.

"There you are my horny little minx. Hurry up and come back to bed. I can't wait to feel your throbbing hot body against mine once again," a familiar voice suddenly says.

I stand as still as a statue, my mouth wide open in shock. Lucia is walking sexily towards Aunty, wearing nothing but a smile!

Oh Lordy!

The End

Printed in Great Britain
by Amazon

60894511R00218